Freedom of Expression and the Media

Nijhoff Law Specials

VOLUME 79

The titles published in this series are listed at brill.nl/nlsp

Freedom of Expression
and the Media

Edited by

Merris Amos, Jackie Harrison and Lorna Woods

Published under the auspices of the
Clemens Nathan Research Centre

CLEMENS NATHAN
RESEARCH CENTRE

MARTINUS
NIJHOFF
PUBLISHERS

LEIDEN · BOSTON
2012

Library of Congress Cataloging-in-Publication Data

Freedom of expression and the media / edited by Merris Amos, Jackie Harrison, and Lorna Woods.
p. cm. -- (Nijhofff law specials ; v. 79)
"Published under the auspices of the Clemens Nathan Research Centre."
Includes index.
ISBN 978-90-04-20774-5 (pbk. : alk. paper)
1. Freedom of expression--Great Britain. 2. Freedom of speech--Great Britain. 3. Mass media--Law
and legislation--Great Britain. 4. Freedom of expression. 5. Freedom of speech. 6. Mass media--Law
and legislation. I. Amos, Merris. II. Harrison, Jackie, 1961- III. Woods, Lorna. IV. Clemens Nathan
Research Centre.

KD4110.F78 2012
342.08'53--dc23

2012013031

This publication has been typeset in the multilingual "Brill" typeface. With over 5,100 characters
covering Latin, IPA, Greek, and Cyrillic, this typeface is especially suitable for use in the
humanities. For more information, please see www.brill.nl/brill-typeface.

ISSN 0924-4549
ISBN 978 90 04 20774 5 (paperback)
ISBN 978 90 04 22940 2 (e-book)

Copyright 2012 by Koninklijke Brill NV, Leiden, The Netherlands.
Koninklijke Brill NV incorporates the imprints Brill, Global Oriental, Hotei Publishing,
IDC Publishers, Martinus Nijhoff Publishers and VSP.

This book is printed on acid-free paper.

CONTENTS

FOREWORD

The Clemens Nathan Research Centre has held a series of one-day conferences here at the International Institute for Strategic Studies to highlight different issues in human rights. We were pleased that Lord Guthrie was our keynote speaker, together with an excellent team of others, on Terrorism and Human Rights; Sir Jeremy Greenstock led a conference on foreign policy and human rights and Professor Paul Collier headed up the discussion on development policy and human rights. We have also held several other meetings through our sister-organisation, the Consultative Council of Jewish Organisations (CCJO), with Robert Badinter, former Minister of Justice of France and former President of the French Constitutional Council, with General Sir Rupert Smith, and with Rolf Ekéus, who between 1991 and 1997 was Director of the United Nations Special Commission on Iraq after the Gulf War.

The aim of these meetings is to achieve an analysis of current situations and perhaps provide some recommendations of what could be done. We often publish the proceedings of the meetings so that the fruits of our labour are available to a wider audience.

The founder of the CCJO, the late René Cassin, was instrumental in the drafting of the Universal Declaration of Human Rights and received the Nobel Prize for Peace for this work. We believe that our modest Research Centre is carrying on in his spirit to help make people more aware of what needs to be done in the field of human rights.

Media and Human Rights is a subject which concerns us all, whether it is due to our wish for privacy or for open dialogue. There have been two outstanding reports based on government communications: the Sir Robert Phillis Report (2003, with revisions in 2004) and the House of Lords Government Communications report at the end of January 2009. Government communications need to be truthful and factual, but it is fascinating to see how the Government has tried to re-assess the whole approach it has to media. This is of course in response to rapidly developing new technologies and ever-larger media made available to the public, who in turn have greater expectations about access to information. It is overwhelming that over 3,000 people are working in the Government Information and Communication Service—let alone all the other national and international organisations, including media companies, voluntary and non-governmental organisations. The impact of this is huge, as it can be exceptionally difficult to develop the skills and tools to reach the public and give them a fair understanding of current issues.

There are so many vested interests in different organisations to promote one view or another. This of course can be healthy in a diverse society and democracy. We all need to know that there is opportunity to express our views, even if they are controversial to others, but we also need to know when these are controversial views, as against clear, truthful and factual information on which to base our own decisions.

The creativity in writing websites is quite outstanding today, and the various methods used to make information attractive to the public in digital and print form is remarkable—even if many of us wish for less of this and instead for more factual information! The growth of the Internet, twitter, blogs and other vehicles available to every citizen is transforming communications between people and governments.

In 2011, the United Kingdom witnessed the 'phone-hacking' scandal. It seemed that many of the issues discussed in the papers that follow came to a head during the summer months, as News International withdrew the *News of the World* newspaper. Employees had sanctioned widespread 'hacking' into the phones of celebrities, crime victims and relatives of service personnel, and the nation was outraged. At the time of writing, a full enquiry has been launched, and we await the outcome. Never before have the issues discussed in this book on media and human rights been more relevant.

With respect to the conference, and this publication, I have to thank particularly our two chairmen, William Horsley and Richard Schiffer. I would also like to thank Merris Amos, Jackie Harrison and Lorna Woods for their enormous help in organising this conference and then editing the papers for this volume, and my colleague Dr Tony Gray who has done much of the work behind the scenes.

INTRODUCTION: FREEDOM OF EXPRESSION AND THE MEDIA

Merris Amos, Jackie Harrison and Lorna Woods

Freedom of expression—particularly freedom of speech[1]—is, in most Western liberal democracies, a well accepted and long established, though contested, constitutional right or principle. Whilst based in ethical, rights-based and political theories such as those of: justice, the good life, personal autonomy, self determination, and welfare, as well as arrangements over legitimate government, pluralism and its limits, democracy and the extent and role of the state, there is always a lack of agreement over what precisely freedom of expression entails and how it should be applied. For the purposes of this book we are concerned with freedom of expression and the media with regard to the current application of legal standards and self regulation to journalistic practice.[2] These applications, it must be said, presume certain views: first and most generally that people should be free to speak their mind; secondly there co-exists within this freedom, a freedom of the press and publication; and thirdly that freedom of expression serves a public good. Each is a contentious matter and subject to revision, constraint and extension as well as much public debate, as—in a slightly different context—the Wikileaks saga has shown. This book is concerned with these issues as they affect the contemporary media, the practice of journalism and why imposed constraints and the extent of the freedoms attached to freedom of expression are managed, and why they may or may not be ultimately regarded as legitimate or not legitimate. It is the practical matter of contemporary journalism and freedom of expression that concerns us. Consequently this is not a philosophical work so much as a work concerned with the way that freedom of expression is evoked and applied and those arguments that support or refute such evocation and application, focussing on areas of tension between freedom of expression and other considerations. In short, this is a book concerned with what the various

---

[1] This chapter will use the terms 'freedom of expression' and 'free speech' as interchangeable.

[2] As such we exclude the entertainment side of the media business, such as films and dramas, game-shows and reality television, though obviously this boundary is somewhat porous.

authors regard as good practice as well as what they regard as problematic and why.

Some background is in order and what follows immediately is a sketch of some theories of freedom of expression that most impact upon the form of regulation, self regulation and the conduct of the contemporary media. Essentially this sketch is comprised of the following overlapping views that: freedom of expression is essential to the discovery of truth and error; that it secures government by discussion; that it requires a vibrant public sphere; enables autonomy and deliberation and that it is an essential condition of a democratic relationship to Government all of which the media should, in part, serve. Combined they frame a space within which media companies—and particularly news journalists—are required or are obliged to operate. While this space is not quite the *mediapolis* of the kind Silverstone[3] desires, namely one concerned to grow a global morality, it is, as Silverstone demonstrates, an ethical space nonetheless which houses both the demands for freedom of expression and its limits; and what one has a right to know and under what circumstances that right does not apply. It is a space in which freedom of expression, public will formation and the responsibilities the media have to its audiences are played out.

One of the earliest arguments on behalf of freedom of expression is that freedom of speech is essential to the discovery of truth and error or is necessary to guide and legitimate political decisions. These positive arguments, as Harrison reminds us in her chapter, received one their first expressions in the work of the seventeenth century, republican and poet John Milton (1608–1674). Milton argued against the licensing requirement on books[4] which stated that 'no book, pamphlet or paper shall be henceforth printed unless the same be first approved and licensed by such, or at least one of such, as shall be thereto appointed,' by distinguishing public prohibition from private choice. He argued: 'all opinions, yea errors, known, read, and collated, are of main service and assistance toward the speedy attainment of what is truest'. Milton did, however, accept the need to have some control over what was published: he accepted the needs of a person's reputation, as well as the validity of copyright and, as Harrison notes, Milton's sense of tolerance and freedom of expression existed

---

[3] Roger Silverstone, *Media and Morality: On the Rise of the Mediapolis.* Cambridge and Malden, MA: Polity Press, 2006.

[4] John Milton *Areopagitica* in *Areopagitica and other Prose Works of John Milton* (J.M. Dent: London, 1927).

alongside his constant insistence that only those who themselves advocated censorship and violence, and were themselves deeply intolerant,
should be censored. The 'proponents of unfreedom—Rome, Charles 1st,
[and] Presbyterians,'[5] were according to Milton, the most deserving of
censorship and worthy of the 'sharpest justice on them as malefactors.'
Whilst much of *Areopagitica* reflects its time, the height of the English
Civil War, its importance as a defence of freedom of expression manifest
through a free press, 'Give me the liberty to know, to utter, and to argue
freely according to conscience, above all liberties,' continues to be pro-
found.'[6] Indeed, J.S. Mill (1806–1873) dedicated a chapter of *On Liberty* to
freedom of expression and of the press.

In this work Mill argues from the basis of a liberal conception of the
individual as sovereign. He argues that the only warranty for interfering
with an individual's 'liberty of action' is self protection and that certain
forms of government, most notably those that represented the 'tyranny of
the majority' over the freedom of the individual, were one of the greatest
threats confronting 'liberty of action.' Significantly Mill believed that liberty of action has as one of its key elements freedom of expression which
consisted of the freedom to think, feel, form opinions and to publish. From
this position Mill argued that freedom of expression carries with it the
responsibility man and government have, namely a duty to form the truest
opinions they can, or as Walter Bagehot[7] summarised this view—government by discussion. Where the actions of government were concerned
Mill argued that,

> the peculiar evil of silencing the expression of an opinion is, that it is rob-
> bing the human race; posterity as well as the existing generation; those who
> dissent from the opinion, still more than those who hold it. If the opinion is
> right, they are deprived of the opportunity of exchanging error for truth: if
> wrong, they lose, what is almost as great a benefit, the clearer perception
> and livelier impression of truth, produced by its collision with error.[8]

In short, and in the words of Bernard Williams, Liberal theories such
as Mill's regard freedom of expression as both an individual right and

---

[5] Harrison p ... citing Christopher Hill *Milton and the English Revolution* p157 (London:
Faber and Faber, 1977).

[6] John Milton *Areopagitica, supra.*

[7] Bagehot argued that "A Parliamentary Government, is essentially a Government by
discussion; by constant speaking and writing a public opinion is formed which decides on
all action and all policy." Walter Bagehot. Physics and Politics Chicago: Ivan R. Dee
Publisher, 1999. xi + 211 pp original 1872.

[8] J.S. Mill 'Of the Liberty of Thought and Discussion' in *On Liberty* (1860) Harvard
Classics Volume 25 (1909 P.F. Collier & Son).

a political good, as it establishes a 'market place of ideas' from which truth can be discovered.[9] This view is encapsulated in the opinion of Holmes, J. in *Abrams* v *US*, in which he said, 'the best test of truth is the power of the thought to get itself accepted in the competition of the market'.[10] However, unless we refer to an idealised or perfect market, what market places actually do is show up imbalances in power and asymmetries in information and access to these ideas and subsequently the means by which to debate them. Consequently, the 'market place of ideas' has two, potentially conflicting, aspects. First, there is what we might call a quantitative aspect where the 'market place of ideas' equates to the acceptance of ideas through popularity, thereby raising the spectre of the tyranny of the (ill-informed) majority, or even mob-rule. Second there is what we might call a qualitative aspect where the 'market place of ideas' equates to democratic deliberation, sound reasoning and rational debate (certainly what Milton, Bagehot and Mill had in mind). Thus, while all these arguments share the idea that some form of public discussion is required, and that public opinion and will formation are desirable so that we might better come to understand the truth of matters, and that such public discussion must be 'unfettered', the metaphor of the market place of ideas is potentially misleading.

Recently the most potent metaphor for public discussion has been that of the 'public sphere' which Habermas defines accordingly:

> The public sphere is a social phenomenon just as elementary as action, actor, association, or collectivity, but it eludes the conventional sociological concepts of "social order." The public sphere cannot be conceived as an institution and certainly not an organisation. It is not even a framework of norms with differentiated competencies and roles, membership regulations and so on. Just as little does it represent a system; although it permits one to draw internal boundaries, outwardly it is characterised by open, permeable, and shifting horizons. The public sphere can best be described as a network for communicating information and points of view (i.e. opinions expressing affirmative or negative attitudes); the streams of communication are, in the process, filtered and synthesised in such a way that they coalesce into bundles of topically specified public opinion.[11]

On the issue of whether there is one public sphere or many, Habermas has this to say:

---

[9] Bernard Williams *In the Beginning was the Deed* (2005 Princeton: Princeton University Press) p140.

[10] *Abrams* v *United States* 250 US 616.

[11] Habermas, J. 1996. *Between Facts and Norms: Contributions to a Discourse Theory of Law and Democracy*, p360 trans William Rehg. Cambridge: The MIT Press.

> Despite the manifold differences [of public spheres] all the partial publics constituted by ordinary language remain porous to one another. The one text of "the" public sphere ... is divided by internal boundaries into arbitrarily small texts for which everything else is context; yet one can always build hermeneutical bridges from one text to the next.[12]

In other words, the public sphere materially links the social practice of public deliberation and freedom of expression together with public opinion and its role—a role that is usually conceived of as the most important mainstay of some contemporary liberal participative democracies.[13]

Dworkin extends this last point and links freedom of expression to 'the freedom of the human being to develop in society' so as to protect a person's autonomy.[14] He suggests that the state should not remove or limit the right of individuals to form their own respective conceptions of the good, and restricting speech would of course violate this, prioritising some views over others and offending against claims for equality of respect.[15] Dworkin expands his position with the claim that individuals should be able to develop their own personality and integrity. At the bottom is the need to respect individuals who are capable of making their own choices. Or, as Isaiah Berlin put it, 'The "positive" sense of the word liberty derives from the wish on the part of the individual to be his own master'.[16] The argument for self-development may be taken further, to acknowledge the significance of human interaction, particularly in regards to each individual's ability to progress and develop. Indeed, this idea may be implicit in Mill's arguments, as he recognised that debate improves capacity. Beyond this, the expression of views may allow an individual to give form or precision to that which was perhaps not previously recognised within him or herself.[17] While not all discussion, public or otherwise, is concerned with matters of truth or concerned with the functioning of a liberal participative democracy, these arguments also emphasise the point that freedom of expression includes speech which may, from the point of view of some, seem trivial, controversial, eccentric or, in some cases, quite bizarre. From this it follows that we encounter the increasing difficulty of establishing

---

[12] Ibid., p374.
[13] Meiklejohn, A., 'The First Amendment is Absolute' [1961] *Supreme Court Rev* 245.
[14] Dworkin, R., *Taking Rights Seriously* (1978), p 272.
[15] Some speech may itself violate respect for equality of others.
[16] Berlin, I., 'Two Concepts of Liberty' in *Four Essays on Liberty*, (Oxford: Oxford University Press, 1969) p 131.
[17] Moon, R., 'The Scope of Freedom of Expression' (1985) 23 *Osgoode Hall LJ* 331 at 348, citing C Taylor, *Hegel and Modern Society* (1978).

boundaries to opinions in terms of what is acceptable and what is not acceptable, what views should be aired publicly and what views should not; and even whether all expressions are worthy of protection.

One way forward is to say that freedom of speech is more or less confined to what, in the context of news journalism, Inglis calls[18] 'our unassuageable hunger to know what on earth is going on' or, as Bernard Williams argues,[19] is centred on the fact that: 'Neither the citizens themselves nor anyone else can answer the question "What is actually going on?" without true information and the possibility of criticism.' In short, freedom of speech is effectively the power of critique orientated toward 'to any reasonable conception of the individual's interest.'[20] Speech which does not meet that standard is not automatically protected by freedom of speech, whether such speech is seen as not falling within the scope of expression, or—more likely—because the limitations on speech in such a case are seen as justified.

Another way forward is adopted by Scanlon[21] who argues that rather than focussing on the rights of the speaker, we should consider the position of the mediated audience. According to Scanlon, a person is only free or autonomous whilst s/he is free to weigh and to choose the arguments put before him or her. Consequently, a government should not seek to limit speech on the basis that it would harm the audience. There are clear links with Mill's arguments again, though Scanlon does not argue that the output of this process would be truth; rather than looking to the consequence of the process, Scanlon focuses on the individuals and their rights. Freedom of expression is not limited to political discourse, but to all speech which provides information and opinion, though it does distinguish between communication relevant to the formation of moral or political beliefs and technical information. The latter may be limited. The fundamental weakness of this position is the ascription to all of the ability to comprehend and to weigh all forms of information in all circumstances. As an approach, it might also seem to overlook to some degree the interests or rights of the speaker but never the less does bring to our attention the relationship, pursued in the subsequent chapters, between audiences

---

[18] Inglis, Fred *Peoples' Witness* (New Haven and London: Yale University Press, 2002), p376.
[19] Bernard Williams *In the Beginning was the Deed* (Princeton: Princeton University Press, 2005), 74.
[20] Ibid.
[21] T. Scanlon, 'A Theory of Freedom of Expression' in Dworkin (ed.) *The Philosophy of Law* (Oxford: Oxford University Press,1977).

and media organisations. In short, the rights of the audience have had and continue to have an impact on reasoning about the regulation of the media, especially in the context of public service broadcasting.

To summarise, the above sketches simply describe an ethical space within which the media reside and which require that the relationship between the media and freedom of expression covers the terrain of matters to do with the discovery of truth and error; legitimate political action; government by discussion; the public sphere; individual autonomy and enabling public deliberation as well as being free from Government corruption and intimidation. Indeed, in many cases the approach taken by the courts is to emphasise the role of the media in a democracy. Policy documents reflect this, and the need to ensure representation and, in terms of the famous mantra that defines the BBC, to inform, educate and entertain the audience.[22] These issues are contentious, and whilst the different approaches noted may produce different regulatory terrains, these theories cannot be assessed in isolation. In short, our sketches simply show that justifications for freedom of expression do, in the end inevitably involve the conduct of the media and it is this that concerns our authors. It is the activities of the media relying on freedom of expression inner change technological and economic environment with which this book is concerned.

Most of the chapters in this book assume a UK regulatory framework; which, influenced by the EU requirements, imposes a differentiated burden on the broadcast media by comparison with the press and, to some degree, content on the Internet. The appropriate regulatory burden for each type of medium (insofar as clear distinctions can be made) has been the subject of as much debate as freedom of expression itself. While the press (and various internet groups) typically relies on a simplistic argument that regulation is bad as it infringes freedom of expression, the regulation of broadcast media has been accepted, however reluctantly. There are four main arguments that support the regulation of the media in one form or another,[23] but each reflects to a large degree the perceived relationship between media, public debate and an instrumental view of freedom of expression. These can be summarised as follows:

---

[22] BBC Charter, October 2006, Cm6925, Article 5.
[23] For a fuller discussion of other possible arguments, see Hoffman-Riem, *Regulating the Media: The Licensing and Supervision of Broadcasting in Six Countries* (New York: Guildford Press, 1996), pp 267–80; for more on the four categories, see for example Barendt, E., *Broadcasting Law: A Comparative Study* (Oxford: Clarendon Press, 1995), pp 3–10.

(1) *Airwaves are a public resource*: while it is debatable whether airwaves are in fact a public resource and, assuming that is so, whether that fact in itself justifies regulation, it is much less contentious to argue that regulation is necessary to avoid overlapping signals and interference;

(2) *Spectrum scarcity*: this phrase encapsulates the idea that where a limited amount of content was possible (because of technological limitations) some regulation to ensure either a fair playing field or to counter market failure so as to ensure a balanced range of content, was acceptable. Some argue that with the development of different delivery platforms and the use of digital technology which allows a greater amount of content to be sent over the same bandwidth, the spectrum scarcity argument no longer holds good. On this view, we are in an age of plenty, where the consumer can choose from a wide range of content. It is, however, a view which assumes that content is wide-ranging in subject matter and also includes new programming, rather than providing content limited to just the mainstream and the popular and/or repeated content. As regards the latter point, public debate is unlikely to arise in a dialogue with a tape recoding of the past. A view espousing the age of plenty argument, if it is to cater for public debate, also assumes any such content is generally available.

(3) *Power of broadcasting*: it has often been argued that the broadcast media, particularly television because of its visual impact, has a greater influence due to its immediacy and place in the home. The impact of modern media, specifically the internet, is not directly addressed by this argument. This point now has more force given that the boundaries between television and internet have increasingly become blurred as the same consumer devices can be used to access different services.

(4) *Compensation for the failings of the press*: it has been argued that taken together the (unregulated) press and the (regulated) broadcasters form a complete system where the characteristics of each—influenced by its respective relationship to the regulatory environment—complements the other. This view has also been criticised[24] and from a theoretical perspective it is hard to justify a regulatory regime to one form of media and not another, particularly if we are concerned with the quality and range of information available to the viewer or reader, a point Feintuck makes in chapter 4 in relation to impartiality rules.

---

[24] Barendt E., Ibid.

While this distinction may be used to argue against the regulation of the broadcast media, equally it can be used to argue for the extension of a regulatory regime to currently unregulated (or self-regulated) media, albeit one which needs to satisfy the usual requirements of good governance. Indeed, we see this direction of travel in the discussions regarding the revision of the Television without Frontiers Directive, as it became the Audiovisual Media Services Directive.[25]

The above arguments emphasise the role of the speaker and only to a lesser extent the role of the audience perceived as a public of citizens. The dominant theme in jurisprudence has been the scope of speakers' rights. This unidimensional conception of freedom of expression and the way it is reflected in regulatory thought, is emphasised as policy makers increasingly regard broadcasting as a consumer service rather than a public service, as a market based product rather than a merit good and, as such, increasingly approach regulatory matters with regard to their economic rather than civil or political consequences. This policy direction is further reinforced by the response of policy makers to a changing technological and economic environment, in which more platforms exist, different ways of using and interacting with technology have developed and cross-border media is more easily available.

Against this background Gibbons argues that we need to make a reinvigorated case for government regulation in the interests of speech and protection of a space in which speech may take place despite the libertarian impetus of a commercialised, multimedia environment. Gibbons suggests it is necessary that the components of free speech should be identified, and a clearer understanding of the nature of the right delineated. He starts from Lichtenberg's suggestions about the purposes of speech and Berlin's distinction between the freedom from and the freedom to—in short, a distinction between a negative and positive conception of the right. Gibbons then discusses the scope of the speech activity and the objectives of speech before considering the specificities of the media environment. Of necessity, we must consider the different nature of impediments to speech; indeed, this aspect is often the focus of discussion within a traditional approach to free speech. Physical and normative interference with speech then become central to the discussion, but Gibbons argues that this results in a narrow and arguably useless

---

[25] Although the press is not regulated by the directive, some internet services are.

conception of the right; what should be protected is its practical enjoyment. While there may be distinctions between public and private interference with speech, there nonetheless appears to be some justification for some state action. From this Gibbons moves to consider the agents of speech which naturally enough includes individuals, but to which can be added media organisations, a step which raises the question of whether organisations have speech rights capable of being subjected to interference. If media organisations' communication activities interfere with individuals' attempts to speak, is state intervention to prevent that interference itself an encroachment on the organisation's freedom of speech? This question reflects the classic recognition that rights are not tidily compartmentalised in separate boxes but overlay and sometimes conflict with one another. Gibbons concludes by exploring the implications of a strong conception of speech activity, including the consequences for regulatory action.

For Amos, we need a clear justice support framework with regard to freedom of speech, one we can rely upon to protect ourselves from the encroachments of others. In the UK, this framework is provided by the Human Rights Act 1998 (HRA) which incorporates the European Convention on Human Rights (ECHR) into the British legal order. Of specific relevance here is Article 10 ECHR. Crucially, Article 10 is not an absolute right to freedom of expression. Amos notes that whilst the incorporation of Article 10 via the HRA has made it possible for the media to seek to vindicate their right to freedom of expression in the domestic courts, as well as to use it as a shield when interferences with that right arise, there are also clear limitations to the protection that Article 10 provides. Amos argues that freedom of expression cannot be used to put those in the media above all other laws in all circumstances. Further, despite media complaints, it is not possible for them to put forward a convincing case that, in the interpretation and application of the HRA, the British judiciary has been biased against media defendants or applicants. The case law has developed in the way it has as a direct result of the nature of Art.10 ECHR which is, and has always been right qualified by other rights and interests. Here, as an aside, it is interesting to note that in this the European position can be contrasted with that in the United States. Not only is the structure of the respective provisions, Article 10 ECHR and the First Amendment, different but some in the American context have put forward arguments that content neutrality means an approach which balances free speech against other values is impossible, because the act of balancing imports an evaluation of content in to the decision-making process.[26] The structure of Article 10, however, (as with a number of other rights in the Convention) indicates clearly that balancing is the way to deal with conflicts between rights and other interests. Thus, as Amos points out, the British courts' approach reflects the requirements of the HRA and the underlying Convention. It, moreover, reflects the arguments of some of the earlier theorists noted above. Nevertheless, where the subject matter is a matter of public interest and 'responsible journalism'— whatever that might mean—has been exercised, the case law demonstrates that the courts are almost always willing to find in favour of the media. Nonetheless, the media is a powerful lobby and Amos notes the planned review of the law on defamation so as to protect freedom of expression, which seemingly has arisen as a result of a consistent and arguably one-sided media assault. As other commentators have suggested, the media lobby's insistence on the first amendment jurisprudence of the United States underplays the fact that that the United States is more or less alone in the world in taking this approach to freedom of expression and other interests. While the law of defamation and privacy are no doubt due for review, in part as a result of technological developments it is important, as Amos points out, that such changes also remain respectful of the rights and interests which, must be placed in the balance against the media's freedom of expression.

While much of the discussion in the media focusses on the threats posed by other individuals seeking to exercise their rights—to reputation or to privacy—freedom of expression may also be balanced against other interests. One key interest which is cited to justify some of the most severe restrictions on freedom of speech is that of security. Security is normally seen as being a right of the group as against individual freedom situated where the government speaks for the group's interest. Returning to our earlier discussion, mistrust of Government can be seen to justify speech rights and would do so the more where individual freedom is particularly curtailed—for example through detention.[27] One of the most pressing current issues is the 'War on Terror' and its consequences for our daily lives. Whether the threat is real or not, we see many governments introducing legislation to wage this war and, as Noorlander notes, the attempts to preserve safety and security have had an adverse impact on

---

[26] Alexander, L., *Is There a Right of Freedom of Expression?* (Cambridge: Cambridge University Press, 2005), 20–21.

[27] See generally, Spigelman, J., 'The Forgotten Freedom:Freedom from Fear' (2010) 59(3) *ICLQ* 543.

many freedoms. Within the overarching framework of a concern about the threat to the liberties of individuals in general, Noorlander considers freedom of expression and the position of the media in general. He understands freedom of expression as a traditional a negative freedom, that is, it is founded on the liberal and pluralistic view that 'freedom from' is a vital element of our personal liberty. It also reminds us that those who would seek to restrict this freedom (for whatever reason) are usually governments and that the traditional position of distrust may well be justified even where their actions are for very well intentioned reasons, such as matters of secrecy where the protection of the nation is at risk. Temporary restrictions become permanent and powers are used in unintended situations, and the rights of an ever-increasing group seen as 'other' become undervalued. While we might persuade ourselves that we live in a liberal democracy, Noorlander surveys the various restrictions that have been introduced, specifically those with an impact of the media, which might otherwise hold governments to account in the context of the War on Terror. Thus in Noorlander's survey, we see restrictions on access to information and the way information may be gathered as well as limitations on what can be published, especially through the use of broadly drafted and vague offences, such as those relating to 'incitement'. As a general view, where offences are vaguely defined, they may be used in an increasingly broad range of circumstances, as the example of the use of the Regulation of Investigatory Powers Act to check whether people are living in school catchment zones illustrates.[28] Even liberal democracies may face interference with speech rights in (perceived) times a threat. The media may play a crucial role in a healthy democracy in putting forward alternative viewpoints and in ensuring Governments are held to account even in difficult times and as such may be peculiarly at risk. Noorlander questions the extent to which the traditional safeguards against abuse of state power, as provided under constitutional and international human rights law, have been sufficient to protect media freedom. In this, Noorlander focusses on the UK given, as he remarks, "its self-proclaimed place in the vanguard of the war on terror", though given the international nature of the problem, the discussion takes place against the backdrop of international norms and the practice of the European Court of Human Rights.

The press has long been known for adopting political agendas in the stories it covers and in the way those stories are told; even the 'regulated'

---

[28] *Ms Jenny Paton v Poole Borough Council* (IPT/09/01/C-IPT/09/05/C) decision of the Investigatory Powers Tribunal. 2nd August 2010.

broadcast media tend to cling to the mainstream agendas. We can see that although the media organisations may be doing no more than exercising their respective freedoms of expression, problems in terms of the consequences to the public sphere or informational market (the proper functioning of which is often used to justify the speech rights in the first instance) arise and there are potential conflicts with the speech rights of others. In short, those with the power to disseminate content may engage in propaganda (whether this be directly at the behest of public authorities or as their own choice), censorship and exclusion. In this context, broadcast media regulation has at least recognised the problems of 'partisanship' and has addressed the matter through rules on impartiality,[29] which is based on the assumption that an audience should hear different views on matters of importance rather than allowing only dominant or conventional views to be expressed, though the extent to which impartiality rules and the objectives of plurality are natural bedfellows has also been question (see e.g. Feintuck). In the UK, for example, we see rules requiring the impartiality of news reporting and current events, at least as far as the broadcast media are concerned. The extent to which impartiality rules address all the issues raised, or the extent to which they are undesirable or ineffective has been the subject of much debate, both in terms of the legal framework and its effectiveness in journalistic practice, especially in a information age of plenty. Questions have been raised as to the need for regulation in general terms to reflect a range of positions, but specifically, the impartiality rules have been challenged in terms of their desirability, their workability and their necessity. It has even been suggested that impartiality gets in the way of engagement for certain disengaged groups in society or limits journalistic ambition.

Barnett considers the arguments against the impartiality rules critically, putting forward five fallacies which he suggests these arguments contain and concludes with a case study on impartiality in the UK, in the context of the attempts by BSkyB to merge with ITV and in the changing approach of the BBC to impartiality. He introduces and endorses the notion of 'radical impartiality' and the internal BBC report 'From See-saw to Wagon Wheel' whose editorial guidelines he finds to be a radical reassessment of impartiality and one that goes some way to solving the problem as to what should and what should not be tolerated under the banner of 'letting everyone have their say.' Feintuck also explores the problem of

---

[29] Hitchens, L., *Broadcasting Pluralism and Diversity: A Comparative Study of Policy and Regulation* (Oxford: Hart, 2006), 35–6.

impartiality only this time though through an examination of the legal framework in the UK. He approaches the matter through a specific example of problems that the BBC has had to face—the Disasters Emergency Committee appeal for humanitarian assistance for the people of Gaza—before considering in the light of the problems raised by this example, what the future holds for impartiality. Here we see the discussions of the House of Lords Select Committee on the Ownership of the News placed against the bigger picture of a changing regulatory environment, questioning whether other mechanisms might better achieve the desired policy objectives. Whether one sees impartiality is desirable or otherwise, certainly—as Feintuck shows—the application of the rules in practice gives rise to difficulties.

Concerns about multiple viewpoints, the heterogeneous nature of the audience, and an imbalance in storytelling power, which are all interwoven in discussions about impartiality, surface again when we look at the questions relating to minority access to the media and media representation of minorities. McGonagle reviews the three most salient Council of Europe treaties with regard to the issue of minority protection: the European Convention on Human Rights (ECHR), the Framework Convention for the Protection of National Minorities (FCNM) and the European Charter for Regional or Minority Languages (ECRML). He analyses the extent to which they form a complete system of protection. An underlying problem, as it is for Gross, is the difficulty of defining clearly the groups which we wish to protect. A further crucial issue for both is whether when we talk of representation, we mean direct representation by the group or, as Gross demonstrates, via intermediaries. In McGonagle's analysis, there is a second question: whether representation rights relate only to content/output or whether it requires involvement in the supply chain and institutional changes. The stronger of these options, in both instances, seem more than the governments or the media are prepared to concede, though this refusal arises in different contexts. McGonagle argues that the ECHR, as interpreted by the Strasbourg court, has significantly recognised the importance of minority participation in pluralist democratic society and in public debate, including via the media, as well delineated principles for the putting into practice of such access claims, subject to the comments already noted. As such he demonstrates the flexibility of Article 10 ECHR in the hands of a concerned judiciary. As he also shows, there are limitations to the impact of this provision, partly because of the inherent constraints of developing the law through case law. By contrast, for their respective parts, the FCNM and ECRML are legislative instruments which focus more specifically on the position of minorities, especially as regards freedom of expression, media access, participatory and cultural rights, though these two are broad frameworks which leave much to their interpretation. The ECRML, in turn, brings the linguistic dimension to questions of media access and functions to the fore. While much has been done in this regard, the effectiveness of those conventions is compromised insofar as they do not provide legally enforceable rights. Essentially, the legal framework even where directly focussed on the position of minorities is practically incomplete in terms of its scope and level of precision in drafting, and in terms of its enforcement.

Gross turns to the issue of media practice to ask specifically about the extent to which media outlets, in the absence of regulation, will fill the gaps. He is particularly concerned with the practicalities of the position of those groups that cannot lay claim to any form of news access rights. Refugees and asylum seekers are difficult to define in the terms required by the legal frameworks as described by McGonagle. The inherent heterogeneity of refugees and asylum seekers, beyond their shared experience of the asylum application process, makes it difficult to define them as a coherent minority group with regard to the media. Consequently, refugees and asylum seekers are difficult to legislate for with regard to systematic media access, though we must also concern ourselves with to the extent that such groups are protected and simultaneously the state of journalistic ethics and practice with regard to the way they are reported. Gross, drawing from an Oxfam-funded study into the representation of refugees and asylum seekers on British television news,[30] suggests that often these vulnerable groups are portrayed in negative terms. These findings confirm those in a number of other research projects which have analysed their portrayal by parts of the British media and have found it often to be problematic.[31] Certainly refugees and asylum seekers have little control over all access to the media machine, so even in McGonagle's narrower conception media practice seems insufficient. In this context it seems that these groups are denied freedom of expression by the exercise of that freedom

---

[30] B. Gross, K. Moore and T. Threadgold, 'Broadcast News Coverage of Asylum, April to October 2006: Caught Between Human Rights and Public Safety' (Cardiff School of Journalism Media and Cultural Studies, Cardiff University, Cardiff 2007).

[31] Cf S. Buchanan, B. Grillo and T. Threadgold, 'What's the Story? Results from research into Media Coverage of Refugees and Asylum Seekers in the UK' (Article 19, London 2003); ICAR, 'Media Image, Community Impact: assessing the impact of media and political images of refugees and asylum seekers on community relations in London' (Information Centre about Asylum and Refugees in the UK, 2004).

by the media and its own predilections in terms of whose views it chooses
to present and the way it articulates them.

Finally, the changes wrought by new technology are portrayed by some
as a solution to issues of freedom of expression, diversity, representation
and minority access. While the cyber libertarians of the 1990s might have
viewed the internet in particular as a jurisdiction-less, regulation-free
space in which all could communicate, the truth of the matter has proved
somewhat different, and especially if we seek to assess the functioning of
the Internet by reference to democracy and the public sphere. While there
may be "goodly people"[32] contributing to this brave new digital world,
there is also much that is biased; vicious, inaccurate or barking mad, as
both Harrison and Woods note. In itself, the internet is not a public sphere
in the terms conceived of by Habermas and others who follow him, nor a
substitute for regulation seeking to achieve such a sphere, even if user generated content (UGC) adds different perspectives to the debate aired by
the main stream media. As Woods demonstrates, whilst individuals may
have rights just as much, if not more so than, companies, it is at this point
that the freedom of the individual becomes entangled with the regulation
of the mass media, as legal systems impose liability on media companies
and liability considerations mean they act as censor, a problem compounded by the fact that the scope of the relevant legal regimes is in no
case clear, leading to caution on the part of the media institutions as to
what UGC to accept, adopt and retransmit. The media then act *de facto* if
not *de jure* as censors. While journalists may themselves be freedom
of expression minded, they are also informed (one would hope) by the
journalistic ethics of their training. This is then a key distinguishing
factor between 'professional' content and UGC, and the acceptance or
verification of the ethical pedigree of UGC may be as much an issue for the
professional media as content itself. As Harrison shows, the use by the
professional media of UGC presents the professional media with a conundrum. On the one hand UGC appears, or is presented as a form of civil
engagement with people exercising their freedom of expression, on the
other hand UGC appears to actually reinforce a tendency toward soft
journalism and human interest, as exemplified by the rise of stories centred on crime, calamities and accidents. If content of this nature leads to a
decline of political and economic coverage and journalistic interpretation
then there is likely to be an attendant decline in public knowledge, the

---

[32] Shakespeare, *The Tempest*, Act V, Scene 1.

consequences of which could well be to diminish the quality of civil debate and limit civil engagement. In short, there may then be a tension between the content as provided by the user and that which qualitatively adds to 'the market place of ideas' or the public sphere. In practice, it seems that UGC is not a substitute for traditional media practices backed up by media ethics; it may in the general run provide additional material of no great significance and with regard to the freedom of expression simply reinforce the view that not everything reported is worthwhile or indeed should be listened to too carefully. While equally being forms expression, UGC should not replace the critically minded journalist in the functioning of democracy.

In sum, Woods' and Harrison's discussions of UGC bring us full circle: to the recognition that the media has a distinct and central role in the functioning of a democratic society, the question being where do we draw lines as to appropriate behaviour so as to create a regulatory space in which the media may achieve this and where the public interest is not secondary to the shareholder interest in media conglomerates.[33]

---

[33] The papers were submitted at Easter 2010, and the editors are aware that much has changed and developed since then. However, the main arguments and cases discussed remain current and relevant, laying important groundwork for future discussion.

FREE SPEECH, COMMUNICATION AND THE STATE

Thomas Gibbons

INTRODUCTION

Contemporary trends in the media and communications sector are challenging the need for its continued regulation. Given the close association between freedom of speech doctrine and the media, there has always been a need for convincing reasons in favour of regulation, as an exception to the widely held principle that there should be no interference with speech. Yet, some of the strongest arguments for regulation relate to the protection of speech itself. Measures to promote pluralism, whereby positive measures to increase diversity are regarded as consistent, or at least not inconsistent, with free speech values,[1] are an example. So, too, are rules to enable access to the media, or to improve the accuracy and quality of discussion, or to enable rights of reply.

Yet the transition from mass media broadcasting to digital interactive distribution has led to increasing diffidence about the case for special treatment. The more that users and consumers of media services can make their own choices about if and when to receive content, the more compelling the argument for allowing normal principles of law to govern media and communications activity. The effect of the exercise of choice will be to re-assert the prominence of a libertarian approach to freedom of speech doctrine, one which disapproves of state intervention to promote media policies, including those to enhance speech itself. A number of current media policy issues reflect this tension: should television news be allowed to become partisan or remain impartial? should political advertising be allowed in broadcasting? how much Internet content should remain deregulated? should press intrusions and distortions be constrained?

Within mainstream free speech doctrine, the general assumption is that non-interference by the state is the most beneficial course of action.

---

[1] Lesley Hitchens, *Broadcasting, Pluralism and Diversity: A Comparative Study of Policy and Regulation* (Oxford: Hart Publishing, 2006) chapter 2; Rachael Craufurd Smith, *Broadcasting Law and Fundamental Rights* (Oxford: OUP, 1997) chapter 7.

Yet there is a growing trend in human rights doctrine to recognise what are described as 'positive' freedoms and to recognise that the state may have a supporting role in realising such freedoms.[2] This is an opportune moment, therefore, to reassess the strength of the traditional doctrine and its resistance to state intervention. The main discussion in this chapter is concerned with arguments about the nature of the liberty which is involved in speech. It is argued that an intelligible conception of the activity of speech entails a wider scope for the liberty, with the consequence that a stronger version of freedom of speech requires safeguarding in law and regulation. The final section of the chapter considers the role of state action in providing safeguards for freedom of speech in a democratic environment.

THE TRADITIONAL APPROACH TO FREEDOM OF SPEECH

Freedom of speech has an unusual status in political and legal theory. When controlling and balancing interests, the prevailing liberal perspective is to say that, when an activity causes 'harm', that is a sufficient reason for regulating it. By way of modifying this perspective, however, a separate doctrine has come to dominate discussion of the appropriate way to respond to harms which result from speech or other forms of communicative expression. The 'free speech principle' requires special and additional justification for interfering with expression, because it is accepted that some kinds of expression are worth preserving despite the fact that they cause harm. Typical justifications for such a principle are that freedom of speech assists the discovery, appreciation or reliability of the truth, or that it promotes participation in a democracy, or that it is essential to an individual's right to self-fulfilment, including the manifestation of one's basic identity.[3] The very breadth of those rationales suggests that the principle is less coherent than may be supposed, and that it may represent no more than shorthand for an important set of reasons for valuing freedom of speech. Furthermore, it has long been recognised that the rationales themselves have difficulties. The arguments based on truth and democracy are essentially consequentialist, so are vulnerable to objections that

---

[2] S. Fredman, *Human Rights Transformed: Positive Rights and Positive Duties* (Oxford: OUP, 2008).

[3] The first three are discussed in E. Barendt, *Freedom of Speech* (2nd edn OUP, Oxford. 2005). The identity refinement is elaborated by J. Raz, "Free expression and personal identification" (1991) 11 *OJLS* 303.

truth or democracy are not intrinsically valuable and may be outweighed by other worthwhile goals, or that neither may be dependent solely on free speech for their realisation. The argument based on personal fulfilment is difficult to establish as a ground for protecting self-expression that is separate from wider conceptions of autonomy.

Yet, there continues to be a strong belief that free speech and the reasons supporting it have a preferential status in political and constitutional theory, and this creates a need to articulate a principle which is independent of the broader idea of liberty and which can lend some unity to the differing strands of justification reflected in the rationales for freedom of speech. Apart from having some rhetorical appeal, at its most basic, the particular freedom may be seen as a principle of caution against too ready a willingness to accept claims of harm caused by speech. But, for some, what unites the rationales is a deep distrust of governments' ability to make distinctions between what speech should and should not be regulated, a suspicion that reflects the fallibility of politicians and wider distrust of government power in general.[4] Once this view is accepted, it becomes easier to characterise freedom of speech as almost being defined in terms of the absence of government interference—with the double implication that possible benefits of government action are beyond consideration, and that other kinds of interference do not matter. Indeed, it is possible to go further and to claim that the defining feature of a right to freedom of speech is the absence of regulatory evaluation of the truth or value of a message's content.[5] Whether it is possible or not ultimately to defend such a right, the general effect is naturally to associate freedom of speech with the libertarian end of a spectrum of liberal thought. If this statement is regarded as altogether too obvious—are we not discussing *freedom* of speech?—the point needs to be made that free speech doctrine has become characterised precisely in terms of a right to a particular freedom. As a consequence of this way of thinking, there has been inadequate consideration of what can or should be allowed to be said, and by whom.

PURPOSIVE OR INTEREST-BASED APPROACH

The established view has not gone without challenge. An exemplar is the important essay by Judith Lichtenberg, published three decades ago but

---

[4] F. Schauer, *Free Speech: A Philosophical Enquiry* (Cambridge: CUP, 1982).
[5] L. Alexander, *Is There a Right to Freedom of Expression?* (Cambridge: CUP, 2005) 11.

still salient, in which she argued for a re-orientation of debate about freedom of speech to take account of what she regarded as the two main goals at the core of our interest in freedom of speech.[6] One is indeed the idea that people should be able to communicate without interference, but the other is that there should be 'many people communicating, or at least many different ideas and points of view being communicated'. These are reflected in what she describes as two principles: 'noninterference' or 'no censorship'—'one should not be prevented from thinking, speaking, reading, writing, or listening as one sees fit'; and 'multiplicity of voices'— 'the purposes of freedom of speech are realized when expression and diversity of expression flourish'.[7] The multiplicity of voices principle is 'positive', in the sense that 'something (talk, conversation, debate) happens,' but it is neutral about the value of the content of such expression. For Lichtenberg, it should not be assumed that it takes second place to the negative, noninterference principle. She acknowledges the latter as the core and prior concern in protecting a fundamental aspect of our interest in freedom of speech: a personal right to think, speak, listen and read—without hindrance. However, its scope is relatively narrow, beyond which, she maintains, it is as important to enhance the multiplicity of voices. That may well involve law and regulation, and her essay shows that, where such regulation encroaches on the interests of the media, the non-interference principle does not apply to them in the same way: such a fundamental right cannot be claimed by the press and media under the guise of a right to editorial autonomy to publish. For her, freedom of the press (and the media) is only an instrumental good, which is contingent on the extent to which it promotes the basic values that underpin freedom of speech.

This standpoint has not been accepted by traditionalists. They claim that the purposive approach is not really concerned with liberty at all but with other values such as equality and welfare. They do not suggest that such values should not be promoted, but they do assert that the individual's liberty has priority. The implication for speech is that the state should adopt a minimalist, non-interventionist stance in matters of expression and that, if policies are promoted to enhance the effectiveness and worth of speech, such policies should not interfere with anybody's desire to

---

[6] J. Lichtenberg, "Foundations and Limits of Freedom of the Press" (1987) 16 Philosophy & Public Affairs 329–55.
[7] Ibid., 334.

speak. However, the traditional perspective rests on a rather narrow conception of the scope of speech activity. When the components of freedom of speech are analysed, it is possible to identify a more plausible and expanded notion of speech activity, one which provides a liberty-based rationale for at least some purposive regulation.

THE COMPONENTS OF FREEDOM OF SPEECH

Initially, it is useful to note variations in the terminology of freedom and speech which are apt to create confusion. It is important to distinguish two sets of ideas. One is 'free speech', in the sense of an empirical state of affairs in which there is uninhibited expression. The other is freedom of speech as a normative doctrine. It consists of freedom from unjustified censorship, entailing a balancing of individuals' liberty claims against each other or against other values. There is potential for confusion if the 'right of free speech' is used to imply, at least rhetorically, an absolute claim, drawing on the powerful appeal of the idea that unrestrained action is necessarily good. Similarly, the doctrine of freedom of speech is not diminished by the fact that most speech is not, literally, free but reflects the outcome of the balancing processes.

Schauer draws on the distinction between negative and positive liberty, most notably drawn by Berlin,[8] to make a point about the scope of the freedom involved. He believes that, in concentrating on freedom *from* and freedom to *do*, 'we can clarify some sticky problems in free speech theory'.[9] In relation to 'freedom from', he distinguishes physical prevention of action and normative penalty (whether directed at a specific act of speech or a general class) that allows action but creates disincentives to take it. In relation to 'freedom to do,' he mentions ways in which speech or communication is prevented from being done, for example, by way of absence of a forum, physical disability such as lack of voice, disinterest from audience, and competing noise. Yet, it is not clear what the point of the distinction is here, other than to enable the assertion that the negative element should dominate. The mention of 'freedom to' allows the question to be asked, whether freedom of speech might be more than freedom from governmental sanction or control, but that serves only to stress

---

[8] I. Berlin, "Two Concepts of Liberty" in I. Berlin *Four Essays on Liberty* (Oxford: OUP, 1969).
[9] Schauer (n 4), 114.

that positive freedom is to be seen as an exception to what he takes to be
the norm.

In a well known essay,[10] Gerald MacCallum suggested that, to claim that
there are two basic 'kinds' of freedom, negative and positive, and that one
is somehow better than the other, distracts attention from the important
issues at stake. The use of the concept of freedom is only intelligible, he
maintained, when it is appreciated that it involves freedom '*of* something
(an agent or agents), *from* something, *to* do, not to do, become or not
become something; it is a triadic relation.'[11] To concentrate on only two of
these relations (as is typically done), with the distinction 'freedom from'
and 'freedom to', is not to distinguish between two different freedoms, but
is to emphasise one relation against the other, without acknowledging
that both (together with the third) are features of every case of agents'
freedom. MacCallum argued that such an approach leads to the wrong
questions being asked. Instead of asking what the nature of 'freedom' is, it
will be more illuminating to investigate what constitutes the components
of the triadic relation: agents, the character or actions which they seek to
obtain, and the impediments or obstacles to achieving them. Each of
those components will span a range of variables and it is only by assessing
the arguments in favour of a particular conception of each of them that it
will be possible to evaluate the relative merits of different social and political arrangements.[12] Not only does any claim about liberty involve these
three dimensions, there are a number of permutations for each.[13]

While these insights seem to have been accepted in political theory
more generally, they are not prominent in the discussion of freedom of
speech. A curious feature of the traditional approach is that it does not
begin with the nature of the actions which we might be free to engage in.
While there are discussions of the definition of speech, and its relationship with action and other forms of expression, the scope of the expressive activity is taken for granted or not articulated. Instead, there is an
excessive focus on what is regarded as the 'negative' aspect of interference. A fuller consideration of freedom of speech requires attention to all
three elements. To avoid circularity, the 'free' quality of speech cannot be

---

[10] Gerald C MacCallum Jr., "Negative and Positive Freedom" (1967) 76 (3) *The
Philosophical Review*, 312–334.
[11] Ibid., 314.
[12] Ibid., 320–27.
[13] This point is emphasised by Swift: A. Swift, *Political Philosophy: A Beginners' Guide for
Students and Politicians* (Cambridge: Polity Press, 2006 2nd ed) 52–54.

defined in terms of minimal regulation. It will be helpful to proceed for the purposes of exposition, therefore, by analysing the components of speech in terms of each component of the triadic relationship. It is appreciated that this kind of disaggregation is not easy to maintain and is exactly what MacCallum counselled against. But a re-assembly of the components at the end will result in a stronger conception of freedom of speech than the traditional view can provide.

THE OBJECTS OF SPEECH

The Scope of Speech Activity

The traditional approach to freedom of speech encourages a rather abstract way of thinking about the liberty. It is a weak conception of speech activity because the substance of the activity does not need to be conveyed. The major consideration is non-interference. Yet the nature and significance of non-interference can only be understood once it is known what it is that is being prevented from happening. Freedom of speech is actually determined by the way the 'active' element[14] is defined, and such definitions are formulated by reference to what an interest in speech might be and why it might be considered valuable and worthy of protection. The intelligibility of 'freedom of speech' depends on what would make sense to the agent who is claiming the freedom. In turn, its appeal will depend on the plausibility of the way agents are characterised.

Concretely, at its most basic, a person will value speech or other forms of expression because it is through language and symbolic forms that thought can be articulated. Since our thought is the manifestation of our very identity, it is easy to understand why its articulation can be claimed to be an overriding interest or a fundamental right.[15] But the relevant overriding interest is usually taken to extend beyond the mere freedom to articulate. With the exception of those recluses who choose to ignore or reject human contact, agents typically inhabit a social environment where it is the possibility of interaction with others which gives meaning and

---

[14] The term 'active' is used to avoid the kind of confusion that MacCallum highlighted. However, many writers do use the term 'positive' in describing the objects and purposes of liberties and rights. For example, Joseph Raz says that "negative freedom is valuable in as much as it serves positive freedom and autonomy": *The Morality of Freedom* (Oxford: Clarendon Press, 1986), 410. Fredman's book, subtitled 'positive rights and positive duties' has been mentioned already (n 3).

[15] See Lichtenberg (n 6).

purpose to lives. Whether (to provide only a few examples) it is the simple display of personality, the ability to persuade others to our point of view, the opportunity to learn from those others, or the indication of emotional connections or fissures, the possibility of communicating our thoughts appears crucial to establishing and maintaining our identity as agents.[16] This social nature of agency is most strongly emphasised in the work of Charles Taylor.[17] But, it is no longer a controversial proposition in liberal theory, which has clearly distanced itself from the image of a political culture inhabited by 'atomistic' individuals.[18]

The traditional approach to freedom of expression, however, seems to be targeted at just such an abstract representation of humans. For its condition for the existence of speech that is free seems to be only this: that there should be no interference in (metaphorically) the making of noise, whether intelligible or not. The implication is that there exist agents who believe that their interest in speech is satisfied when such a condition is met. At the same time, most discussion of freedom of speech contains the implicit assumption that 'speech' does involve more than merely making a noise. The general expectation is that speech will be communicated in discussion or debate. As Lichtenberg pointed out, all the arguments for freedom of expression demonstrate the 'centrality not of speech simply but of discussion, debate, diversity of ideas and sources of information'.[19] Indeed, without such an expectation, the rationales for giving special protection to speech would not make sense. They are based on the belief that speech is valuable because of the indirect benefits which it provides through the exchange of ideas and opinion: facilitating the discovery of truth or participation in democracy, or in enhancing autonomy. There is an assumption that it will be used to communicate—J.S. Mill, for example, clearly values debate, and the 'market place of ideas' is predicated on the clash of viewpoints. Indeed, to the extent that the autonomy rationale does not necessarily require communication, it is considered to be the weakest rationale for special protection by Schauer. But even that, as

---

[16] In principle, there should be no limit on the content of such communication which is embraced by the claim to the liberty. Whether such a claim is justified, or whether it may be justifiably limited in the interests of other values, is the question which takes up the bulk of freedom of speech doctrine. But it is beyond the scope of this chapter.

[17] C. Taylor, *Sources of the Self: the making of the modern identity* (Cambridge, Mass.: Harvard University Press, 1989).

[18] W. Kymlicka, *Liberalism, Community and Culture* (Oxford: OUP, 1989); J. Rawls, *Political Liberalism* (New York: Columbia UP, 1993).

[19] See Lichtenberg (n 6) 348.

again Lichtenberg has demonstrated, depends on the symbolic expression of intentionality and meaning.[20]

The curious feature of the traditional approach is that its foundation is a conception of speech which has such a narrow scope. While there is some discussion of the definition of speech (whether it includes some kinds of activity, or whether it should be characterised in terms of content or purposes),[21] there is no concern with what the speaker wishes to achieve through speech. Rather, is sufficient that the state does not interfere with attempts to use speech. The reason why this is curious is that, given the importance of the objects of speech, it might be expected that (however described) they should be an intrinsic part of any overriding interest or right, rather than being contingent on the exercise of a minimalist conception of the interest or right. How then, should 'speech activity' be described for the purpose of recognising what is worthy of protection? As mentioned already, the answer has important implications for the way that interference with that protection is to be defined, and it depends on the way that agents are envisaged.

A highly individualistic perspective would be to take a 'natural' or physical baseline, and to include activity which emanates from the speaker but does not involve others. Thus, a mere utterance would be covered, as would inviting others to listen to one's speech by way of attracting attention to it, as would shouting loudly in order to drown out others' speech. On the spectrum of making a noise to engaging in discussion, the limit to what the speaker can demand would be reached very early, before the point where, to go further, would require others to acknowledge the existence of the speech and at least pay it attention. From the libertarian perspective, the demand for any kind of reciprocation will be seen as an encroachment on others' interests; the optimal situation of liberty entails that freedom to speak is balanced by freedom not to listen or read.

A more social perspective on agency would regard such a depiction as unrealistically narrow. If the meaning and purpose of human activity is indeed identified by reference to interaction with others, the significant freedom to be protected in relation to speech is the freedom to be part of the social interchange which is the point of speech activity. So, what does this imply? At a minimum, it entails the freedom to draw others' attention to the wish to speak, followed by the freedom effectively to extend an

---

[20] Lichtenberg (n 6) 336.
[21] Barendt (n 3) chapter 3; Schauer (n 4) chapter 7.

invitation to pursue a conversation. The philosophical anthropology of a
social conception of agency is that communicative interaction and
exchange is part of the normal way of existence. The issue is not whether
there will be an interaction, but what it is that one is free to do in that
context. It is, therefore, the freedom to 'make a pitch' for further attention
and engagement. This contrasts with a position which starts with a set of
individuals who can do no more than call to each other in the hope that
the process—a conversation—will start at all. But, if the more normal
context for speech is essentially social, where initiating conversation is
not regarded as abnormal, freedom to do precisely what is normal may
be seen as the minimum activity which should be protected against
interference.

How far should the freedom extend in the social context? Is there a
right to be heard, or be read? This seems to go too far: it requires a different kind of cooperation from the listener, or reader, not to consider merely
the request to communicate, but to insist that attention be given and
that dialogue be engaged. However, such attention may well be required
where a conversation has already been joined. The social rules of conversation require that the parties show some reciprocation of involvement.
Furthermore, in more organised settings, such as a discussion group or a
political debate, freedom of speech may imply the freedom to take part in
the dialogue. Here, it is important to understand that it is the 'give and
take' of conversation or dialogue which is the activity in which the agent
is free to engage. It therefore does not make sense from the perspective of
an agent-conceived-as-social to say, as a libertarian might, that the expectation to give way to one speaker is a limit on the freedom of another
potential speaker to speak continuously.

Speech Objectives

A focus on the objects of speech also invites consideration of the purposes
to be achieved. While Lichtenberg sees the limit of the interest in freedom
of speech, in addition to manifesting autonomy, as the facilitating of
diversity of viewpoint, others have gone further, to consider the quality of
outcome. Within this approach, some have suggested that the social
dimension should be given more weight than the individual contribution.[22] Owen Fiss[23] also identifies autonomy as a freedom of speech value

---

[22] For example, A. Meiklejohn, *Political Freedom: The Constitutional Power of the People*
(New York: Harper Collins, 1960).
[23] O. Fiss, "Free speech and social structure" (1986) 71 *Iowa L Rev*, 1405–1425.

but, for him, the other value is 'rich public debate', which he regards as a priority in the interests of collective self-determination. Autonomy may have to be sacrificed for the sake of enhancing the quality of public debate. For him, 'What the phrase "the freedom of speech" in the first amendment refers to is a social state of affairs, not the action of an individual or institution'.[24]

However, as Post[25] has pointed out, in criticism of this perspective, First Amendment doctrine in the United States has not followed this interpretation but has adopted a 'participatory' approach. This involves citizens having individual rights to participate in formation of public opinion, unfettered by restrictions on content (in terms of, for example, its rationality, style, or offensiveness). Direct, active participation, whatever the outcome, takes priority over the regulation of public discourse designed to maintain the integrity of collective thinking processes.

These are quite differing views of the objectives of speech, and the contrast cannot be resolved here. One potential difficulty with the specification of the objects of a liberty is that it invites open-ended divergences of viewpoint about its ultimate aspirations.[26] For present purposes, it is notable that both perspectives are based ultimately on a thin, weak version of speech activity. The underlying attitude is essentially passive. If speech is considered to be so valuable for what it can achieve, one might expect some characterisation of the sense of engagement which is required. Instead, we are presented with either a participatory citizen who takes part in activity whose purpose is seemingly not appreciated, or an abstract situation of public debate in which the interactions of speech activity are unspecified. For both perspectives, to make sense of freedom of speech, a stronger specification of the speech activity is required.

Speech Activity in Publications and Media

Up to this point, the discussion has emphasised the interactive nature of personal conversation and, by extension, public debate. However, it is

---

[24] Ibid., 1411. The general theme is also developed in O. Fiss, "Why the state?" (1987) 100, *Harvard Law Review*, 781–94 and O. Fiss, *The Irony of Free Speech* (Cambridge: Harvard University Press, 1996).

[25] R. Post, "Reconciling Theory and Doctrine in First Amendment Jurisprudence" (2000) 89, *California Law Review*, 2353.

[26] It is beyond the scope of this chapter, but it may be noted that Berlin was especially concerned about the dangers of allowing (totalitarian) states effectively to redefine liberty, in a 'positive' way, as a mental construct in opposition to physical confinement.

implicit that the same points can be made about writing, publishing and dissemination in other media. The underlying principles of traditional free speech doctrine apply similarly to oral speech, writing, media content, or other kinds of expression, both literal and symbolic. Whatever the form, the issue is whether the activity expresses the sentiments of the agent who instigates it. The 'speech' activity of agents-conceived-as-social, therefore, includes their writing and publishing with a view to attracting the attention of readers and audiences. The mechanisms for inviting attention are obviously different from the use of the spoken word. But that only becomes significant for the objectives of speech activity if they require the use of resources which do not belong to the 'speaker,' or where a request to communicate with others has the effect of demanding their concentration. The question of resources will be discussed in the course of the next section, and some wider implications will be considered in the concluding part of the chapter.

IMPEDIMENTS TO SPEECH

This is the dimension of freedom of speech which is emphasised in the traditional approach. Furthermore, the discussion usually proceeds by adopting a narrow version of impediment, the notion of 'interference', and usually that imposed by the state. For Schauer, for example, freedom of speech is generally agreed to involve immunity from direct government coercion or punishment. The approach implies that other obstacles or constraints are a matter of indifference from a freedom of speech perspective. However, it is based on a series of contestable contrasts: natural and socially constructed resources, availability and effectiveness, the public and the private. The effect is to define various activities as not constituting impediments, implicitly restricting the scope of the liberty to be protected and thereby challenging, at least indirectly, the claims made for purposive objects of speech.

Physical and Normative Interference

Deliberate interference with speech, whether through physical coercion or a normative means, such as the imposition of a sanction for breach of law or regulation, is not controversial as being an impediment to its free exercise. More debateable are indirect interferences, such as social and economic structural constraints (which will be discussed below), and omissions to take remedial action. The latter is significant both for the state and for private institutions, such as the media, which may be thought to have public roles. For Raz,[27] for example, harms may be perpetuated as much by the refusal by the state to take action as by direct action. Where individuals' action has the effect of causing harm by preventing a desirable state of affairs from existing (for Raz, it is the conditions for autonomy), the state will be justified in interfering with individuals' behaviour to prevent such harm (consistent with the wider, libertarian 'harm principle'). On this view, it is the failure to intervene which perpetuates the impediment to liberty, and the intervention actually involves a removal of the impediment. Generalising this logic, it is increasingly accepted that the state should take positive steps to protect important rights.[28] The human rights doctrine of horizontal effect already reflects this idea: the consequence of a claimant's action to enforce the state's duty to protect such rights may be to require the state to provide remedies against private individuals or organisations which do not have a direct duty to the claimant.[29] In relation to freedom of speech, there is no default position whereby interference with speech only takes place by government, and there is no reason why such interference should be condoned by the state.

Availability and Effectiveness

The traditional approach reflects a narrow, minimalist and, arguably relatively useless, conception of freedom of speech. As Rawls observed, the important matter for most individuals may not be the civic status of being free but the practical enjoyment of the liberty—its worth.[30] In the case of speech, a minimalist conception can be enhanced only by providing opportunities to take advantage of it in conversation and discussion with others. But the absence of such opportunities is characterised by Schauer as a matter of practical ability and effectiveness. Failure to provide facilities cannot be regarded as an interference with the availability of the liberty if that has not been withdrawn.[31] Furthermore, it is said that the argument for positive enhancement of the exercise of free speech proves

---

[27] Raz (15).
[28] Fredman (n 3).
[29] See H. Fenwick & G. Phillipson, *Media Freedom under the Human Rights Act* (Oxford: OUP, 2006) 123–144. A topical example is the development of a remedy for the protection of personal information, as a means of enforcing Article 8 of the European Convention on Human Rights under the Human Rights Act 1998.
[30] J. Rawls, *A Theory of Justice* (Oxford: OUP, 1971) 204.
[31] Schauer (n 5), 114ff.

too much: if facilities are to be made available, should they be confined to the provision of a discussion platform, or should they extend to a good education and financial support? These arguments appear compelling in their own terms, yet there is unease about their impact. The typical way to reconcile this is to say that positive policies, reflecting the purposes of freedom of speech, may encourage favourable conditions for speech to take place, and they should not be regarded as inimical to the liberty. Thus, media pluralism and public service broadcasting are commended, but not imposed and, given the narrow conception of the liberty, they cannot be regarded as interfering with individual claims to be free to speak. Alternatively, as Barendt has more recently argued, the value of equality can be invoked to ensure at least fair provision of opportunities to speak where control of platforms to speak is not evenly distributed.[32] Barendt sees this solution as rather exceptional, in contrast to Fiss, who acknowledges that inequality of resources, reflected in the structural features of society (socio-economic patterns, and property rights enshrined in law and regulation), are systemically implicated in the effectiveness of speech. However, the traditional approach is inclined to view this simply as a matter of the 'natural' allocation of public and private competencies, rather than being socially constructed.

Public and Private Resources

Again, it is Schauer who has articulated most fully a set of reasons for distinguishing between public and private interference with freedom of speech.[33] He stresses that the free speech principle is focused on government action rather than private action. While private actions may well have the effect of preventing speech from taking place, they are not the same as government coercion; it is a different in kind and not just degree. Furthermore, Schauer claims that what is described as 'private censorship' is more usually an example of necessary social choices about the way that resources are used. We choose how to respond to and evaluate speech, and we have to make necessary choices about which guests to allow into our homes (to speak). As editors of newspapers or broadcasting stations, we have to choose what content to include, just as members of the audience choose what to read or receive. Where choices are necessary to the purposes of an institution (for example, the criteria which are essential to

---

[32] Barendt (n 4) 106.
[33] Schauer (n 5) 116–25.

running a media outlet, a library, an academic journal, or a government), interference with freedom of speech is not usually an issue.

The difficulty with this attempt to rationalise the public-private distinction is that it takes for granted the existing pattern of social structures. But such patterns, including private property rights, reflect a complex of interests. They are the product of policy choices over time and their current configuration is not inevitable. This means that free speech choices are not always necessary. It also means that government should not be absolved from reconfiguring relationships between private individuals or institutions where liberties or interests are at stake.

In relation to the media, it is not credible to maintain that private organisations do not have a public function in addition to their private activities. The media's claims to have a special role in democratic life, together with their close affiliation with freedom of speech, are predicated on the belief that they are serving public purposes. Even without those claims, the ubiquity of modern media in everyday transactions demonstrates that they are not an optional mode of communication but are integral to social life. Their choices to restrict access to their platforms will have the power, therefore, to restrict conversation and debate.

Taking these considerations into account, together with the idea that state omissions may themselves constitute interference with liberty, there is a case for intervening in private media activity in order to prevent its negative impact on freedom of speech. As Lichtenberg has remarked, why should corporations be trusted over governments to make the correct decisions about whom to allow access? The case is more compelling when a strong, active conception of speech activity is deployed. For it seems to imply that there should be a form of universal access to potentially accessible audiences, and there is no reason why private structures should be immune from that requirement.

Is State Action to Remove Impediments Itself an Impediment to Free Speech?

There appears to be justification for at least some state interventions in speech activity, whether it is a matter of purposive policy, or of positive action to prevent interference with speech. But the traditional approach to freedom of speech is reluctant to acknowledge a role for the state in protecting speech. Two sets of argument are deployed by defenders of a traditional approach to free speech, neither of which appears convincing, however.

a) Antipathy to any State Action in General

Antipathy to state action in general seems unsophisticated. After all, it is the state which guarantees and enforces rights and liberties. The problem stems from an unwillingness to distinguish the political power of government from legitimised constitutional power. The latter is necessary for the law and its system of rights, however defined. From a libertarian perspective, it is not usually considered justifiable to interfere with speech simply because the government disagrees with the content. However, it does not necessarily follow that all state interference is not justified. It is not only libertarians who tend to believe that, since is it not easy to know whether government can make the distinction, the more prudent approach is to limit state interference. But modern democracies employ legal and regulatory structures to implement, with appropriate checks and balances, various policies for the public good. It does not seem logical to exclude regulation of speech.

b) Evaluative Neutrality is Particularly Relevant to Speech.

Alexander has argued that evaluative neutrality is the core of free expression.[34] This entails that no point of view can be privileged and that, therefore, government cannot be partisan in promoting the values it endorses. He claims that government cannot, in fact, maintain neutrality, because it operates within a liberal normative framework that values certain kinds of speech over others. This leads him to conclude that a right to freedom of expression cannot be defended.[35] From a different perspective, Fish has argued that there is no such thing as free speech, because all speech is constrained by the values of the societies or communities in which it takes place.[36]

For our purposes, both perspectives are of interest because they imply that any state involvement in speech regulation will necessarily constitute an impediment to free speech. The assertion is that a commitment to protecting speech will necessarily involve censorship of views which are contrary to that commitment. There is an engaging paradox here: how can the state allow content to be voiced which disapproves of free speech? Furthermore, free speech doctrine never permits any speech

---

[34] A view shared by Schauer.

[35] L. Alexander, *Is There a Right to Freedom of Expression?* (2005).

[36] S. Fish, *There's No Such Thing as Free Speech, and It's a Good Thing, Too* (Oxford: OUP, 1994). See also M. Robertson, "Principle, pragmatism and paralysis" (2003) 16 *Legal Theory*, 287.

unconditionally; some kinds of speech are always valued over others, notwithstanding attempts to impose strict scrutiny for content neutrality.

Attractive as the assertion first appears, it is based on two related but mistaken assumptions. One is that state facilitation of the expression of viewpoints is the same as endorsing them. The other is that state decisions about permissible speech content have implications for the institution of free speech itself. Alexander's theory describes a one-step process, whereas at least two are involved. If the institution of free speech is valuable, we can still tolerate advocacy of the abolition of free speech, without conceding that the institution should be removed. Freedom of speech can be protected by the state in a neutral way in the first part of the process, which endorses a set of values unrelated to content: a context of fair play, fair discussion, moral agency, respect for what a speaker brings to a non-violent interaction. The second part of the process involves a decision about what should be done; here it may well be decided that free speech should be overridden for justifiable reasons. It follows that regulation to remove impediments to somebody's freedom to speech should not be characterised as an act of partisan support for the sets of speech otherwise not favoured.

AGENTS OF SPEECH

This third dimension of liberty of speech has not received as much attention as the objects of speech and the nature of impediments to speech. Agents of speech obviously include individuals, and the agency dimension is significant because the purpose of recognising the liberty is to enable speakers to identify themselves as holding or endorsing particular points of view. In relation to the media, however, it raises the question of whether organisations have speech rights capable of being interfered with. If media organisations' communication activities interfere with individuals' attempts to speak, is state intervention to prevent that interference itself an encroachment on the organisation's freedom of speech?

Traditionally, the exercise of governmental power has been regarded as the major threat to freedom of expression. But it is no longer controversial to note that the media also wield considerable power over the environment in which free speech can take place. The media present both opportunities and problems for personal expression and the deliberative process. They provide platforms, but not for everybody or every viewpoint. They have strong emotional power, exemplified by the immediacy of impact of television and radio, and the human interest sensationalism of the press. They provide information, but not comprehensively—they can be inaccurate and they are selective. These features extend to new media and new forms of communicative interaction, which themselves raise additional issues. For example, in general, the aggregation of popularity and other kinds of preferences may take priority over reflective consideration and, in particular, social networking websites may exacerbate problems such as invasions of privacy, bullying, defamation or discriminatory speech. Yet, for all that, user content distributed through new media has at least the potential to complement, and even provide appropriately subversive corrections to, the mainstream. The difficulty in determining how much latitude should be given to the media is that, as organisations, media perform significant public functions in addition to their commercial enterprise, yet they have considerable control over individuals' speech activity.

The traditional approach to freedom of speech displays some ambivalence here. Media are not accorded special rights as organisations. But individuals within the media—proprietors, editors and journalists—enjoy the same freedom to speak as other individuals. At the same time, the special value of media activities for democracy is recognised in freedom of speech doctrine.[37] It is easy to believe, therefore, that the beneficial role of the media would be diminished if their freedom to provide positive contributions to speech and communication were to be restricted. It then seems easy to go further, and to suggest that the media should be able to claim that their speech activities merit special protection.

However, as O'Neill has noted,[38] the idea of freedom of speech was typically developed and articulated in the context of small scale publications or meetings. It was not intended to apply to institutions or organisations but to individuals. We value media power because it can be strong enough to resist political power, whether through rational debate or by puncturing personal affectations. But it is not unconditional—freedom for proprietors to use their media and communications property is not same as freedom of expression. The problem is that the media's business model often requires the delivery of kinds of speech that might be

---

[37] This has been reiterated time and again. Examples include: *Observer & Guardian v UK* (1991) 14 EHRR 1537; *Bergens Tidende v Norway* (2001) 31 EHRR 16.

[38] O. O'Neill, *A Question of Trust* (BBC Reith Lectures 2002) (Cambridge: CUP, 2002) chapter 5.

thought democratically unacceptable in order to subsidise the offer of more acceptable speech. When speech is deployed by a speaker who commands the resources of a large media organisation, it takes on a different character. Rather than being a manifestation of expression, it becomes an incidence of the ownership that reflects the property right.[39] This does not mean that the media's 'voice' cannot be identified; editorial decisions are likely to reflect substantive viewpoints. Indeed, Fiss regards those as worthy of constitutional protection, since, as he puts it, the media are soapbox (a forum) and speaker.[40] At the same time, the relative balance of the media's power over others' resources to speak, as against their facilitating the personal speech of owners, editors or journalists, suggests that the latter cannot prevail when the wider protection of freedom of speech is at stake. This is especially the case where media accept a public role for themselves.

It may nevertheless be objected that any interference with choices about the content that the media communicate is necessarily an infringement of the personal liberty of speech of the owners, editors or journalist, because it represents the belief that reports of others' views are worth conveying and, as an expression of that belief, must attract the same protection as directly-held personal opinion. The choice could be considered analogous to the manner and form of expression, a matter which should generally be left to the speaker's discretion.[41] The analogy breaks down, however, because the object of the protection, and the values that it supports, is not to consolidate power to control resources but to provide opportunities for autonomous communication and the circulation of opinion. Those are not necessarily compromised by constraints on the deployment of media organisations' resources. In any event, requiring media outlets to publish something (for example, providing for speakers to have access, or structuring the way that material is presented to achieve balance or impartiality) does not mean that they are unable to publish their own different viewpoint. Nor, as discussed above, would such requirements entail editorial endorsement. Generally, the media should not be able to raise a purported liberty to speak as a defence against state action to protect freedom of speech more broadly.

---

[39] See also Barendt, (n 4) 421.

[40] Fiss, (n 24) 1410.

[41] Examples of judicial endorsement of this point are: *Jersild v Denmark* (1994) 14 EHRR 1; *AG v English* [1983] 1 AC 116.

IMPLICATIONS OF A STRONG CONCEPTION OF SPEECH ACTIVITY

This analysis of the three dimensions of freedom of speech suggests that the traditional approach is unconvincing because it does not reflect an intelligible conception of the value that speech holds for moral agents. By contrast, a strong conception of freedom of speech holds that: the significant interest to be protected is the freedom to seek out speech activity; that the state is justified in intervening to secure that protection; and that such intervention should extend to the private control of speech activities. As already indicated, one implication is that some degree of access to the media may be justified insofar as the media provide opportunities for seeking out speech activity. Another implication is that policies intend to enhance interaction and discussion between speakers should be regarded in a positive light. Whether state action is necessary to implement such measures is a different question, and it may depend on how successful other methods, such as self-regulation, can be.

Access to the Media

What would this entail in practice? At the personal level, striking up conversation with other individuals is regulated by informal rules for social interaction but, where a wider audience is sought, a public platform is needed. That much is recognised in what Fiss has described as the 'street-corner' tradition in free speech doctrine,[42] and in the closely related doctrine of freedom of assembly.[43] Insofar as the media have a public role in communications, for speech which takes place through the media, the analogous need is for a facility for speakers to solicit audience interest. This does not amount to a claim for full access to the media.[44] However, it does entail that editors give serious attention to speakers' wishes to connect with their audiences or readerships. Such minimal access rights might involve, for example, editors informing the audience that they have received requests for a range of viewpoints to be conveyed, perhaps providing a representative sample of viewpoints, and inviting responses— which might lead to no more than a blog, but which might merit some detailed treatment of the issue. Once such a conversation or discussion is

---

[42] Fiss, (n 24) 1410.
[43] Barendt, (n 4) chapter 8.
[44] Most notably advocated by Jerome Barron: J. Barron, *Freedom of the Press for Whom? The Right of Access to the Mass Media* (Bloomington: University of Indiana Press, 1973).

joined, there is a need for some structuring of exchanges to allow the parties to make a contribution. Again, just as this applies to face-to-face encounters, so there is an analogous requirement in the media for the presentation of different points of view.

The question of how such protection of speech is funded is a separate question. The implication is that private media organisations should be prepared to modify their behaviour sufficiently to support the minimal level of accessibility to an audience which is required. In response to market demand, much media is already an integrated experience for some users, with the use of web sites to complement newspaper or broadcast material with comments, forums and blogs. Such facilities make it easier, and with low additional marginal costs, for private operators to provide the minimal access that a strong conception of free speech activity requires. There continues to be a case for provision of such access through public service content. Indeed, one consequence of accepting this strong conception of freedom of speech is that it enables aspects of public service to be recognised as a liberty of speech issue as well as one of democracy and social inclusion. Furthermore, insofar as Internet communication provides the opportunity for speakers to become known to audiences and users, the provision of universal broadband is also a liberty of speech issue.

Positive Policy Measures

These are minimal requirements. Some aspirational improvement of freedom of speech is also desirable and the strong version of free speech may work, not so much to create new rights, but to limit what can be seen as a constraint on speech. Hence, if there is a policy to enhance speech, through positive action, that need not be seen as an interference with somebody else's speech.

The values that justify the special status of speech (truth, democracy, self-fulfilment) and which characterise its purposes (communicative autonomy, multiplicity of viewpoints and enhancement of public debate) are the ones that justify active policies measures to ensure that it is worthwhile. In order to enhance the worth of speech, state regulation can take measures to increase the amount of speech available. Structural regulation, such as media ownership rules or merger rules, are intended to increase the plurality of sources of information, allowing others to speak and enabling audiences to experience more speech. Content regulation may be used to increase the diversity of material (for example, requirements for a variety of genres and the reflection of a range of views, requirements about impartiality and context, and rules providing for access to the media in general or at least during elections). All these are consistent with a stronger conception of freedom of speech. The other general approach is to attempt to improve the quality of free speech. This may involve interference in the way that a particular speaker (or media outlet) exercises the freedom, a limitation on the freedom for the sake of achieving a better quality of communication overall. Examples are the rules about accuracy, impartiality and fairness in broadcasting regulation. However, such limitations will not be regarded as being too intrusive if a strong conception of freedom of speech is accepted, since that entails access to a conversation or dialogue. One further implication is that the press and other non-broadcasting media should not regard themselves as immune from such regulation where they acknowledge a public role in facilitating engagement between speakers. Finally, although it typically does not involve close regulation, speakers may be encouraged to speak, and speak effectively, through education and media literacy programmes.

Self- or Co-regulation as Alternatives to State Power?

Even if the argument for 'positive' regulation is accepted, it may be objected that such regulation need not involve state power, and that some variation on self regulation will be adequate to meet public policy objectives. Self regulation may be favoured for the following reasons: it enables industry expertise to be deployed to achieve effective compliance with standards; its costs may be more efficient and are not met by the public purse; it can provide speedier and cheaper complaints procedures and remedies; they command the respect of the industry which is more likely to comply. However sceptics may ask: whether an industry can be trusted to formulate adequate standards and police them effectively to serve public objectives; whether informal procedures are sufficiently fair; whether the process can be sufficiently accountable.[45] It is not always appreciated that a necessary condition for successful self regulation is that there is a coincidence of interest between the industry and public objectives. Without that, there will be a tension which, in the absence of state power, will tend to resolve itself in favour of the industry.

---

[45] See generally, R. Baldwin, M. Cave & M. Lodge *Understanding Regulation: Theory, Strategy and Practice* (Oxford: OUP, 2nd ed. 2012, chapter 8).

In the media, the BBC has been a relatively successful model of self regulation. It invented the broadcasting norms that are now used to judge it and its peers. It is perhaps ironic that it has recently had regulation imposed on it (except for its duties relating to impartiality),[46] whereas the press industry has not. Indeed, until recently (that is, until the expansion of providers that media convergence has stimulated), broadcasters in general have shared a core of values that seemed to be endorsed by the public. By contrast, the press has not displayed the conceptual uniformity of aims that a successful system of self regulation requires. It has successfully exploited an apparent tension between the public objective of protecting freedom of expression and other public objectives such as requiring accuracy, respect for privacy, and the fair administration of justice. It does not acknowledge that the two sets of objectives may be consistent. At a practical level, it may be an empirical question as to whether the Press Complaints Commission (PCC) delivers an adequate level of regulation. Current criticisms, from Parliament and others suggest that it does not.[47] The onus seems to be on it to demonstrate that the system is not just self-serving, but is legitimate and deserving of public trust. Calcutt's reports, in the early 1990s, threatened statutory supervision if a self regulatory scheme were to fail in the press industry.[48] Since then, the industry has exploited an understandable reluctance to impose state control by claiming the PCC's complaints mechanism to be a viable alternative, but its willingness to provide an effective scheme remains open to doubt.[49]

The experience of the PCC contrasts with that of the Advertising Standards Agency, where public objectives and those of the advertising

---

[46] Communications Act 2003, s.198; Department for Culture, Media and Sport, *An Agreement Between Her Majesty's Secretary of State for Culture, Media and Sport and the British Broadcasting Corporation* (London: HMSO, 2006) Cm 6872, clauses 43–63.

[47] Culture, Media and Sport Committee, "Press standards, privacy and libel" HC, (2009–10) 362-I & II; Media Standards Trust, *Can Independent Self-Regulation Keep Standards High and Preserve Press Freedom?* (Media Standards Trust, London 2010) available at http://mediastandardstrust.org/wp-content/uploads/downloads/2010/08/Reforming-independent-self-regulation.pdf (accessed 1 May 2012).

[48] D. Calcutt (Chairman), *Report of the Committee on Privacy and Related Matters* (London: HMSO, 1991) Cm. 1102; D. Calcutt, *Review of Press Regulation* (London: HMSO, 1993) Cm. 2135.

[49] Independent Governance Review (Vivien Hepworth, Chairman), *The Governance of the Press Complaints Commission: an Independent Review* (London 2010) available at http://www.pccgovernancereview.org.uk/index.html (accessed 1 May 2012). The review was based at the PCC's offices and its separate website uses the PCC's house style. The Leveson Inquiry, set up in 2011 in the wake of a major phone-hacking scandal involving News International, is currently examining the culture, practices and ethics of the media: see http://www.levesoninquiry.org.uk/ (accessed 1 May 2012).

industry do appear to coincide: both favour honest and truthful advertising, if possibly for different motives. At the other end of the spectrum between voluntary and enforced regulation, in the broadcasting sector, statutory regulation has been imposed to force the industry to work within a framework of public objectives and that appears to have been successful in maintaining the appropriate standards.[50] A contemporary trend is to consider more flexible arrangements between industries and the state, and to provide for various permutations of voluntary and imposed regulation, encapsulated by the notion of 'co-regulation'.[51] It has been adopted in relation to broadcast advertising, for Channel 3 programming promises and, recently, for television on demand.[52] In other areas of the new media, such as the Internet and mobile telephony, the prospects for self regulation look poor, because there is no coherent body of industry opinion and support that could sustain it.

These considerations may lead to the conclusion that self-regulation or co-regulation need to be used selectively in protecting free speech activity, because they are likely to have varying degrees of success according to the nature of the media industry which adopts them. But that conclusion assumes that state restraint in this area is the default position. In doing so, it takes for granted the traditional approach to freedom of speech and the minimalist conception of speech activity that it envisages. As discussed earlier, a strong conception of speech activity requires that the state should not avoid responsibility for the protection of speech, in particular, access to the audience and fair participation in dialogue. In such a case, the presumption should be the other way, that the state will indeed intervene to protect an interest as basic and important as freedom of speech. That does not mean that forms of self-regulation have no role to play, but that the media industry cannot be tolerated to specify the public objectives at stake. State regulation is justifiably the starting point for enforcing

---

[50] A notable example relates to premium rate telephone services relating to games and voting on programming: Ofcom, *The Communications Market 2007* (London: Ofcom, 2008) para. 215, available at http://stakeholders.ofcom.org.uk/market-data-research/market-data/communications-market-reports/cmr07/tv/ (accessed 1 May 2012).

[51] See Hans-Bredow-Institut, Hamburg & the Institute of European Media Law, *Final Report: Study on Co-Regulation Measures in the Media Sector* (European Commission, Brussels2006) Study for the European Commission, Directorate Information Society and Media.

[52] The Association for Television On-Demand was designated as Ofcom's co-regulator for on demand programme services on 18 March 2010. See http://stakeholders.ofcom.org.uk/broadcasting/tv/video-on-demand/ (accessed 1 May 2012).

the democratic interest in freedom of speech and the role of the industry should be, at most, as part of some form of co-regulatory scheme.

STATE ACTION TO FURTHER PROMOTE FREE SPEECH

If it is accepted that the primary interest in the freedom to speak is the capacity to engage in dialogue with others, this has wider implications for the doctrine of freedom of speech. It suggests that, in deciding what might be a justifiable interference in speech, the impact on exchange and dialogue should be a major consideration. It does appear that, within our core moral and political framework, considerable value is given to the process of deliberation—rationality is valued, both in itself and as part of the democratic process. This implies that, prior to decision making, no viewpoints should be ruled out of consideration merely because of their content or their source. Nor should there be constraints on at least seeking to reopen a decision process. In this sense, open-mindedness, neutrality and a respect for others' points of view are key characteristics of the speech 'environment' that we value, one which enhances the legitimacy of the democratic process. But this does not mean that such a 'neutral' process cannot or should not lead to decisions about speech itself, including the prioritisation of some kinds of speech as more important than others. We do not allow 'free' speakers to incite to violence, at one end of a spectrum, and we can equally ask for media reporting to be accurate and to reflect a diversity of viewpoints, at the other. Both reflect a conception of democratic deliberation where, ultimately, the force of reflective argument is valued as the way to achieve progress. Within that context, we have to choose what contribution we want the media to make to freedom of expression. Indeed, we already do so, for example, in contemporary debates about public service broadcasting, the problem of differential audiences for news and current affairs, the role of partisan reporting, the relationship between emotional and rational coverage of events, the quality of children's programming, the influence of celebrity culture, the status of fundamental beliefs, and more. New and different forms of media power require a similar, substantive theory of free expression by way of response. To the extent that the state is the manifestation of democratic expression, it is too crude to say that there is no place at all for state power to be used to secure the kind of speech that we consider appropriate for our society. Its legitimacy certainly depends on the extent to which there exist sufficient checks and balances to enable citizens to control undue exercises of power. We recognise state intervention in many areas of social policy on this basis and, while the free speech principle requires much pause before action, it does not rule out legislation or other forms of regulation. Rather, and especially under a strong conception of speech activity, it requires positive awareness of the impact on speech not only of state intervention but also state failure to become involved.

IMPOSITION OR EMPOWERMENT? FREEDOM OF SPEECH, BROADCASTING AND IMPARTIALITY[1]

Steven Barnett

INTRODUCTION: THE EUROPEAN VERSUS THE AMERICAN APPROACH

Is it possible to reconcile the notion of an unqualified freedom to speak your mind—the bedrock of any definition of democracy—with a statutory obligation imposed on broadcasters by central government to ensure that TV and radio output is impartial?

For those who adhere rigorously to the letter of the American Constitution's First Amendment—that "Congress shall make no law ... abridging freedom of speech, or of the press"—the answer to this philosophical question is easy: no law means no law, even if such lack of intervention places certain voices or commercial institutions in a position of greater power and influence. American sociologist Michael Schudson recounts the story of a candidate for political office in Florida in 1972 who demanded a right of reply to critical coverage in the Miami Herald, was refused, and whose case eventually went to the US Supreme Court. In a unanimous judgement, America's highest court found for the newspaper's freedom to make its own judgement rather than run the risk of government intrusion. In Schudson's words: "if the marketplace is to be the censor, that may be regrettable, but it is fully in accord with the Constitution. It is *state* censorship that the Constitution forbids" (2003:202, italics in original).

This fundamentalist approach to the First Amendment was reinforced during the 1980s by a deregulatory market-led approach to communications policy-making. It was encapsulated by Mark Fowler, the Reagan-appointed Chairman of the Federal Communications Commission (FCC) from 1981–7, who famously expressed the view that television was "just another appliance.... a toaster with pictures" (Horwitz, 1989; Barnett, 2008; Freedman, 2008). Under Fowler, the FCC voted to abolish the "Fairness Doctrine", which had been America's equivalent to the impartiality

---

[1] Research for this chapter has been supported by the Arts and Humanities Research Council.

obligations still in place throughout Western Europe. At the heart of this decision, as with the Miami Herald case related by Schudson, was a deep-seated antipathy to any notion that the state might intervene to prescribe content. Such a course of action, argued the FCC, would "increase the government's intrusion into the editorial decision making process of broadcast journalists" and would "enlarge the opportunity for governmental officials to abuse the doctrine for partisan political purposes" (quoted in Bollinger, 1990:358).

Europe historically has been more comfortable with state intervention as a means of promoting the public interest, a difference that is rooted in cultural and philosophical differences between the two continents. Writing about two different traditions in respect of jurisprudential attitudes to privacy, for example, one author commented recently:

> What is at stake are two different core sets of values: on the one hand, a European interest in personal dignity, threatened primarily by the mass media; on the other hand, an American interest in liberty, threatened primarily by the government. On both sides of the Atlantic, these values are founded on deeply felt sociopolitical ideals, whose histories reach back to the revolutionary era of the later eighteenth century (Whitman, 2004:1219).

This particular conclusion was predicated on an examination specifically of France and Germany, and more wide-ranging studies have shown that media systems can differ substantially within Western Europe.[2] Hallin and Mancini's classic comparative study (2004) distinguished between what they called the Polarised Pluralist Model (loosely found in southern Europe), the Democratic Corporatist Model (Northern Europe), and the Liberal Model, essentially the US, Britain and Ireland. While the Corporatist model would quite happily accommodate, for example, press subsidies for threatened newspapers (as in Norway and Sweden), these would be inconceivable in the UK. Despite these manifest inter-nation differences, however, Hallin and Mancini can correctly contrast "the European tradition of the active state" with the First Amendment absolutism of the United States which instinctively turns its face against any state-sponsored intervention in the free market. In broadcasting, an integral element of this political philosophy has been the imposition of public

---

[2] By contrast the media systems of most of the former Soviet Bloc East European countries are still evolving from the totalitarian centralised monopolies of the communist era when state intervention was precisely synonymous with propaganda and state censorship.

service obligations, including a requirement on broadcasters to provide coverage of important public affairs in an impartial and balanced manner.

IMPARTIALITY IN BRITAIN

Impartiality was only formally incorporated within the BBC Licence in 1996, but had been accepted as an integral aspiration for the BBC since it first started reporting in the 1920s. With regard to commercial broadcasting, the impartiality requirements were imposed by statute at its inception in 1954. The easy passage of impartiality requirements during parliamentary discussions of how commercial television would operate was facilitated by discontent within the Labour Party opposition that a private enterprise approach to news would inevitably bring a right-wing bias to coverage of politics.[3] Section 3 of the 1954 Television Act therefore placed a duty on the new regulatory body, the Independent Television Authority (ITA), to ensure that "programmes maintain a proper balance in their subject matter"; that "any news given in the programmes (in whatever form) is presented with due accuracy and impartiality"; and that due impartiality must be preserved on "matters of political or industrial controversy or relating to current public policy".

This statutory obligation was reinforced not only by the oversight of a powerful regulatory body, the ITA, but also by ensuring that a senior member of the ITA attended all meetings of the commercial news supplier "to watch the operation of the news through the eyes of the Act" (Lindley, 2003:9). With very little change these statutory obligations have continued through the years, appearing most recently in sections 319 and 320 of the Communications Act 2003 which require that "news included in television and radio services is presented with due impartiality" and that this applies to "matters of political or industrial controversy" and to "matters relating to current public policy". Interpretation and implementation of the law has over the years been left to the successive regulatory bodies, which have provided a series of codes to guide broadcasting practice and against which any alleged transgressions can be measured. This duty now falls to the converged regulator Ofcom, and Section 5 of its Broadcasting Code (last updated in December 2009) provides a detailed exposition of

---

[3] Their fears were exacerbated further when two of the first three consortia to be awarded contracts for commercial television licences featured newspaper groups with long-standing Conservative affiliations.

how the notion of "due" impartiality is interpreted to cope with the multi-plicity of broadcast outlets in a multi-channel world:

> "Due" is an important qualification to the concept of impartiality. Impartiality itself means not favouring one side over another. "Due" means adequate or appropriate to the subject and nature of the programme. So "due impartiality" does not mean an equal division of time has to be given to every view, or that every argument and every facet of every argument has to be represented. The approach to due impartiality may vary according to the nature of the subject, the type of programme and channel, the likely expectation of the audience as to content, and the extent to which the content and approach is signalled to the audience. (Ofcom, 2009:23).

While these requirements have historically been accepted as an integral element of the licence to broadcast, they have not always met unanimous approval and have prompted some deep-seated hostility at both ends of the political spectrum. Radicals of left and right have periodically bemoaned what they see as the chilling effect of a statutory regime which disqualifies polemicists and—depending on their political leanings— either provides a platform for an institutionalised left-liberal view of the world, or upholds a comfortable establishment perspective which silences serious dissent. One of the UK's great television documentary makers, John Pilger, has frequently railed against the restrictions of impartiality describing the word itself as "almost Orwellian in the perversity of its opposite meaning" (quoted in Knightley, 2001:72).[4] More recently, he has continued to condemn the "journalistic myths of a neutral, non-political centre" which he believes underpins an essentially right-wing market liberalism and is all the more dangerous for its lack of acknowledgement (Pilger, 2002).

In his scathing assessment of the establishment view of impartiality, Pilger's criticisms echo those made in the 1970s and 1980s by a number of critical media scholars in the wake of television coverage of industrial conflicts such as the miners' strikes. They argued that a cloak of impartiality actually concealed a fundamental in-built establishment bias in which industry leaders, government ministers, and "official" voices

---

[4] Through his personal and committed journalistic style, Pilger has found himself at odds not just with commercial television's regulator but with the British television establishment. The venerated doyen of British television journalism, Robin Day, refused to present him with BAFTA's Richard Dimbleby award for his contribution to factual television on the basis that it should be reserved for practioners who respected the tradition of due impartiality in British television (Hayward, 2001).

were privileged. Radical perspectives that did not fit within this consensual framework were, it was argued, not entertained; and the labels of impartiality and balance disguised the implicitly ideological nature of television news in favour of powerful elites (Hall et al, 1978; Philo, 1990; Eldridge, 1993; Pedelty, 1995). The same arguments were summarised more recently by the former television current affairs producer turned distinguished academic, Brian Winston, who argued that the due impartiality requirements, when first introduced in 1954, were "nothing but a threadbare attempt on the part of our political masters to curtail free expression by limiting the range of acceptable opinions on air", and that little has changed in the intervening period (2004:22). His view that it is time to "let go of nurse" chimes with the First Amendment approach of the United States.

Meanwhile, different oppositional arguments have been fuelled by the libertarianism of the free-market right, prompted both by aversion to any government-sponsored inhibition and by the exponential rise in the number of television and radio channels. Increasingly, these arguments coalesce around the concept of consumer sovereignty, and a conviction that the proliferation of new electronic news sources—including online versions of the print media—vitiate old arguments about spectrum scarcity, and render the long-standing distinction between print and broadcast media superfluous. These arguments were forcefully articulated by James Murdoch, during his 2009 MacTaggart lecture at the Edinburgh Television Festival, when he said that the effect of a system which imposed impartiality was "not to curb bias... but simply disguise it". He went on:

> We should be honest about this: it is an impingement on freedom of speech and on the right of people to choose what kind of news to watch. How in an all-media marketplace can we justify this degree of control in one place and not in others?... [The free press] is driven by the daily demand and choices of millions of people... why do we continue to assume that [a different] approach is appropriate for broadcasting: especially as one communications medium is now barely distinguishable from another? (Murdoch, 2009)

Questions have of course been raised about the commercial self-interest of such protestations, and the extent to which Rupert and James Murdoch simply want to clear the path for an ideologically committed and unencumbered version of Fox News in the UK (e.g. Petley, 2003). It is certainly true that Rupert Murdoch has expressed his desire to see Britain's Sky News move closer to the Fox model. When asked by the *New York Times* in 2003 whether Sky News had begun imitating Fox, Murdoch's reported response was: "I wish. I think that Sky News is very popular and they are doing well, but they don't have the entertaining talk shows—it is just a rolling half-hour of hard news all the time." (Kirkpatrick, 2003). However, he made it clear to a visiting delegation from the House of Lords Communications Committee in 2008 that his quarrel was with the presentational style and pace of the channel rather than the need to abide by impartiality rules.

Whether the Murdochs' approach to impartiality requirements is rooted in commercial self-interest or ideology, their objections reflect a growing trend over the last ten years towards scepticism about the continuing relevance of an impartiality regime in the age of convergence, online news, social networking and twitter feeds. In fact, doubts were being expressed by disinterested commentators even before the most recent technological innovations began to take hold. One media law scholar wrote in 1998 that "it is now difficult to find convincing arguments to justify the imposition of a rigorous impartiality standard on private commercial broadcasters, when none is applied to the print media", and went on to suggest that perhaps the best argument for its continuation was simply tradition (Barendt, 1998:110). Another suggested that "[t]he end of 'objectivity' and 'impartiality' as the guiding principles of an ethic of public service may soon be in sight" (Allan, 1997:319). The rest of this chapter examines the core arguments now being advanced for removing impartiality requirements and the inherent flaws in all those arguments; it examines the crucial and continuing role of impartiality in buffering the impact of industrial consolidation and concentration of media ownership; and it outlines how a reconfigured and more sophisticated definition of impartiality from the BBC has both shored up the relevance of the concept and should help to ensure its survival;.

Questioning the Impartiality Regime

Ironically, one of the first indications of an intellectual shift was prompted by a complaint of bias against Fox News to Ofcom's predecessor regulator, the Independent Television Commission (ITC). Because the channel was available in the UK via Murdoch's BSkyB satellite platform, it was licensed to broadcast by the ITC and therefore obliged to abide by the ITC's editorial code. In June 2003, in one of its final judgements before being folded into Ofcom, the ITC found in favour of Fox News on the basis that its cultural origins were elsewhere and that the phrase "due impartiality" allowed for a flexible interpretation in such cases. It was a pragmatic decision, but illuminated the dilemmas being posed for policy makers who themselves started to question whether such rules were relevant, enforceable or, indeed, potentially damaging for democratic pluralism. There was a growing sense that impartiality had become a far more complex aspiration in a world no longer isolated within parochial national boundaries, and where politics had moved beyond the binary left versus right incarnation of the Cold War era. Fukiyama's "end of history" had given way to a more complex and multi-layered maelstrom of competing ideas and political priorities: from environmentalism to ethical trading, from animal rights to assisted suicide, from Euroscepticism to internationalism, the politics of the 21st century could no longer be squeezed into the classic political straitjacket of two opposing ideologies. It was therefore perhaps not surprising that, as technological changes accompanied a greater political complexity, the regulator itself started to wonder aloud about whether the impartiality regime was still "fit for purpose".

The first overt rumblings of dissent came from the ITC before its dissolution. Writing in 2002, its Director of Policy Dominic Morris emphasised that impartiality was not value-free and comes with usually unspoken baggage of "assumptions, values and principles" which, in a postmodern, multi-ethnic and increasingly globablised society, were subject to new and different sets of interpretative frameworks. He argued that new distribution platforms in television allowed room for the full diversity of opinions to be aired and that clearly identified "opinion channels" should be permitted. The multichannel era was, he said, "the occasion for Britain's regulatory regime to re-assert the values of Locke, Voltaire and Mill. We should trust the robust common sense of all the communities on our Islands to hear a diverse range of views, to tolerate that diversity, and arrive at their own right answer" (Morris, 2002:48–9). This conceptual distinction between "opinion" and "news" was predicated on treating niche television channels as akin to a polemical printed press, with appropriate labelling safeguards for the unsuspecting viewer.

This critical approach to the universal applicability of impartiality in television was reinforced in an official ITC study on News commissioned from Cardiff University and published in the same year. The main author at Cardiff, Ian Hargreaves—a seasoned journalist who had occupied very senior editorial positions at the BBC, the Independent and Financial Times—was to play a highly influential part in the debate as a founding member of the Ofcom board. The study, a comprehensive examination of consumption and content as well as policy options in television news, was explicitly contextualised in terms of "a perceived crisis in journalism. ...

which is blamed for the decline in levels of political engagement and
voter participation in advanced democracies" and was timed to coincide
with the debate on the Communications Bill that was to culminate in
the 2003 Act (Hargreaves and Thomas, 2002:9). It therefore introduced
a different rationale for questioning the impartiality regime. They argued
that anxiety over democratic engagement where particular demographic groups—in particular, ethnic minorities and young people—were
deserting political news and eschewing political participation could be
somehow linked to a journalistic culture of impartiality in television.
Despite the flimsiest of empirical evidence (as I argue below) either that
there was indeed a crisis of democratic engagement or that any link could
be made between engagement and journalistic impartiality, the authors
made the following policy recommendation:

> ..... [T]here is among Britain's ethnic minorities and indeed other groups,
> such as the young, a sense that mainstream broadcast news does not repre-
> sent them or their interests well, fairly or with insight. It may be that a more
> opinionated style of broadcast news, originated from well outside the UK
> broadcasting mainstream, is helpful in the overall news mix, so long as con-
> sumers are aware what they are getting and which services conform to
> impartiality rules and which do not. The time has come when a range of
> experimentation should be encouraged.....(Ibid.:105)

Other voices from the industry echoed these sentiments, sensing a changing tide of professional opinion and themselves becoming anxious about
a lack of diversity in television news agendas. Interviewed for the ITC
report, the Head of News and Current Affairs at Channel 5, Chris Shaw,
argued that Fox News was striking because "it feels passionate.... Their
anchors engage—they call it like they think it.... What annoys me is how
same-ish all this news is. We're all covering the same stories in pretty
much the same way. That's something that the establishment welcomes
and it's fostered by a tough climate of regulation" (Ibid.:98).[5] Shaw's analysis was endorsed the following year by the then head of BBC television
news, Roger Mosey. Interviewed by the Guardian, Mosey argued that "In
my personal view, the right way forward is to ensure that some clearly-
designated services have an obligation to truth, decency and the representation of a diversity of views; but the rest should have the freedom to take

---

[5] Shaw reiterated his views a year later in the Guardian: "I feel very strongly that this is
the way forward for television news. It upsets me that we have genuine diversity in the
printed press and very little diversity in the TV news world." (Wells and Cassy, 2003).

any view within the law of the land.... [Fox News Channel] is feisty, provocative and engaging: a stone chucked into the pool of the broadcasting consensus.... [T]hat is the joy of the new broadcasting environment: choice rules" (Wells and Cassy, 2002).

The notion of consumer choice was a seductive refrain, but suffered from one enduring drawback: surveys of public opinion showed consistently, in the words of Hargreaves and Thomas themselves, "very strong public support for the existing regime of broadcasting impartiality". Viewers reared on a medium entrusted with values of unbiased truth-telling were not convinced of the case for letting it go. Other voices, particularly those well acquainted with the opinionated style of Fox and American radio shock-jocks, warned against the overweening power of certain well-funded voices to distort the range of available opinions. One particularly influential opponent of change was Lord David Puttnam, who chaired an all-party review of the Broadcasting Bill and was instrumental in achieving some key amendments as it passed through its legislative stages in the House of Lords. He argued at the time: "The idea that loosening regulation would enhance diversity is.... a fool's bargain. In practice, it's likely that one very well-funded partisan voice, probably a deviant version of Sky News, would drown out most of the others." (Puttnam, 2003) This certainly represented a majority view in Parliament as well as amongst the public, a unity of purpose between the political classes and the electorate which ultimately ensured that impartiality rules remained intact.

It was left to the new regulator Ofcom to adopt a form of words in its Broadcasting Code (outlined above) which allows for the same flexible interpretation of "due impartiality" as originally applied by the ITC, varying according to the type of programme and channel as well as to "likely audience expectation". The discretion thus afforded to and liberally interpreted by the regulator clearly signalled a genuflection to the array of niche channels available through various global transmission systems (including the web), and is the basis on which culturally specific channels like Fox, Russia Today and Al Jazeera can be licensed by Ofcom without objection. This discretion does not, however, extend to blatant editorialising, and Ofcom has demonstrated its willingness to censure broadcasters who clearly breach the code, including the threat of sanctions for further violations.[6]

---

[6] An example of such intervention was the action taken by Ofcom in 2007 against the TalkSport radio station in respect of a broadcast by the then Respect MP George Galloway.

Even the adoption of a flexible code did not, however, prevent Ofcom from revisiting arguments around disengagement and impartiality. In 2007, in anticipation of the switchover to digital television in 2012, its comprehensive examination of television news again attempted to create a causal link between declining interest in news, disengagement with politics, and the impartiality regime in television journalism.

Once again, the regulator's approach was characterised by a tendentious use of empirical data which raised serious questions about its neutral approach to "evidence-based" policy making. A chapter headed "Disengagement, trust and impartiality" was designed to examine "the public policy questions arising from increased disengagement from news; and whether due impartiality is still relevant as a core value in television news"—thereby connecting two entirely separate issues. (Ofcom, 2007:59). There was no effort to deconstruct what was meant by "disengagement" from news, nor to theorise how removal of impartiality requirements might promote a greater interest in either political affairs or television news.[7] The report simply reiterated unsubstantiated claims from those opposed to maintaining the status quo, that "relaxation of impartiality rules for channels other than the main PSBs might encourage the emergence of new and alternative voices [which] might encourage greater engagement" (Ibid.:65). Nevertheless, the regulator felt justified in raising two policy-related questions arising directly from its own flawed logic:

> For channels other than the main PSBs, is impartiality still important, or is it a barrier to diversity in an era with a wide range of services available to viewers? Subject to changes in legislation, should other channels be allowed to offer partial news in the same way that newspapers and some websites do at present? (Ibid.:71).

What emerges on a careful reading of Ofcom's report—and, to a lesser extent, its predecessor document from the ITC—is some serious intellectual confusion about the continuing relevance of impartiality for television journalism and its contribution to diversity, democracy and public

---

Galloway attacked the political and ministerial record of another MP whose constituency he was targeting for the next election, but neither his programme nor the station offered any alternative perspective.

[7] In fact, the "evidence" for disengagement from television news seemed to rely on responses to one statement in an attitude survey that "much of the news on TV is not relevant to me": those agreeing had risen from 34% to 55% since 2002, but it was unclear (and unexplored in the Ofcom report) to what extent the change was attributable to different methodologies or to different stories breaking during the period of fieldwork.

life. By unpicking the different strands of this debate, it is possible to identify five different fallacies implicit in the arguments being propounded for
dismantling the current policy apparatus.

The fallacy of increased political engagement. As we have seen, there is a
lazy tendency to associate impartiality rules with a commonly held theory
that young people, in particular, are becoming disillusioned with politics
and are disengaging themselves from the political process. At its most
extreme, this fallacy holds that democracy itself is endangered by the
imposition of rules on broadcast journalism. The corollary of such an
argument is that, once such impositions are swept away, the flowering of
unrestrained political debate on our TV and radio sets will galvanise the
nation's youth and send them flocking to the voting booths.

Of the many fallacious assumptions here, two stand out. First, there is
plenty of evidence that citizens, both young and old, are very much
engaged informally in the political system without necessarily casting
votes or belonging to a political party. A comprehensive analysis of political engagement in Britain published in 2006 found that "37% of non-
voters were members of, or active in, a charity, community group, public
body or campaigning organisation", and pointed to the massive member-
ship increase in organisations like Friends of the Earth, Greenpeace, the
National Trust and the Countryside Alliance as illustrations of how single
issues or less traditional concepts of politics were now captivating large
numbers of people (The Power Report, 2006). A BBC study four years
earlier similarly reported on a "disconnection" between the public and
national politics as represented by the formal mechanisms in Westminster and Whitehall. (BBC, 2002).

Second, there is no evidence that a highly partisan and committed
media serve to increase voter interest or participation in public affairs.
The UK is renowned for a vocal and fiercely partisan national press which
boasts ten daily national newspapers and a national readership rate which
is the highest in Europe. Why should a partisan television environment
succeed where a partisan newspaper environment has manifestly "failed"?
The US, as we have seen, had its television restrictions removed in the mid
1980s and the emergence of at least one vociferous cheerleader for the
Republican cause in Fox News. Yet concerns in America for the health of
participatory democracy have scarcely abated, even with the "Obama

bounce" of the 2008 presidential election. In the absence of any clear indication to the contrary, it is difficult to find any reliable proof that the removal of impartiality rules will make the slightest difference to citizen involvement in the political process.

The fallacy of greater relevance. There is certainly a prima facie case that certain groups—in particular the young and ethnic minorities—find television news unengaging and unfulfilling for their own purposes. Ofcom's qualitative research amongst Asian, Afro-Caribbean and Muslim groups suggested that many members of these groups were dissatisfied with mainstream UK news bulletins. To some extent, this returns us to the dominant framework thesis developed by critical approaches to television news in the 1970s and 1980s and what Golding and Elliott called "the development of news as a service to elite groups" (1979:209). Critiques of television news grounded in theories of hegemony and the "unconscious" bias inherent in the organisational structures of news have become less popular over the last 20 years, but there are still shades of a television agenda which leaves certain population groups feeling marginalised and certain frames of reference uncovered.

Such critiques, however, were founded on a different conception of impartiality than the imposition of professional news values grounded in notions of accuracy, fairness and objectivity; they argued essentially for wholesale organisational changes in broadcasting and in society. Contemporary arguments about relevance are more narrowly founded on a vague conviction—unsupported by empirical evidence—that allowing broadcast news to be opinionated or partisan would somehow inspire those disaffected groups, particularly the young, with a greater sense of the relevance of television news for their own lives. For younger generations, this is an issue of life-stage: they tend to be less interested in the ramifications of a new economic deal for house prices, or of nuclear treaty negotiations with North Korea for the preservation of world peace. That is a long-standing demographic issue, and certainly not adequate cause for removing the responsibility of broadcasters to report without promoting a pre-determined political agenda.

The fallacy of a more diverse news agenda. A related argument is that television news agendas are almost indistinguishable, demonstrating an unhealthy homogeneity of issues, approaches and reportage (as suggested by Chris Shaw and Roger Mosey, above). My own research has demonstrated that on any given day terrestrial bulletins are unlikely to show much variation: some deviations in running orders, perhaps some different footage, but overall a broad similarity of stories (Barnett et al, 2000). The issue here is not to interrogate the structural or cultural reasons behind such homogeneity, but to question the relevance of removing impartiality restrictions. The notion that somehow allowing broadcasters to approach their editorial agendas unburdened by the need to impose balance will suddenly transform their news agendas is simply fanciful. Even those who support relaxation of existing rules accept the fallacy of this argument. Thus Tim Suter, the senior Ofcom executive responsible for content regulation when its study was published in 2007, wrote a year later:

> [I]t is worth observing that the rules around impartiality only affect the way any given story is presented: they have no bearing on a channel's choice of stories. It is therefore entirely possible that a news service could pursue a policy to exclude particular types of story without triggering any breach of the impartiality rules (Suter, 2008:117).

There is also 20 years of evidence from America where market imperatives have ensured an even more marked homogeneity of output than in the UK. Such an argument also ignores the evidence of broadcast news which emanates from different cultural perspectives or which is specifically designed to reach particular demographic groups. Al-Jazeera's news agenda might offend some viewers in the west, but it does not require a licence to be partisan to prioritise a different set of economic, political or cultural issues. Similarly, the news output from BBC3 or BBC Radio 1— both aimed at young people—can pursue different news agendas without compromising the Corporation's statutory commitment to impartial reporting.

The fallacy of greater ambition in editorial approaches. Some professionals believe that removing impartiality obligations will unleash a creative torrent that might somehow overcome the natural confines of the television medium. This assumption is usually linked to a frustration with the undoubtedly uniform narrative forms adopted by most television journalism. In fact, the last 25–30 years of British television have seen a number of innovations in approach, form and content in news and current affairs: news bulletins have lengthened to half an hour; Channel 4 and Five have provided, respectively, more depth and more dynamism; news analysis programmes like Panorama have provided more context; and even daily news bulletins tend now to offer background detail beyond straight reporting on at least one item each day. These innovations have been enabled— rather than encumbered—by a regulatory framework which mandates both space and investment for television news. Concerns about lack of ambition or adventure in journalistic approaches are attributable more to lack of investment than lack of imagination. There is certainly no evidence that an opinionated free-for-all stripped of traditional editorial values of accuracy and fairness will generate more innovative forms of television journalism.

The fallacy of technological preclusion. A common argument, perhaps the modern incarnation of technological determinism, holds that any attempt to restrict the flow of new, feisty, opinionated channels is condemned to Canute-like failure. This problem of enforceability was Tim Suter's main objection:

> With some 750 or so channels broadcasting under an Ofcom licence, the regulator's ability to monitor output, even if it wished to, would be severely limited. Furthermore, that output includes a large number of channels.... targeting either non-UK audiences or specific linguistic and ethnic communities within the UK (Op. cit.:118).

This did not preclude Ofcom's predecessor the ITC from revoking the licence of Med TV, a channel aimed at Kurdish viewers, for failing to conform to impartiality rules in 1999. Since Ofcom responds to complaints about breaches of its codes rather than relying on round-the-clock monitoring, there is no technological reason why such complaints relating to impartiality cannot be scrutinised ex post facto. Appropriate warnings and fines may follow, as they do for breaches of harm or offence codes, followed by the ultimate sanction of licence revocation. It is certainly possible that alternative web-based transmission mechanisms will challenge the regulator's authority, and there is no question that convergence of traditional television and computer poses awkward regulatory questions. But for the moment, and certainly for the foreseeable future, consumer approaches to television remains distinct from the computer in terms of its audience reach, impact and visibility. As long as television journalism can be properly distinguished from web-based journalism, there is no reason why medium-specific codes cannot continue to be applied.

IMPARTIALITY AS A SAFEGUARD FOR PLURALITY—A CASE STUDY

Having rebutted the most common arguments for abandoning impartiality, it is also necessary to underline an increasingly important reason for its retention: the institutional protection which impartiality rules offer against proprietorial intervention. It has long been accepted within the print media that newspaper and magazine owners can and do exert significance influence over the editorial direction and content of their publications. In the UK, such editorial impact has been manifested in a number of ways from the Murdoch newspapers' passionate support for the Iraq war and the Telegraph newspapers' hostility towards a European single currency to ownership agendas which deliberately prioritise issues such as immigration, "family values" or crime stories (Greenslade 2003, Hastings 2002, Davies 2008). In the United States, both theorists and empirical scholars have adduced evidence for corporate intervention which has materially affected journalistic agendas and output in both print and broadcast media (Baker 2007, Bakdikian 2004, Barnett 2002). Although such influence is partly dictated in the corporate world by the drive towards profitability and therefore a need to pare back higher areas of expenditure (such as foreign bureaux and investigative reporting), these and other writers have provided abundant evidence that the whims of individual owners can and do significantly alter the journalism being practised.

This creates particular problems for promoting a plural media as media companies consolidate and homogenise. By the first decade of the 21st century, long-standing media business models were coming under huge pressure from a combination of new interactive technologies, a severe economic downturn, and changing consumer approaches to news. As television audiences fragmented and advertising revenue shifted from traditional media to online, media enterprises desperately sought ways of avoiding large-scale redundancies and even permanent closure. For many companies this meant consolidation into larger media entities as a means of trying to sustain some investment in original journalism while inevitably having to reduce the number of their news outlets. The mounting economic crisis was particularly harsh for smaller, privately owned companies, and was felt throughout Europe. In the words of one analyst: "Globalisation has largely pushed traditional family owners and other long-standing media champions out of the European marketplace" (Horsley, 2008:43).

While the internet offers a myriad number of voices and sources, it produces virtually no original newsgathering and current research suggests that the great majority of online news and information is essentially recycled from traditional media institutions (Fenton, 2009). In the print media, it is very difficult to intervene in mergers and acquisitions to protect pluralism. But in broadcasting, where impartiality rules still apply, the diminution of outlets offering properly funded, professional journalism can be ameliorated by ensuring that those left standing are not pulled in a particular editorial or political direction.

That impartiality rules can offers some protection for pluralism was recognised by the competition authorities in Britain in a 2006 merger case between BSkyB, (part of Rupert Murdoch's News Corporation empire), and ITV, Britain's largest free-to-air commercial public service broadcaster. Concerned about rumours of a possible merger between the UK's leading cable company NTL (subsequently rebranded as Virgin Media) and ITV, and the threat that a unified ITV/NTL would pose to BSkyB's supremacy in the pay TV and sports rights market, the satellite company suddenly announced in November 2006 that it had spent £940m to acquire 17.9% of ITV. Not only had it thus become ITV's largest shareholder overnight, but it also forced NTL to abandon its interest because the newly inflated share price was too high. The following February, the shareholding was referred by the Department of Trade and Industry (DTI) to Ofcom to investigate the "public interest issues" raised about plurality of ownership. The Office of Fair Trading (OFT) was also asked to look at competition aspects.

In April 2007, both regulators reported concerns: Ofcom that "there are public interest issues, in relation to sufficient plurality of news provision for both cross-media and television news in the UK", and the OFT that ITV was no longer "independent" (Tryhorn, 2007). A month later, the government referred the acquisition to the Competition Commission (CC) on both grounds, to the very public annoyance of BSkyB's chairman Rupert Murdoch. In December 2007, the CC published its findings which ruled against BSkyB on competition grounds and ordered it to sell its stake down to below 7.5%. Crucially, however, it found in favour of BSkyB in terms of news and editorial plurality. In one of the most important passages of its report, it concluded that "the regulatory mechanisms, combined with a strong culture of editorial independence within television news production, are likely to be effective in preventing any prejudice to the independence of ITV news" (Competition Commission 2007: par 5.75). It cited in particular three internal and regulatory constraints which were likely to limit a shareholder's influence on news: that final decisions of editorial judgement on particular stories are made by programme editors at ITN; that ITV is subject to impartiality requirements; and that the "reputational risk" of compromising this impartiality in response to a shareholder's request would be very substantial. The CC's argument was seemingly endorsed a few months later by Michael Grade, then chairman of ITV, when giving evidence to a House of Lords select committee inquiry into news and media ownership. Asked whether it might be possible for an iconoclastic new owner "to completely degrade and change the news agenda" of ITV, Grade responded:

> Should some less scrupulous owner of ITV decide that they wish to turn the news to their own commercial advantage or whatever, they would first have to find some decent journalists who were prepared to do that.... Let us assume they could, then they would run foul immediately of the regulatory and statutory rules, and I think they would have the devil's own job to do it. (House of Lords, 2008: Q991)

We should, however, be a little more circumspect in taking this as categorical evidence that impartiality rules will always protect against overweening proprietorial power. When the matter was taken to appeal, the Competition Appeals Tribunal (CAT) confirmed the CC's original competition ruling that the merger was anti-competitive, but disagreed with its findings on plurality. It argued, first, that the nature of media plurality was fragile and, once lost, may be impossible to restore. Second, it recognised the importance of plurality to the proper functioning of a democracy. Third, it acknowledged that degrees of control or influence under a single owner may change once a green light has been given and "there may be a creeping influence over time" (Competition Appeals Tribunal: par 263).

The CAT could also have made reference to other evidence given to the House of Lords inquiry which suggested that editors of television news bulletins, while certainly operating according to professional and statutory codes of conduct, do so within an editorial framework loosely laid down by the client (the television company). For historical reasons, commercial stations in the UK subcontract their news rather than supply it themselves, and there are clear editorial agreements which define what is expected from different news bulletins. This was described by the Chief Executive of ITN, who supply ITV and Channel 4 news, as a contract in which "we provide a service to our customers around their requirements and we agree with them in quite intense coordination of what kind of news service they want" (House of Lords, Op. cit.: Q12). In other words, there are potentially large areas of an impartial news agenda which would still be vulnerable to executive interference: the trade-off between serious and light coverage, for example; or the level of investment in investigative journalism; or whether more emphasis should be placed on crime or immigration issues at the expense of, say, health or transport. Nor will impartiality requirements help journalists to resist subtle pressure from their clients to "go easy" on a negative story about a major advertiser or key shareholder. Such protection that impartiality affords, then, keeps the broadcast medium away from overt attachment to a political cause or party. But given the subtle ways in which news agendas can be manipulated, it remains a qualified rather than comprehensive safeguard against a consolidated media environment.

IMPARTIALITY, THE BBC AND A FRESH APPROACH

In contrast to the growing debate about impartiality on commercial stations, there is no debate about whether or not the BBC should still be subject to impartiality requirements. Given a reputation forged over 80 years of broadcasting history, and given its status as an independent and publicly funded institution, the BBC's commitment to impartiality is axiomatic. Before the second world war, under the leadership of Lord Reith and with news reporting heavily circumscribed by the need to placate newspaper interests, the BBC attempted to distance itself from government. As BBC historian Asa Briggs and others have written, this was at best a compromised independence in which the BBC was formally separate from the state, but maintained very close ties to the government and the establishment. During the 1926 General Strike, Reith famously wrote an unambiguous memorandum describing the fledgling BBC's position: "Assuming the BBC is for the people, and that the Government is for the people, it follows that the BBC must be for the Government in this crisis too" (quoted in Schlesinger, 1987:18). As the BBC turned from private company to public corporation, Reith tried to maintain a delicate balancing act that would neither upset the established order nor allow it to become an explicit arm of the State. To some extent it was sleight of hand—and the BBC was certainly not impartial in the sense we understand it today—but it also provided the basis for a genuinely independent entity to emerge with a more holistic approach to impartial journalism.

As BBC journalism evolved out of the war, no longer hampered by restrictions on when and under what conditions it could provide a news service, its political reporting carefully mirrored the bi-polar nature of Westminster politics. Given that post-war Parliaments were dominated by the Labour and Conservative parties, the institutional assumption was that equal time given to each party on matters of policy would satisfy in most people's minds the BBC's claim to be impartial. The first real test of these claims arose during the Suez crisis of 1956 when the government-sponsored invasion of Egypt to "liberate" the Suez Canal was bitterly opposed by the Labour opposition. When Conservative Prime Minister

Anthony Eden was afforded the right to a ministerial broadcast, the Labour leader Hugh Gaitskell demanded a right of reply. In the teeth of furious pressure from Eden—including threats to take over the BBC— the BBC Board of Governors agreed to broadcast Gaitskell's dissenting view. Thereafter, despite predictable spats with individual politicians, Prime Ministers, and minor political parties who often felt excluded, the BBC's commitment to "formal" impartiality in terms of Westminster politics was generally accepted.

At a more informal level, a serious intellectual debate within the academy questioned both the practical and theoretical limits of a "value-free" approach to news, and argued that news was necessarily a social and professional construction rather than some kind of objective view of the world. Moreover, scholars argued that the BBC's construction was part of an established social order. According to one radio reporter interviewed at the time for Philip Schlesinger's seminal study in the early seventies, "The Corporation's view is middle-class liberalism. Strikes, Communists, Black Power, Fascists are all bad. Social Democrats and Tories are good" (Ibid.:166). This notion of the BBC sustaining an essentially conservative consensus was also a key theme of the Glasgow Media Group studies of the 1970s and is still occasionally heard today. One commentator, for example, recently described the BBC as "from top to bottom, in structure and staffing, in history and ideology.... a conservative organisation, committed to upholding Establishment values and protecting them from challenge" (Hasan, 2009). More commonly heard in the first decade of the 21st century, though, were complaints from the right (and in particular the right-wing press) that the BBC has an inbuilt left-wing bias which infects its coverage and corrodes its judgement. Paul Dacre, editor-in-chief of the Daily Mail, has been a particularly colourful exponent of this view:

> [the BBC] exercises a kind of "cultural Marxism" in which it tries to undermine that conservative society by turning all its values on their heads.
>
> Of course, there is the odd dissenting voice, but by and large BBC journalism starts from the premise of leftwing ideology: it is hostile to conservatism and the traditional Right, Britain's past and British values, America, Ulster Unionism, Euro-scepticism, capitalism and big business, the countryside, Christianity, and family values. Conversely it is sympathetic to Labour, European Federalism, the State and State spending, mass immigration, minority rights, multiculturalism, alternative lifestyles, abortion and progressiveness in the education and the justice systems (Dacre, 2007).

Notwithstanding those highly politicised and polarised versions of whether the BBC practises impartial journalism, the principle of a BBC

64 STEVEN BARNETT

dedicated to an editorial code which *aspires* to impartiality as a journalistic ideal has never been seriously questioned. By the turn of the century, however, the *practical* implications of that aspiration was becoming recognised as increasingly difficult. It was this practical issue of impartiality in a changing world (and, by implication, a world whose priorities had been transformed by the terrorist attacks of 9/11 and its aftermath) which were broached by the then BBC Chairman Michael Grade in May 2005:

> Social attitudes have changed. Many new groups have entered British society, bringing with them their own cultures, and religions, and value systems—all of them legitimate expressions of belief. Now, when legitimate value systems compete, the BBC must act impartially. That applies to areas of cultural controversy, just as much as to the traditional areas of political and industrial debate as defined in the impartiality regulations (Grade, 2005)

Grade's speech presaged a new period of serious examination by the BBC into both specific areas of its coverage and to more general definitional arguments. The governors commissioned a series of impartiality reviews on BBC coverage of the European Union, of the Middle East, and of its business reporting. More significantly, Governors and Management jointly commissioned a study to examine the implications for the BBC of the cultural and technological changes articulated by Grade. Its aim was to deliver "a set of principles underlying impartiality in the 21st century" and "a list of broadly identified implications for the BBC".[8] While the author tasked with that particular study was conducting his analysis, the BBC's thinking was further elaborated by its Head of News, Peter Horrocks, in a significant lecture in 2006.

Horrocks couched his argument partly in terms of declining audiences and the need to ensure that the BBC was editorially attuned to the distinctive tastes of its different audiences. But he also argued, in the context of an increasingly fragmented and segregated society, that "we will need to look again at what we mean by impartiality and transform editorially to re-find our lost audiences". He rehearsed the old definitions of impartiality in terms of balancing interviews between Left and Right, arguing that the defining moment of change came as the interactivity of email and then red-button technology allowed the audience to express their own reactions. This, combined with more sophisticated and detailed research

---

[8] BBC Impartiality Project Terms of Reference, accessed at http://www.bbcgovernors-archive.co.uk/docs/reviews/rev_impartiality_termsofreference2.pdf.

into how audiences respond to specific news stories, permitted a more nuanced audience-based perspective of impartiality rather than a paternalistic top-down approach. The new purpose of BBC journalism in such an environment was described by Horrocks as:

> to provide the widest range of information and views.... so that the bulk of the population sees its own perspective reflected honestly and regularly. We must also provide the opportunity for people to regularly come across alternative information and perspectives that provide a wider viewpoint. We need to provide that information and opinion in forms and styles of sufficient appeal to attract all users. That attraction must be based on delivering to their individual interests and information needs (Horrocks, 2006).

Thus, the old arguments about engagement were now being enhanced by new ones about widening the range of views being transmitted—including views which, said Horrocks, many might find "abhorrent". He labeled this a "radical impartiality" in which interviews with members of the Taleban and the far-right British National Party would sit alongside those speaking out against Europe or against immigration. This wider embrace would, in his view, restore some lost credibility amongst those who felt that their views had been neither represented nor respected. It would not fall victim to "commercial" approaches to television journalism which was concerned solely with maximising audiences (and particularly audiences with high disposable income). But it would appeal to broader constituencies by acknowledging that there was no longer a shared vision of the world.

"FROM SEESAW TO WAGON WHEEL"

This theme was explored and extended in a groundbreaking report on Impartiality inherited by the new BBC Trust when it succeeded the BBC Governors in January 2007. Its title "From Seesaw to Wagon Wheel" was designed to convey the new complexities of the contemporary political world: where once it was conceived as a simple bi-polar division of political opinion, "in today's multi-polar Britain, with its range of cultures, beliefs and identities, impartiality involves many more than two sides to an argument" (BBC Trust, 2007:5). It argued that the old two-dimensional seesaw should be replaced by the wagon wheel borrowed from television's diagrammatic coverage of a batsman's innings in cricket "where the wheel is not circular and has a shifting centre with spokes that go in all directions". This somewhat clumsy symbolism was arguably a belated recognition of arguments being iterated by critics and academics during the 1970s and 80s that significant voices—and in particular, those detached from the mainstream for ethnic, economic, regional or political reasons—had been systematically marginalised in television's representation of reality. It was, however, a timely articulation of aspirational principle and practice within an institution dedicated to the pursuit of rigorous, accurate and independent journalism. At the heart of the report were twelve "guiding principles" designed to complement the internal Editorial Guidelines on impartiality:

1. Impartiality should be a "source of pride" rather than a legal or institutional requirement. It had been conceived and developed culturally rather than legalistically, and must continually evolve to meet the needs of a more diverse society.

2. The audience should be an integral part of determining impartiality, and the growth of user-generated content should be welcomed as an additional resource (subject to checks on authenticity).

3. Impartiality should be applied beyond political and industrial controversy to embrace a broader range of opinions, appreciating that contemporary political activity and expression had moved outside the confines of Parliament and Westminster.

4. Reporting from the centre ground is "often the wrong place to be" and impartiality can be breached by omission. There should be space for rational or honest opinion, however out of the mainstream.

5. There should be room for controversy, passion and polemic; impartiality need not be a recipe for bland or insipid programming, as long as authorship is clear and a balance is provided over time. On the other hand, the integrity of BBC journalism requires that its reporters do not compromise their own authority by voicing their own opinions.[9]

6. Impartiality applies beyond journalism to the whole spectrum of BBC output, including drama, comedy and entertainment. Plot

[9] The report quoted a typically colourful description from the BBC's former Political Editor Andrew Marr: "the first thing that happens to you as a BBC journalist is that you're taken down into a dank basement to have your trousers pulled down and your organs of opinion removed with a pair of secateurs by the Director-General and popped in a formaldehyde bottle. You're told you're allowed them back when you leave."

lines of soap operas can be as imbued with one-sided meaning as the most partisan political coverage.

7. Campaigns should be treated with particular care when they appear to be uncontroversial but may have a political subtext. This care must be balanced with the BBC's involvement with major national events that capture the imagination.[10]

8. Individual journalistic dilemmas will always be hotly contested. There is no "template of wisdom" but the BBC's journalistic experience is an invaluable resource.[11] The institutional position of the BBC will sometimes clash with professional journalistic instinct, and these must be carefully balanced.

9. Programme-makers, editors and producers should constantly be challenging their own positions and guard against "shared assumptions". It would not be surprising within such a large organisation to find programme-makers inhabiting "a shared space, a comfort zone, which if unacknowledged may cause problems for impartiality".

10 The BBC must examine its own "institutional values" and be aware that its corporate behaviour may unconsciously convey a message to the audience which affects judgements of impartiality. It must remain aware and self-critical of its own institutional (and essentially western, democratic) perspective.

11 Transparency is fundamental to the process, and any breaches of impartiality should be acknowledged openly and quickly, to secure audience confidence in the BBC decision-making process.

12 It is incumbent on every individual from junior researcher to Director General to apply the principles of impartiality at every stage of the programme-making process, across platforms and from the earliest stage of idea creation.

This report stands as a welcome antidote to two opposed but commonly articulated theoretical arguments against impartiality: that either it is a

---

[10] Similar issues were involved when covering the Live8 concert in July that year, designed to raise awareness of worldwide poverty and timed deliberately to take place just before a summit meeting of the G8 leaders in Scotland.

[11] Potential editorial dilemmas debated at a preceding seminar, such as whether an interview offered by Osama Bin Laden in a mountain village in Pakistan should be accepted, produced some fascinating divisions of opinion between cautious BBC editorial figures and their more journalistically ambitious commercial counterparts.

futile ambition whose imposition constrains free debate and unencumbered journalism; or that it is such a self-evident set of professional practices that it barely needs elaboration. By acknowledging the complexity of 21st century political and cultural life, and by recognising the many voices which have arguably felt excluded from the cultural mainstream of BBC journalism, this report cements the BBC's position as holder of the impartiality flame as well as offering a self-referential template for any institution seeking to turn ideal-type theory into professional reality.

CONCLUSION

Implicit in the BBC's report was a sense of how professional and institutional values in journalism ultimately come down to notions of intent: what are the prime motivations of the programme editors, on-screen journalists, off-screen producers and researchers who are responsible for creating today's broadcast journalism? What are the normative expectations of the institutions for which they work? If their prime purpose is to maximise ratings, pursue a single-minded ideological vision, create publicity or elevate an individual on-screen personality, then journalistic rigour as well as balance will most likely be compromised or at least be relegated to a second-order consideration.

To take one hypothetical example, a programme or in-depth news item on climate change and the environment can take several routes: it can offer dramatic and apocalyptic images of flooding, starvation and forest fires, linking them inexorably to CO_2 emissions and reckless profiteering by oil companies; it can furiously denounce the proponents of man-made climate change as lunatic left-wingers intent on undermining capitalism; it can have a 20-something autocutie in the studio introducing beautifully shot pictures of cuddly polar bears struggling to survive in a diminishing polar ice cap. It can be emotionally driven, ideologically driven, picture driven—or it can be journalistically driven, weighing up the scientific evidence, explaining the context of the debate, providing pictures to illustrate particular arguments, but ultimately designed to leave the viewer better informed and better placed to make intelligent judgements than before. If we pursue the notion of intent, then perhaps the fundamental difference in those approaches can best be characterised as "integrity": a state of mind which requires decision-makers to interrogate themselves about their purpose. Writing about the myriad pressures on television journalists in the 21st century, one of Britain's most experienced foreign reporters (and briefly an MP) Martin Bell wrote:

> It does no harm for all journalists.... to ask ourselves a simple question: What do we believe in? If it is only making money, then we are clearly in the wrong business because money can deflect, if not corrupt, us. But if we have standards and values and principles, then we should stand by them because they are what we believe in and what sustains us. There is actually a word for it. The word in *integrity* (Bell, 1998:108)

This is, perhaps, the most helpful way in which to interpret the BBC Trust's report, the continuing statutory safeguards on impartiality, and the associated Ofcom codes: as sophisticated instruments for institutionalising integrity not only in the BBC but in the practice of all television journalism. In a world where journalism is increasingly distrusted, where the public are increasingly sceptical of information sources and are poorly served by the accuracy and reliability of many of those print sources that have survived, television still stands out as a beacon of dependability. In the UK, ever since the BBC's self-imposed mission was embedded by law into the commercial sector, television has been understood to be different and still commands—even in the digital era of fragmented audiences— easily the highest levels of credibility and consumption of national and international news. That public trust is inextricably linked to impartiality requirements which remain a powerful and effective safeguard of the public interest.

Moreover, the continuing relevance of those requirements are recognised and endorsed by the vast majority of viewers: Ofcom's own research in 2007 found that 87% believe that impartiality is important for radio and TV news, a pretty convincing vote of confidence in a regime which applies to the medium rather than individual channels. To surrender it for what would be—despite protestations to the contrary—no more than commercial pragmatism would be to disturb the clarity of professional television journalistic practice as well as running counter to the wishes of the vast majority of citizens. While first amendment purists will always baulk at any attempt to impose statutory restrictions on commercial organisations, I hope that this essay demonstrates how such obligations—rooted in ideal journalistic norms of accuracy, fairness and integrity—can empower rather than suppress those forms of journalistic expression which will leave citizens better informed and democracy better served.

References

Stuart Allan, (1997) "News and the Public Sphere: Towards a History of Objectivity and Impartiality", in M. Bromley and T. O'Malley (eds.) *A Journalism Reader*. Routledge, pp. 296–327.

BBC, "Beyond the Soundbite": BBC research into public disillusion with politics, BBC, 2002.

BBC Trust, 2007, "From Seesaw to Wagon Wheel: Safeguarding impartiality in the 21st century", BBC.

Ben Bakdikian, 2004, *The New Media Monopoly*, Beacon Press.

C. Edwin Baker, 2007, *Media Concentration and Democracy*, Cambridge University Press.

Eric Barendt, 1998, "Judging the Media: Impartiality and Broadcasting" in *The Political Quarterly*, Vol 69, pp. 108–116.

Steven Barnett, 2008, "TV news and the echo of Murrow" in *British Journalism Review*, Vol 19 No 4, pp. 37–44.

Steven Barnett, 2002, "Impartiality redefined: protecting news on commercial television in Britain" in Damian Tambini and Jamie Cowling (eds.) *New News? Impartial broadcasting in the digital age*. London, IPPR. Chapter 4, pp. 51–64.

Steven Barnett, Ivor Gaber and Emily Seymour (2000) "From Callaghan to Kosovo: changing trends in British television news 1975–1999". London, University of Westminster.

Martin Bell, 1998, "The Truth Is Our Currency" in *Harvard International Journal of Press/Politics*, 3(1):102–109.

Lee C. Bollinger, 1990, "The rationale of public regulation of the media" in *Democracy and the Mass Media*, ed Judith Lichtenberg, Cambridge University Press.

Competition Appeals Tribunal, 2008, Judgement on BSkyB v Competition Competition and Virgin v Competition Commission, 29 September.

Competition Commission, 2007, *Acquisition By British Sky Broadcasting Group PLC of 17.9 per cent of the shares in ITV PLC*, Report sent to Secretary of State (BERR), 14 December.

Andrew Currah, 2009, *What's Happening to our News?*, Reuters Institute for the Study of Journalism, Oxford.

Paul Dacre, 2007, The Hugh Cudlipp Lecture, London College of Communication, 22 January.

Nick Davies, *Flat Earth News*, Chatto and Windus.

John Eldridge, ed, *Getting the Message: News, Truth and Power*, Routledge.

Owen M. Fiss, 1990, "Why the state?" in *Democracy and the Mass Media*, ed Judith Lichtenberg, Cambridge University Press.

Natalie Fenton, 2009, *New Media, Old News: Journalism and Democracy in the Digital Age*, Sage.

Des Freedman, 2008, *The Politics of Media Policy*, Polity Press.

Peter Golding and Philip Elliott, 1979, *Making the News*, Longman.

Michael Grade, *Goodman Media Lecture: The Future of Impartiality*, Institute of Mechanical Engineers, London, 11 May.

Roy Greenslade, 2003, "Their Master's Voice", in The Guardian, 17 February.

Stuart Hall, C. Crichter, T. Jefferson and B. Roberts, 1978, *Policing the Crisis*, Macmillan.

Daniel Hallin and Paolo Mancini, Comparing Media Systems: Three Models of Media and Politics, Cambridge University Press.

Ian Hargreaves and James Thomas, *New new, old news*, Independent Television Commission, 2002.

Mehdi Hasan, "Bias and the Beeb" in *New Statesman*, 27 August.

Max Hastings, 2002, *Editor: An Inside Story of Newspapers*, Macmillan publishing.

Anthony Hayward, 2001, *In the name of Justice: The Television Reporting of John Pilger*, Bloomsbury.

William Horsley, 2008, "Europe: media freedom in retreat" in *British Journalism Review* Vol. 19, No. 2, pp. 39–45.

Peter Horrocks, 2006, "Finding TV News' lost audience", lecture at St Anne's College and the Reuters Institute, Oxford, 28th November.

Robert Horwitz, 1989, *The Irony of Regulatory Reform: The Deregulation of American Telecommunications*, OUP.

House of Lords, 2008, Select Committee on Communications, *The Ownership of the News*, HL Paper 122-II, Minute of the House of Lords select committee visit to the United States: Appendix 4, par 47.

David D. Kirkpatrick, 2003, "Mr Murdoch's War" in *New York Times*, 7 April, Section C.

Philip Knightley, 2001, "Is he a poet or a journalist?" in *British Journalism Review*, Vol 12 No.2 pp. 71–3.

Richard Lindley, 2005, *And Finally...? The News from ITN*, Politicos.

Dominic Morris, 2002, "Impartiality in the multi-channel age: a personal view from the trenches" in Damian Tambini and Jamie Cowling (eds.) *New News? Impartial broadcasting in the digital age*. IPPR, Chapter 3.

James Murdoch, 2009, "The Absence of Trust", Edinburgh International Television Festival MacTaggart Lecture, 28 August 2009.

Ofcom, 2007, *New News, Future News: The challenges for television news after digital switchover*, 4 July.

Ofcom, 2009, *The Ofcom Broadcasting Code (Incorporating the Cross-promotion Code)*, Ofcom, December.

Mark Pedelty, 1995, *War Stories: The Culture of Foreign Correspondents*. Routledge.

Julian Petley, 2003, "Foxy Business" in *Index on Censorship*, Vol 32, No 2, pp. 17–22.

Greg Philo, 1990, *Seeing and Believing*, Routledge.

John Pilger, 2002, column in *New Statesman*, 2 December, pp. 15–16.

The Power Report, 2006, *An Independent Inquiry into Britain's Democracy*, Joseph Rowntree Charitable Trust, March 2006.

David Puttnam, "News: you want it quick or good" in *British Journalism Review*, Vol. 14, No. 2, 2003, pp. 50–57.

Philip Schlesinger, 1987, *Putting Reality Together*, Routledge.

Tim Suter, 2008, "Impartiality—the case for change" in Tim Gardam and David A.L. Levy (eds.) *The Price of Plurality: Choice, Diversity and Broadcasting Institutions in the Digital Age*, Reuters Institute for the Study of Journalism.

Chris Tryhorn, 2007, "Ofcom flags up Sky-ITV worries in The Guardian, 27 April 2007, accessed 15 March 2010 at http://www.guardian.co.uk/media/2007/apr/27/ofcom .citynews.

Matt Wells and John Cassy, 2002, "Ungag us", in *The Guardian*, Media Section, 14 April 2003.

James Q. Whitman, 2004, "The Two Western Cultures of Privacy: Dignity Versus Liberty" in *Yale Law Journal*, Vol 113: pp. 1151–1221.

IMPARTIALITY IN NEWS COVERAGE: THE PRESENT
AND THE FUTURE

Mike Feintuck

Introduction

It can reasonably be expected that impartial or balanced news reporting
can contribute significantly to the well-informed and active citizenry on
which democracy is generally expected to thrive. Thus, at one level, impartiality in news coverage may seem to fall into the same category as "moth-
erhood and apple pie"—uncontroversial and unmitigated goods that are
near impossible to argue meaningfully against.

However, even the briefest second thought, reveals the potential conflict between the imposition of requirements of impartiality on news
media and the democratically fundamental expectation of freedom of
expression in the media. Closer inspection still reveals that impartiality in
news, at least as presently implemented in the UK, is far from uncontroversial, and in particular, may seem to cohabit uneasily with its apparently natural partner, diversity of news output. The scene is still more
complicated when it is acknowledged that, in addition to the significant
tensions between the values of impartiality on the one hand, and diversity
and freedom of expression on the other, any attempt to justify current
duties of impartiality on broadcast news services becomes problematic
when we are faced with technological convergence that serves to blur traditional demarcation lines between media sectors, and the simultaneous
development of new forms of news media, via the internet, including user-
generated content which may lack any editorial oversight. In addition, in
the absence of strong and current justifications for the continuing imposition of requirements of impartiality, it may prove difficult or near impossible to defend such requirements given the hegemony of market-driven
values, which place faith in the exercise of individual choice to determine
what goods and services will be provided. In such a context, any "public
interest" in ensuring impartiality in certain news provision will require
the strongest foundations if it is to be perceived as legitimate.

In the first part of 2009, two issues developed which provide useful
contexts in which to discuss questions of impartiality. The first was a

relatively narrow, specific illustration of the sort of issues that can arise, and concerned the BBC's reaction to the Disasters Emergency Committee (DEC) appeal for humanitarian assistance for the people of Gaza. The second was much broader, and related to questions over the extent to which the imposition of impartiality requirements on commercial Public Service Broadcasters (PSBs), and UK commercial broadcasters (non-PSB) more generally, were justifiable or sustainable post-Digital Switch-over (DSO).

There is also a third, less obvious or immediate, but possibly more interesting question, of how requirements of impartiality placed on UK broadcasters can be justified at all, when no such requirements exist in relation to print media, international media or internet news sources, in an era of technological development which allows UK citizens and residents access to global media sources, and in which technological convergence leaves distinctions between traditional media sectors increasingly blurred. In such circumstances, on what basis might regulatory interventions in pursuit of impartiality be justified? Before addressing these questions, it is first necessary to set-out the regulatory provisions, and their interpretation, on which existing requirements of impartiality are based in the UK.

STATUTORY PROVISIONS AND THEIR INTERPRETATION— UK COMMERCIAL BROADCASTERS

At present, all UK broadcast news is subject to the requirement of impartiality. In the case of commercial broadcasters this is imposed by statute, as implemented in practice by Ofcom's Broadcasting Code. In the case of the BBC it arises from the BBC Trust's enforcement of principles arising from duties under its Charter.

Section 319(1)(b) of the Communications Act 2003 (CA03) requires Ofcom "to set, and from time to time to revise, such standards for the content of programmes to be included in television and radio services as appear to them best calculated to secure ... [*inter alia*] ... [s.319(2)(c)] that news included in television and radio services is presented with due impartiality and that the impartiality requirements of section 320 are complied with."

Section 320(1)(b) requires "the preservation, in the case of every television programme service, teletext service, national radio service and national digital sound programme service, of due impartiality, of all ... matters [320(2)] (a) of political or industrial controversy, and (b) relating to current public policy", though under s.320(4)(a) this requirement "may be satisfied by being satisfied in relation to a series of programmes taken as a whole".[1]

Thus, while commercial PSBs (Channel 3, Channel 4 and Channel 5) are subject to specific licensing requirements relating to quantity, quality and scheduling of news, *all* UK broadcasters are subject to requirements of "due impartiality".

Ofcom's Broadcasting Code[2] explains "due impartiality" as follows:

> "Due" is an important qualification to the concept of impartiality. Impartiality itself means not favouring one side over another. "Due" means adequate or appropriate to the subject and nature of the programme. So "due impartiality" does not mean an equal division of time has to be given to every view, or that every argument and every facet of every argument has to be represented. The approach to due impartiality may vary according to the nature of the subject, the type of programme and channel, the likely expectation of the audience as to content, and the extent to which the content and approach is signalled to the audience. Context, as defined in Section Two: Harm and Offence of the Code, is important.

Beyond this, Ofcom's Code does little more than restate the statutory provisions, though it does helpfully seek to clarify the definition of "series of programmes taken as a whole". The intention here seems to be to permit the requirement of due impartiality to be met across the entirety of a linked series rather than in each single broadcast programme within such a series, permitting a more sustained and developed analysis than could be developed within a rigid framework of requirements of balance for each individual programme:

> 5.5 Due impartiality on matters of political or industrial controversy and matters relating to current public policy must be preserved on the part of any person providing a service (listed above). This may be achieved within a programme or over a series of programmes taken as a whole.
>
> *Meaning of "series of programmes taken as a whole":* This means more than one programme in the same service, editorially linked, dealing with the same or related issues within an appropriate period and aimed at a like audience. A series can include, for example, a strand, or two programmes (such as a drama and a debate about the drama) or a 'cluster' or 'season' of programmes on the same subject.

---

[1] Section 320(5) requires Ofcom's standards code to contain provisions setting out the rules to be applied in relation to s.320(1)(b) requirements, and interpretation of the s.320(4)(a) provision.

[2] October 2008. Section 5.

5.6 The broadcast of editorially linked programmes dealing with the same subject matter (as part of a series in which the broadcaster aims to achieve due impartiality) should normally be made clear to the audience on air.

THE BBC AND IMPARTIALITY

The provisions of Section 5 of the Ofcom Broadcasting Code, set out above, do not apply to BBC services which are regulated on these matters instead by the BBC Trust. The Framework Agreement accompanying the BBC's 2006 Royal Charter states that the BBC "must do all it can to ensure that controversial subjects are treated with due accuracy and impartiality in all relevant output. The BBC Trust has sole jurisdiction over issues concerning accuracy or impartiality... in all the BBC's services/programmes".[3]

The BBC's decision-making in this area is structured by a series of principles set-out in Editorial Guidelines[4] complemented by principles established in its document "From seesaw to wagon wheel".[5] In the forward to this document it is stated that "Impartiality has always been (together with independence) the BBC's defining quality. It is not by chance that all BBC staff carry an identity card which proclaims as the first of the BBC's values that they are independent, impartial and honest."[6]

The Report goes on to acknowledge, in relation to its traditional focus on values of impartiality, a shift from a traditional "seesaw" model of party politics to a more dynamic model (the wagon wheel used in analysing a batsman's scoring pattern in televised cricket coverage) "where the wheel is not circular and has a shifting centre with spokes that go in all directions" (p.5)! This rather stretched analogy is meant to indicate a changed relationship with audiences, whereby the BBC has to adapt to a more diverse range of interest groups and user patterns, in a world of many more (unregulated or lightly regulated) sources of "news", and which end users have more control over their news and information agendas. "Twelve Guiding Principles"[7] are also set out. These supplement or complement the existing Editorial Guidelines.

---

[3] BBC Trust/Ofcom Board, Memorandum of Understanding, July 2008.

[4] June 2005.

[5] BBC Trust, *From seesaw to wagon wheel—safeguarding impartiality in the 21st century*, June 2007.

[6] Ibid., 2.

[7] Summarized at Ibid., 6–8.

Of course, the BBC can never win in this regard. In Keane's words, "The public service claim to representativeness is a defence of *virtual* representation of a *fictive* whole, a resort to programming which *simulates* the actual opinions and tastes of *some* of those to whom it is directed. That is why the public service claim to 'inform all of the people all of the time' triggers a constant stream of complaints."[8] The challenge of this situation has traditionally been met with BBC programme makers claiming success is achieved when an equal degree of criticism emerges from both ends of the political spectrum. However, in the same era that has seen the BBC acknowledge the diverse range of its audience perspectives, since the Blairite revolution moved the Labour Party away from its Socialist traditions and accepted the triumph of Thatcherite politics, there has developed in Britain a dominant, mainstream politics based around the individual and the market. Given the absence of significant philosophical difference between the main political parties, there is a sense in which the media in general, and perhaps the BBC in particular has slipped into what Lloyd describes as "acting as an opposition, not so much to one party or the other, but to government: even to politics."[9] It is not necessary to agree or disagree with, or to applaud or deprecate such a phenomenon; the media's status as "Fourth Estate" does seem to imply a role within, rather than simply commenting on, our polity. However, it is important to understand the implication of this, namely, that that the BBC may remain wholly impartial in a party political sense, while very much maintaining a particular world view which may, or may not, be viewed as adequately "impartial" by its viewers and listeners, or politicians. There remains, however, a risk associated with the BBC's position here which Lloyd goes on to highlight. If the BBC's position on politics becomes simply one that "politicians are inherently objects of suspicion",[10] it serves only to echo the kind of approach adopted by the Daily Telegraph in its 2009 "outing" of MPs' abuses of the expenses system, which, for better or worse served to discredit our mainstream politics.

Coleman et al find that "the BBC continues to perform the role of trusted reporter and interpreter for some people; certainly more so than any other news institution, but less, we suspect, than would have been the

---

[8] Keane, J., *The Media and Democracy* (Cambridge: Polity Press, 1991), 122, original emphasis.
[9] Lloyd, J., *What the Media Are Doing to Our Politics* (London: Constable, 2004), 126.
[10] Ibid., 177.

case twenty years ago."[11] And if the BBC cannot find a position which successfully distinguishes it from the commercial media and which serves to
enhance its credibility in the eyes of the more disengaged sectors of the
community, despite any apparent or alleged increased or excessive influence or presence on the world stage,[12] it really will struggle to find a role
as its dominance of 20th century broadcasting in Britain increasingly
challenged.

THE BBC AND THE GAZA APPEAL

The BBC's application of its "impartiality principles" was, subjected to
close scrutiny following its decision in January 2009 not to broadcast the
DEC appeal relating to Gaza. Sky News also chose to adopt the BBC's
approach, refusing to screen the appeal, and this will be returned to,
briefly, later.

The thrust of the D-G's decision had been that, in relation to the Israeli-
Palestinian conflict, "it was in this case impossible to separate the political
causes of the dispute from its humanitarian consequences", and that
screening the appeal would have "implied a level of BBC endorsement" of
the Palestinian position, even if a disclaimer had been broadcast making
clear that the material in the appeal did not represent the BBC's views.
Interestingly, the D-G had originally referred to a reason for not broadcasting the appeal by reference to the likelihood, or not, of aid resulting
from the appeal actually reaching the people of Gaza given the military
and political realities. Though this was subsequently marginalised by BBC
spokespersons, and the Trust found that the D-G had not relied on this
factor in taking his decision, initial discussion of this factor perhaps served
to confuse the issue, and certainly did not help sceptics to believe in the
BBC's good faith in this matter. The Trust was also satisfied that no bias
against the Palestinian people had been created by not broadcasting the
appeal, and that the BBC "had covered both the humanitarian situation
and the DEC appeal controversy itself at length on its news bulletins".[13]
In relation to the BBC's Director-General's decision not to broadcast the

[11] Coleman, S., Anthony, S. and Morrison, D., *Public Trust in the News: a constructivist study of the social life of the news* (University of Oxford/Reuters Institute for the Study of Journalism, 2009), 34.

[12] Douglas Bicket and Melissa Wall *Media Culture Society* 31 (2009), 365.

[13] BBC Trust, *Determination of an appeal against the decision of the Director General of the BBC not to broadcast the DEC Gaza Crisis Appeal*, February 2009, 4.

appeal, or to uphold complaints regarding this decision, the Trust's assessment was "that the Director-General's decision not to uphold the complaint was a reasonable one for him to reach",[14] based on advice received
and without taking into account any irrelevant considerations. In conclusion, however, the Trust did ask the D-G "to explore any wider lessons that
may be drawn from this episode", and to take a view on whether the 1971
agreement with the DEC and the associated criteria for considering
appeals "are still appropriate for today's broadcasting environment".[15]

DEC Appeals have regularly been broadcast by the BBC since the DEC's
inception in 1963, including, interestingly, in 1967 an appeal for donations
for Palestinian and Syrian refuges from the "Six Day War". However, as The
Times reports,[16] not all such proposed appeals have been broadcast by the
BBC. One such refusal occurred in relation to an appeal for aid for victims
of the 2006 Israel/Hezbollah conflict, and refusals have also previously
been made in relation to an appeal for starving people in East Africa being
declined on the basis that it did not believe agencies could successfully
deliver aid, and it initially declined to broadcast an appeal for victims of a
cyclone in Burma because of limits on access to that country imposed by
the governing regime there. While it might be thought desirable that the
BBC and commercial PSBs would adopt similar practices in this area, the
different outcomes available under the different schemes were revealed
starkly in this case. As The Times went on to report, "The decision to screen
messages from the DEC is usually made by consensus between the BBC,
ITV, and Sky, who provide free airtime. However, the BBC's refusal ...
sparked such intense debate that ITV has decided to transmit the appeal
without its two usual partners. Instead Channel 4 and Five will also carry
the message."[17]

Of course, few political issues reveal such deep-seated and divergent
and apparently irreconcilable positions as the state of Israel and in particular its relations with the Arab world. In a decision relating to commercial broadcaster Press TV,[18] Ofcom has noted, in finding a programme

---

[14] Ibid.
[15] Ibid.
[16] 26 January 2009.
[17] Ibid.
[18] See Ofcom Broadcast Bulletin 139, 3 August 2009. http://www.ofcom.org.uk/tv/obb/
prog_cb/obb139/ Press TV receives funding from advertising revenue; Iranian tax-payers;
sales from services provided in respect of the technical and engineering industry; and sales
from its archives.

presented by George Galloway MP to be in breach of Rules 5.11 and 5.12, that in relation to matters of high controversy,

> There must be a place for ... programming which gives air to highly opinion-ated and vocal reaction on issues of such importance. However, in order to comply with the Code, broadcasters must ensure that, when discussing mat-ters of major political or industrial controversy or a major matter relating to current public policy, a real range of significant views are included in a pro-gramme. Further, in such cases, when presenting any significant alternative view, it must be given due weight and consideration.

Ultimately, there remains a real sense that the BBC's position on the DEC Gaza appeal was tenuous to the point of implausibility; at the very least, the BBC could not be said to have covered itself in glory in this case. Its reasoning would indicate, logically, that short of wholly natural disaster (and even then there is likelihood that some of the potential recipients of aid would be party to ongoing political dispute, in which, by implication, the BBC could be viewed as taking-sides by broadcasting an appeal), there can be no foreseeable circumstances in which the BBC will in future broadcast an appeal. On the specifics of the Gaza Appeal case, in terms familiar to British public lawyers, the reasonableness test being applied by the Trust must be at the end of the scale which permits extreme latitude, in the region of determining only that the D-G had not actually taken leave of his senses! The decision may, in such terms, be seen as reasonable, but a decision showing very poor judgement at best, and, under a banner of maintaining impartiality, actually risking alienating a large section of the BBC's audience.

Principle 11 of the BBC's 2007 document[19] states that "Impartiality is a process, about which the BBC should be honest and transparent with its audience: this should permit greater boldness in its programming deci-sions. But impartiality can never be fully achieved to everyone's satisfac-tion: the BBC should not be defensive about this but ready to acknowledge and correct significant breaches as and when they occur." It is not imme-diately apparent how the decision in relation to the DEC appeal for the people of Gaza is consistent with this principle, or how the BBC's reputa-tion for impartiality was in any way enhanced by its decision on this mat-ter or its response to criticism of the decision. While it is clear that, inevitably, the decision and response to challenge certainly failed to sat-isfy everyone, the weak reasoning offered by the Corporation's highest

---

[19] Op. cit., n.4, 8.

officers make it difficult, even for those whose instinct is to defend and support the BBC, to fall behind the decision in this case.

THE FUTURE OF IMPARTIALITY REQUIREMENTS

While consideration of the BBC's reaction to the DEC Appeal on Gaza offers an interesting narrow case study of the application of impartiality in practice, it is also important to examine impartiality in the context of the technological and market change which will arise following the forthcoming switch-off of analogue transmission across the UK. Though simply one more step, in a long sequence of steps away from the comfortable and monopolistic historical position in British broadcasting enjoyed originally by the BBC, a position which was subsequently shared with its PSB competitors, this particular step comes at a time when the pressures of technological and corporate change in media markets have grown to an extent that they now challenge the very legitimacy of a licence fee-funded BBC in the form that we have known it.

Discussion about the post-DSO era consistently involves the coming together of the two values identified earlier—impartiality and diversity. At one level these values seem to spring from a similar heritage, associated with a vision of a public sphere representing and incorporating a maximally wide range of values existing within society, and encouraging participation in society by well-informed citizens. However, as will be seen, discussion of the values in this context seems to bring to the fore the differences rather than similarities between the concepts. This theme will be returned to, but for the moment it is helpful to sketch-out some current thinking on the topic of impartiality.

Ofcom's discussion document "New News, Future News"[20] looks at a series of news-related issues in the post-DSO era. In relation to impartiality, it raises five specific points:[21]

> It is Ofcom's view that television should play its part in encouraging diversity of provision within a core of impartial news on which viewers can rely (in line with viewer expectation).
>
> However, universal impartiality may become less enforceable in a digital environment, where regulated and unregulated services exist side by side on

---

[20] Ofcom, *New News, Future News: the challenges for television news after Digital Switch-over*, 4th July 2007.
[21] Ibid., 71.

the same platform. It follows that consumers who place a high level of importance on impartiality will find it harder to discover channels they can trust.

For these reasons, the requirement for the BBC and Channel 4 to be impartial should continue; and there appear to be no reasons for any relaxation on other channels with PSB status.

For channels other than the main PSBs, is impartiality still important, or is it a barrier to diversity in an era with a wide range of services available to viewers?

Subject to change in legislation, should other channels be allowed to offer partial news in the same way that newspapers and some websites do at present?

Peter Phillips (Ofcom Partner, Strategy and Market Developments), summarised the position in a speech on 5th July 2007:

> One possibility—no more than that—post-2014 might be relaxation of the statutory rules on impartiality. We believe these will remain absolutely essential for maintaining overall trust in key PSB providers, such as the BBC and Channel 4. But might a degree of relaxation for other services enable a wider range of voices to be heard, and for minority groups to feel more engaged? Minority ethnic groups don't see mainstream media (BBC, ITV, broadsheets) as being as impartial as do the rest of the population. C4 performs better among minority ethnic groups than white people for impartiality. Such relaxation could also reflect that, by 2014, convergence may have reached the point where similar-seeming services may reach the same screen in the same way, but from an entirely different regulatory background—regulated 'TV' alongside unregulated press or internet.

Phillips' last point is important, and will be returned to. However, the general direction that Ofcom were looking in had been flagged-up some months earlier, in January 07, by Ed Richards at IPPR Media Convention: "The regulatory framework may help generate the high levels of popular trust in broadcast news compared with other outlets. But the impartiality rules which underpin that trust may come at the price of constraining diversity of viewpoint."

Already, the potential conflict between impartiality and diversity is highlighted, but Richards' view is by no means universally shared by those actively involved in the media. In its response to "New News",[22]

> Channel 4 rejected any suggestion that impartiality rules stifle debate and restrict the range of voices that can be heard on TV. If broadcasters are

---

[22] Ofcom, *New News, Future News: responses to the Ofcom discussion document*, October 2007, 11, original emphasis.

failing to provide enough breadth of opinion generally in TV news then this is an issue that can be addressed without removing the impartiality requirements.

Ofcom suggests that impartiality will become less enforceable in future. But Channel 4 says impartiality is a core regulatory function in UK broadcasting regulation. All content regulation will become increasingly difficult to justify as regulated services exist side by side with unregulated ones, but this does not mean that it will be unenforceable for licensed services. Indeed, it is likely that the fact that a service is licensed, and therefore regulated, will become a valuable sign of trustworthiness for consumers. Arguably, with a plethora of news sources, it is ever more important for viewers to be able to identify who it is they can trust for an objective view.

Ofcom also suggests that relaxing impartiality obligations on some non-PSB channels might attract disengaged youth and members of ethnic communities. Channel 4 is unconvinced. Newspapers, which have clear editorial lines, also have difficulty in attracting these segments of the population. The real answer must lie in how the news is presented and the range of stories covered, not in permitting *news* to be anything other than objective and impartial. What is needed is a national conversation, involving politicians, representatives from 'disengaged groups' and broadcasters and other media to explore ways in which society can involve and reflect the involvement of all of its members.

Channel 4 also observes a further important risk.[23] This relates to the fact that, given that almost 100% of UK television news viewing is to programming from the BBC, commercial PSBs, or Sky News, relaxing impartiality requirements for non-PSB channels would in effect create in Sky News a single, powerful, non-impartial television news provider. Of course, there is no certainty that relaxation of regulation would result in Sky becoming partisan in its news coverage.[24] It can be argued that the very presence of the BBC, and the cultural transfer of values brought about by the fact that many Sky News staff have previously worked in the BBC may reduce the likelihood of such an outcome. However, removing such impartiality requirements would serve to end any regulatory guarantee that the only significant UK news broadcaster then not subject to impartiality requirements might not exercise a significant degree of party-political influence. While such a risk might be perceived as problematic and/or unacceptable in itself, it might seem still more so if we take on board that Sky is a broadcaster which, as Channel 4s evidence to a Lords

---

[23] Ibid.
[24] Curran et al Media System, Public Knowledge and Democracy: A Comparative Study *European Journal of Communication* 24 (2009), 5.

Select Committee noted,[25] is itself controlled by a company that also owns over 35% of the UK newspaper market. Thus, relaxing the impartiality requirements in this way would risk increasing further the already substantial power of News Corporation within the UK media market as a whole.

In relation to non-PSB news, the House of Lords Select Committee was unambiguous:[26]

> We believe that any weakening of the impartiality requirements as they apply to UK broadcasters would have a negative impact in the quality and trustworthiness of the country's news. Such a move would not benefit the public or journalists and could run the risk of undermining the most important medium for news.

It is however, unwise to view the UK news market exclusively in terms of UK-based broadcasters. Viewing figures for overseas-based news broadcasters remain relatively small within the UK, but the likely outcome of any substantial regulatory intervention to require overseas broadcasters to observe requirements of impartiality can be seen as being the suspension of such services, or the broadcaster withdrawing their UK service themselves, which the House of Lords Committee found "would not benefit diversity of voice".[27] As regards non-UK news channels, the Committee noted a witness's observation of the near impossibility of regulating international media such as Fox or Al Jazeera: "all we can do is to try to support an alternative, which would be a strong system of public service broadcasting".[28]

Lord Carter of Barnes, speaking for the Government on the Select Committee Report,[29] indicated an ongoing preference for an agenda of impartiality in television news: "The Government fully endorse the committee's considered view of the importance of the impartiality requirements, especially on, but beyond, public service broadcasters." He stated explicitly that such requirements should continue to extend beyond the BBC: "We may be comfortable as a society with the BBC as the sole purveyor of impartial news in television, in radio or at a local level, but I doubt that many, including the BBC, would see that as an ideal outcome."[30]

---

[25] House of Lords, Select Committee on Communications, *The Ownership of the News: Volume I, Report*, HL Paper 122-I, June 2008, para. 351.

[26] Ibid., para. 353.

[27] Ibid., para. 357.

[28] Ibid., para. 356.

[29] Hansard, 5 November 2008, Col.314.

[30] Ibid., Col.312.

The latter point appears to be correct, given the very clear steer given by the BBC in a June 2007 document.[31] In it, the BBC makes a persuasive case that commercial benefits relating to "reach" and "brand" to PSBs from the provision of impartial news output of good quality, may well be underestimated in cost-benefit analyses undertaken in relation to commercial broadcasters' position on future news provision. It is not impossible that awareness of such matters may have in part informed Sky News's perhaps otherwise surprising decision to position itself alongside the BBC in declining to transmit the DEC appeal regarding Gaza.

In the Lords debate on the Select Committee Report, Lord Carter went on to note that,[32]

> Of course the print media are very different. It is a long-standing principle that the content of the press should be free from state intervention. We continue to believe that robust self-regulation is the best way of ensuring high standards of reporting in the press. In fact, as the traditional media place greater emphasis on the internet to deliver content, we may need to trust more to effective self-regulation.

He went on to conclude that, "However, I would like to put on record that we may therefore need to expect more from this system." For those old enough to remember, this feels rather like the then National Heritage Secretary in the 1990s talking of the press and the PCC "drinking in the last chance saloon"! Clearly, the saloon remains open, and it is difficult to see any likelihood of a government calling "time" at the bar. Greater intervention into the print media remains rather far-fetched, because of the political difficulty of such a move, which would cut-across long-established claims of freedom of expression in the press.[33] However, beyond this obstacle, imposing any additional regulatory burden on the press would seem almost impossible to justify or legislate for at a time when parts of the newspaper industry are fast-approaching crisis point in relation to advertising revenue.[34]

THE BIGGER PICTURE

The concept of impartiality in news coverage is of direct application only to one sector—news broadcast by UK broadcasters. As noted above, there

---

[31] BBC, *The Future of News on the Commercial PSBs*, June 2007.

[32] Hansard, 5 November 2008, Col.314.

[33] For an excellent discussion of arguments in this area, see Keane, Op. cit., n.7, chapter 1. See also Feintuck, M. and Varney, M. *Media Regulation, Public Interest and the Law* (second edition), (Edinburgh: Edinburgh University Press, 2006), 9–14.

[34] See *The Ownership of the News*, Op. cit., n.21, paras. 39–41 and para. 59.

seems significant pressure for this in the future to be limited to PSBs, or even perhaps only BBC and C4, or maybe only the BBC. Ofcom's second PSB Review (January 09) seems not to favour this last option, preferring, like Lord Carter, at least one other serious PSB player, probably based around Channel 4, alongside the BBC. It remains to be seen what route government chose to pursue in relation to this agenda, but such a decision may not be unconnected to any possible decision to top-slice the licence fee to offer support for Channel 4.

However, in terms of the degree of confidence we can attach to the ongoing imposition of requirements of impartiality, at present we can see developing a picture of concentric circles. At the heart is the BBC, then PSB channels, then a third circle of other UK broadcasters. But this image only captures a part, and a shrinking part, of overall media news output. There is a large outer circle which appears to be somewhat detached from the others, namely the rest of the global media broadcast news industry, plus UK print media, plus the internet and an abundance of user-generated content. There is a tangible sense of unreality about any debate which does not consider this broader context, or indeed the context of technological convergence, when reviewing impartiality requirements. Significant obstacles are presented, however, as a result of both the apparent impossibility of regulating news content on non-UK originated material, and the political heresy involved in suggesting regulation of print media.

The political impossibility of imposing such requirements on newspapers has to be accepted as a reality, despite the fact that it is clear that it is the broadcast news sector, regulated for impartiality, remains clearly the most trusted medium by the public. Figures published in the British Journalism Review[35] indicate 61% of survey respondents trust BBC journalists to "tell the truth", with 51% for Channel 4 and ITV, 43% for quality press, 18% for mid-market, and 15% for red-tops. As many have rightly acknowledged, and as Keane emphasises, "Democracy requires informed citizens",[36] and it is clear that public service broadcast news, regulated as it is for impartiality, is perceived widely as the most reliable source of "truthful" news, at least amongst traditionally recognised news sources. However, quoted earlier, was the work of Coleman et al, who note also that "We were struck by the confidence that people expressed in the

---

[35] "Trust and the Media: a BJR/You Gov Poll", *The British Journalism Review*, Vol.19, No.2 (June 2008). Cited in *The Ownership of the News*, Op. cit., n.21, para. 344.

[36] Keane, Op. cit., n.7, 176.

internet generally and Google specifically as the most trusted source of explanation and analysis."[37] Certainly, this might be seen as problematic from the point of view of challenging and developing ideas and positions if there is any truth in theses which suggest that people trust the net because it is a place where they get their prejudices confirmed—by talking to like-minded selves and using like-minded news sources.[38] Of course, reliance on internet sources is hardly a surprising finding for academics, faced daily with the written work of students from "the Wikipedia generation" who seem incapable of, or unconcerned about, critically evaluating the content of material gained from notoriously unreliable sources. It might, however, serve to reinforce a case for the maintenance and enhancement of trust in regulated news outlets on which reliance might reasonably and safely be placed.

Seeking to argue against the maintenance of impartiality requirements, Suter observes that,

> The fact that the requirement for impartiality stretches back to the beginning of broadcasting but not into print journalism, implies that it relates to some specific characteristics of broadcasting. Of these, two are particularly important: the necessity for state intervention to secure access to spectrum and therefore audiences; and, linked to that, the potential of the medium to exert a powerful influence over public opinion.[39]

It is not necessary here to address in detail familiar questions regarding differential levels of regulation between media sectors in an era of convergence. It is sufficient to re-assert that theses such as this, and those based around a partial press being acceptable because of the existence an impartial broadcast media appear to offer, rather than a rational or principled basis for the situation, at best an *ex post facto* rationalisation of a situation which in reality appears to have arisen as a consequence of historical accident—while the press fought for freedom in an earlier era, broadcasting came about in an era of interventionist "big government. And in the digital era, the spectrum scarcity argument can now be essentially relegated to historical interest.[40]

---

[37] Coleman et al, Op. cit., n.10, Ibid.
[38] See, for example, Sunstein *Republic.com 2.0* (2007) and *Going to Extremes: How like Minds Unite and Divide* (2009) and Hindman *The Myth of Digital Democracy* (2009).
[39] Suter, T., "Impartiality—the case for change", in Gardam, T. and Levy, D. (eds.), *The Price of Plurality: Choice, Diversity and Broadcasting Institutions in the Digital Age* (Oxford: University of Oxford/Reuters Institute for the Study of Journalism, 2008), 118.
[40] See Feintuck and Varney, Op. cit., n.33, 57.

In the current era, following the essentially deregulatory CA03, the dominant assumption in relation to media regulation, is that, in general, the market will deliver—diversity of views will emerge and remain in circulation as a result of plurality of outlets and ownership, and hence regulatory intervention is necessary only at the extremes/margins via interventions in respect of takeovers and mergers, frequently leaving oligopoly as the norm. Such limited intervention and reliance on market forces serves as a politically convenient and ideologically preferred surrogate for direct intervention in pursuit of diversity of views as means of protecting democratic interests in news output—interests which are invariably assumed and too rarely spelled-out. Of course, assumptions about the relationship between plurality of ownership and diversity of output should not be accepted uncritically—though there is a clear *contingent* relationship between plurality of ownership and diversity of output, it can be strongly argued that there is no *necessary* relationship between the two. Simply put, it is easy to observe how, in pursuit of audience maximisation, a multiplicity of media owners may still produce output targeted at the lowest common denominator or clustered predominantly around the most popular themes and types of output.[41]

In reality, regulation aimed at plurality of ownership may properly be viewed as a convenient surrogate for what would be more controversial intervention targeted directly at regulation of media output in pursuit of diversity. As has been argued elsewhere,[42]

> Congdon et al. (1995: 70) note that 'The aim of regulation of market share is primarily to restrict influence, but it ought, within a general competition framework, to provide the necessary—though not sufficient—condition for access and for content diversity'. This is important, both in highlighting the absence of any necessary, direct, connection between regulation of market share and ensuring diversity of content, and at the same time emphasising that regulation of market share serves only as a surrogate for regulation focused unashamedly at the ultimate objective, freely available and diverse content.

Yet it is the assumed relationship between plurality of ownership and diversity of output that underlies all recent legislation, and indeed the recent House of Lords Inquiry into "The ownership of the news", referred to above, which focused on the relationship between ownership patterns

---

[41] Ibid., 59–61.
[42] Ibid., 70.

and diversity and "quality" of news output. The agenda for this Inquiry was much broader than simply impartiality, though this emerged as central to it. Broadly put, the agenda which the Inquiry pursued addressed matters of,

(5) *quantity* (broadcast hours, and column inches),
(6) *quality* (accuracy, analysis and timeliness, the latter becoming increasingly important and, maybe on occasion running-counter to the first two!),
(7) *diversity* (including local and sectional perspectives), and
(8) *impartiality* in news output.

Of course, diversity of ownership does not guarantee any of the above, given the essentially contingent relationship between ownership patterns and quantity, quality, diversity and impartiality of news output without regulatory intervention It is worth noting in passing that questions of levels of investment in journalism, and original journalism, emerged as important sub-themes to the Committee's considerations of quality and diversity of news output. Also worth noting is a further approach which the Inquiry touched on—it is possible that journalistic and/or editorial independence is just as important as, or perhaps more important than, diversity of ownership, with the Scott Trust serving as an example of a structure which might offer guarantees in this regard.[43] It is also possible that guarantees of independence written into journalists' contracts might also serve to limit proprietorial or editorial control, and may contribute towards agendas of diversity and impartiality, though it is highly debatable whether any such measure can avoid the likelihood of editors appointing journalists, or owners appointing editors, who share their world view.

It might be thought that impartiality is a curious approach to adopt in relation to news journalism, given the risk of it leading to very bland news coverage—certainly, it could lead towards output very far-removed from the opinionated news agendas which we often find in the very best journalism. However, it can also, as our PSB tradition at its best does, lead to what is often considered to be news output which is reliable and "high quality".

In light of all of the above, it has to be concluded that impartiality requirements for some outlets remain necessary and justified—in their absence, the freedom of expression in mass media that is so often talked

---

[43] *The Ownership of the News*, Op. cit., n.21, para. 155.

about, in the absence of guarantees of editorial/journalistic independence can amount in reality to guaranteeing nothing beyond freedom of expression for those with enough financial power to own media outlets. Of course, some such media owners may demonstrate a strong commitment to contributing to agendas of freedom of expression, diversity of viewpoint and quality of output. Meanwhile, others may not, and in the absence of regulatory interventions requiring such outcomes from at least some media outlets, there is no guarantee that this important expectation will be delivered. As regards ways of reaching the sectors of society currently disengaged from mainstream news provision, as Tait observes, "There is no evidence that relaxing the rules on impartiality would make television news more appealing to hard-to-reach groups such as young and black and minority ethnic viewers."[44]

Whether it would be sufficient to leave only the BBC with obligations of impartiality, or the BBC and Channel 4, or the BBC, Channel 4 and the other commercial PSBs is open to debate. The underlying question, however, is whether the debate will be decided by reference to democratic principles relating to the need for an informed and active citizenry[45] or by pragmatic and reactive responses to technological change and market forces, informed by a belief in the power of the market to deliver what individuals want.

Conclusions

If access to a range of viewpoints and a quantity of high quality news material sufficient to permit an informed and active citizenry remains important, then reliable impartiality also seems to remain important; in its absence, there is no guarantee that the market will deliver such outcomes. That said, the maintenance or enhancement of impartiality requirements will be difficult, indeed increasingly difficult to define and justify, if the general and predominant approach to media regulation is through market-based techniques and values. The combination of factors that have been identified above, have certainly made it increasingly difficult to justify the imposition of impartiality requirements on commercial PSBs. It is even more difficult in relation to non-PSB channels,

[44] Tait, R. "Impartiality—why it must stay", in Gardam, T. and Levy, D. (eds.), Op. cit., n.34, 112.
[45] See Feintuck and Varney Op. cit., 107–111.

approaching impossible in relation to non-UK channels and the internet, and politically unthinkable in relation to the press. Yet these distinctions between traditional media sectors are now all but impossible to defend on any rational basis, and rely on sectoral divides that have rapidly broken-down in the face of technological convergence and cross-media practices and ownership patterns.

Thus there is a pressing need to establish (or re-establish) and assert (or re-assert) a justificatory basis for intervention to ensure impartiality in at least some sections of the mass media. Despite the prominence/dominance of market-oriented approaches to media regulation, the Lords Inquiry does suggest underlying cross-party consensus (in the political mainstream) on the existence of democratic imperatives which can be used as a basis on which intervention can be legitimated.

As has been noted elsewhere,[46] in a quietly radical proposal, the UK's House of Lords Select Committee on Communications in 2008 identified correctly and highlighted an issue which is often neglected or avoided in debates over media regulation. While competition law responses are generally premised on concerns about the market, and the interests of players and consumers, the basis of legitimacy for special measures targeted at media industries is, in reality, derived from arguments regarding the democratic interests relating to citizenship, which extend far beyond those of consumerism

Without going into great detail, it is worth at this point considering how the UK legislative framework relevant to media regulation recognizes explicitly the existence of a potentially significant divergence of interests as between citizens and consumers (perhaps representing, respectively, democratic and market interests). Section 3(1) of CA03 explicitly distinguishes between citizen and consumer interests in establishing Ofcom's general duties, while the statutory provisions which govern media take-overs and mergers[47] identify a range of "public interest" considerations clearly inspired by concern for a range of values relating to citizenship and democracy rather than consumer interests in the marketplace.

In the case of a newspaper merger, the public interest considerations, as defined by the Act, are:

---

[46] Feintuck, M., "Regulating media markets in the public interest—principles beyond competition", *Journal of Media Business Studies*, 6:3 (2009), 63–77.

[47] Section 375 Communications Act 2003, incorporated into Section 58 Enterprise Act 2002.

- The need for accurate presentation of news in newspapers;
- The need for free expression of opinion in the newspapers involved in the merger;
- The need for, to the extent that is reasonable and practicable, a sufficient plurality of views expressed in newspapers as a whole in each market for newspapers in the UK or part of the UK.

In the case of a broadcasting merger or a cross-media merger, the pubic interest considerations as defined by the Act, are:

- The need for there to be a sufficient plurality of persons with control of the media enterprises serving that audience in relation to every different audience in the UK or a particular area/locality of the UK;
- The need for availability throughout the UK of a wide range of broadcasting which (taken as a whole) is both of high quality and calculated to appeal to a wide variety of tastes and interests;
- The need for persons carrying on media enterprises and for those with control of such enterprises to have a genuine commitment to the attainment in relation to broadcasting of the standards objectives set out in Section 319 of the CA03 (for example governing matters of accuracy, impartiality, harm, offence, fairness and privacy in broadcasting).

In essence, the provisions are targeted at maintaining a degree of diversity and quality within media output in the UK. Though at one level these seem quite detailed elaborations of the principles underlying the powers, it is clear that the precise way in which such broad provisions will be interpreted remains subject to substantial regulatory discretion. However, what is important for present purposes is that this regime has unique aspects, as the general system of competition law in the UK is based almost entirely on economic considerations, and, the procedure under Part III of Chapter 2 is the only part of the EA02 which bestows a significant role on the Secretary of State and demands engagement with arguments relating to a vision of "public interest" which extends beyond the pursuit of effective market competition.

In recognition of the divergent interests of citizen and consumer, or democracy and market, the House of Lords Committee recommended explicitly that "When Ofcom considers the public interest considerations of a media merger it should be required to put the needs of the citizen ahead of the needs of the consumer."[48] Of course, great clarity is needed as

---

[48] Op. cit., n.21, para. 275.

to precisely what is intended by "the needs of the citizen". However, though this recommendation is not focused on the present topic of impartiality, in seeking to address the prioritization of citizenship interests, echoing the Puttnam Report's recommendations on the Draft Bill which led to the Communications Act 2003, the Select Committee's Report does represent a relatively rare, but important step in re-confirming the ongoing necessity for, and legitimacy of media regulation in pursuit of citizenship-related values in the face of powerful economic forces associated with technological change and corporate conglomeration and consolidation in the media industries.

The imposition of requirements of impartiality represents an attempt to ensure a minimum standard of balance from the most important and most trusted news sources on the most important issues, facilitating the expectations of citizenship in relation to informed participation in civil society. These requirements also serve as an acknowledgement that the market, even a market regulated by reference to competition concerns and consumer rights, cannot be relied upon to deliver on this agenda. If, as the present author has argued previously,[49] expectations of citizenship are placed at the forefront of the regulatory regime relating to the media, as regards debate about impartiality in news as much as any other issue, it may be possible to start building a regime which can legitimately pursue directly the citizenship-serving objectives of impartiality without being diverted by the sometimes parallel, but sometimes contradictory, issues of diversity of news content and news outlets, and plurality of ownership

Despite some shared heritage within a liberal-democratic tradition, it can properly be argued that there are also some important differences in the lineage of impartiality and diversity. The expectation or requirement of impartiality in news broadcasting appears to derive clearly from an admittedly unfashionable paternalistic, "public interest" perspective, closely related to the PSB tradition that has been so significant in the UK and much of the rest of Western Europe. Meanwhile, diversity appears to be rooted largely in a tradition which emphasises matters such as equality and the representation of minorities, but also relates more closely to an individualistic set of values, and one which can be readily linked to consumerist needs and desires that can be serviced via market formats. In simple terms, while arguments for diversity tend to serve and reflect the liberal element of "liberal democracy", meshing closely with the

---

[49] Feintuck and Varney, Op. cit., n.33, chapter 3.

consumerist and individualistic zeitgeist, impartiality, with its concerns for an informed citizenry is linked much more directly to the democratic aspect of it.

Without doubt, diversity of high quality news output seems desirable, but in the absence of reliably impartial news sources of quality, a diverse media requires the end-user to engage effectively in triangulation of sources in order to obtain an "accurate" perspective. Diversity of available news is therefore not, by itself, enough. To expect end-users to routinely and effectively triangulate sources in this way places major demands on individual citizens and groups—they need to be sufficiently news aware, to be sufficiently media-savvy, and to have the necessary time and energy to engage actively in this process of triangulation. This would be a big assumption to make, and is not one that can safely be made. Thus, while it seems likely that most citizens are now guaranteed access to a reasonably wide range of news source, of differing perspectives and quality, it may yet still be desirable to preserve a reliable, impartial, quality news service (or more than one?) to ensure universal access to a service which can serve as a surrogate for the diligent research and triangulation undertaken by the "ideal-type" citizen. This does imply an unfashionably paternalistic approach, but, it might be argued, a democratically necessary approach.

We do need to remain aware, however that, as noted earlier, impartiality could imply a bland news agenda, or unduly defensive approaches (as, perhaps, exemplified by the BBC's approach to the DEC Gaza appeal), which could lead to alienation from news for many citizens as individuals or groups. Equally, impartiality does not necessarily imply a wide-ranging or inclusive construct of diversity—"narrow impartiality", applied only to the political mainstream, though important, may not help achieve the widest sense of inclusivity in society, or relevance of the mainstream news agenda across the broadest spectrum of social groups, again perhaps illustrated by the BBC's response to the DEC Gaza Appeal. Likewise, the sort of journalism that Lloyd describes,[50] based on "a pervasive contempt for the governing classes, ... a concentration on process at the expense—often the complete obliteration—of policy and outcomes; a privileging of conflict and complaint and a dramatization of ordinary conflict, such as within government as crises" may remain in a real sense impartial, but may prove counter-productive in democratic terms leading to citizens

---

[50] Lloyd, Op. cit., n.8, at 195.

being disengaged rather than active and well-informed. Thus there remains the risk that certain visions of impartiality could actually produce the unintended consequence of furthering the disengagement from mainstream news of large groups; an issue which may well need addressing, but has to be properly seen as an issue quite distinct from arguments about the essential democratic purposes of and justifications for impartiality requirements.

Given the apparent democracy-serving intended function of impartiality in some of our major news sources, it seems crucial that we retain interventions that service this agenda But, diversity of output is also to be valued, and is desirable in itself, if, as suggested above, in pursuit of a related but different sets of values. Ultimately, it seems preferable that we have both. Tait,[51] referring with apparent approval to the BBC's expressed perspective,[52] states that "diversity and impartiality have to work together, not in conflict—in a diverse society with complex problems, true impartiality is about fairly reflecting diversity and not restricting coverage to a narrow and sometimes politically correct view of the world." However, it remains crucial that diversity and impartiality be not confused, and that, where a choice has to made as to which should be prioritised, it should always be impartiality, in the direct service of citizenship and democracy, which should come out on top.

---

[51] Tait, Op. cit., n.38, Ibid.
[52] In "From seesaw to wagon wheel...", Op. cit., n.4.

PACKAGED VOICES: A CASE STUDY ON THE MEDIATION OF
MINORITY VOICES (ASYLUM SEEKERS) ON TELEVISION NEWS

Bernard Gross

"Although "access" [to the media] can hardly be described as a human right
in itself, it can be a crucial factor in rendering the human right to freedom of
expression effective in practice."

McGonagle, this collection

"who gets "on" or "in" the news is important—very important indeed. Whose
voices and viewpoints structure and inform news discourse goes to the heart
of democratic views of, and radical concerns about, the news media."

Cottle, (2000). "Rethinking News Access." *Journalism Studies* 1(3): 427–448.

To have access to, to be part of the media and the news media is essential
in a liberal democracy if one is to be part of the public sphere through
which society attempts to work out what it is, what it is not and decide on
common purposes. Alternatively, this means that to have limited or be
denied access to this sphere "can have far reaching consequences" about
whether "social groups are representationally legitimated or symbolically
positioned as "Other", labelled deviant or rendered speechless".[1] Minorities,
one of the groups identified by Cottle in this context, are prone to be on
the receiving end of such treatment by parts of the media; hence the
development of legislation to safeguard against their being stereotyped or
denied media access. However, as McGonagle points out in this volume
(citing Lichtenberg) there cannot be an unqualified right to access to the
media for everyone, as it would spell chaos and render public discourse
ineffective. The developing set of "contingent" rights of access that have
been established by the Council of Europe in relation to minorities and
media access is trying to strike a balance and in McGonagle's estimate
represent "a string of near-misses and staggered successes". It is important
to realise, however, that even these do not necessarily apply equally to all
minorities. In reference to the *The European Charter for Regional or*

---

[1] Cottle (2000), 428.

Minority Languages, McGonagle writes: "the languages of so-called new minorities and migrants are *presumptively* excluded from the protection and promotion generally offered by the Charter's provisions." So what about groups that cannot lay claim to any form of news access rights? Refugees and asylum seekers, for instance, are difficult to define in the terms required by these legal frameworks. Their inherent heterogeneity beyond their shared experience of the asylum application process makes it difficult to define them as a coherent minority group. A number of research projects have analysed their portrayal by parts of the British media and have found it to be often problematic:[2] Refugees and asylum seekers have often been portrayed in exactly those terms noted by Cottle above. Recently Gross, Moore and Threadgold undertook an Oxfam-funded study into the representation of refugees and asylum seekers on British television news.[3] It is these findings that I now wish to draw upon before analysing one particular instance in more detail.

CASE STUDY: 'BROADCAST NEWS COVERAGE OF ASYLUM SEEKERS'

The main findings of the study[4] were:

1) Asylum and refugee issues are "rarely the main focus of reporting or news .... *Asylum* is, however, regularly mentioned in news stories focussing on other topics.[5]" The voices of asylum seekers and refugees are rarely part of television news. People labelled 'refugees' and 'asylum seekers'[6]—labels that were not always applied correctly—are very rarely used as sources of information in news items.

---

[2] Cf S. Buchanan, B. Grillo and T. Threadgold, "What's the Story? Results from research into Media Coverage of Refugees and Asylum Seekers in the UK" (Article 19, London 2003); ICAR, "Media Image, Community Impact: assessing the impact of media and political images of refugees and asylum seekers on community relations in London" (Information Centre about Asylum and Refugees in the UK, 2004).

[3] B. Gross, K. Moore and T. Threadgold, "Broadcast News Coverage of Asylum, April to October 2006: Caught Between Human Rights and Public Safety" (Cardiff School of Journalism Media and Cultural Studies, Cardiff University, Cardiff 2007).

[4] Between 24th April and 31 July 2006 BBC 1 News, ITV News and Channel 4 News were tracked by a team of researchers from Cardiff University for the use of the words refugee or asylum which was then subsequently analysed quantitatively as well as qualitatively.

[5] Gross et al 2007, 6.

[6] These labels are not always used correctly (for a discussion of labelling see Buchanan et al 2003; Gross et al 2007). However, whether applied correctly or not, these labels identify people within the individual news story, hence data has been selected accordingly.

2) Even though coverage in terms of intensity, use of certain images or negative labels had changed from that observed in previous research[7] the negative discursive framework has remained remarkably stable.[8]

3) When asylum and refugee issues are mentioned but are not the main focus of an item, recurring connections between them and a number of dominant themes, such as terrorism or political crisis, frame these issues "as a largely negative phenomenon"[9]

4) Of the 53 stories on BBC TV News,[10] that mentioned the terms 'asylum' or 'refugee' 8? 6 stories on *Channel 4 News*, 2 stories on *ITV 1 News* and no stories on *BBC 1 News* featured an asylum seeker or refugee as a source.

The first three points highlight how asylum and refugee issues were discursively positioned at that time within the main evening news on three of the five UK public service broadcasters, the three with the largest audience share for news. The fourth point raises two issues which are of particular concern here. One, it indicates that the voices of refugees and asylum seekers are not often part of television news. Two, the low frequency suggested by these numbers does not in itself say anything about the how and what. The how and what become relevant when voice is more than just sound but attains a political dimension as "the expression of a distinctive perspective on the world that needs to be acknowledged".[11] In other words, when these voices are part of a news story, when refugees and asylum seekers are given access, it becomes important to analyse whether their voice counts in the political sense by looking at what they say and how this is incorporated into the discursive structure of a news story.

All but one of the voices of a featured asylum seeker or refugee were embedded in so-called packages, that is, pieces in which a journalist puts together various interview fragments as well as well as footage and graphics, which are usually introduced by a presenter in the studio and accompanied by a running commentary, a so-called voice over by a reporter. It is precisely the selection and interweaving of the different elements into an

---

[7] Buchanan et al 2003.

[8] Gross et al 2007, 9.

[9] Ibid.

[10] These 53 items are those that mention either the term 'asylum' or 'refugee' in a UK or EU context on BBC 1 *News at 10*, the evening Channel 4 *News*, and the late evening news on ITV 1 during 24 April and 31 July 2006. Note: EU context means pertaining to the EU-level not to other EU countries.

[11] N Couldry, *Why Voice Matters: Culture and Politics After Neoliberalism* (London: Sage 2010), 1.

ordered and hierarchical "web of voices"[12] that establishes the discursive
structure and potential meaning of an individual piece. Because of the
high level of construction inherent in this type of news item—compared
for instance to the broadcasting of a full-length interview—I call this
occurrence of voice a *packaged voice*. The *packaged voice* positions the
migrant in his or her own words as an integral part of the structure of an
individual piece. The key characteristic of the *packaged voice*, however, is
the tension between content and meaning, the content of the migrant's
utterance and its meaning within the particular news story. Media professionals have the ability to define meaning and to direct interpretation
through the selection of particular fragments and their con-/re-
/entextualisation,[13] packaging as part of the item. This process is inherent
to standard and acceptable processes of journalistic production from
beginning to end. When journalists approach a topic, they do not start
from scratch. Besides their general knowledge and understanding of the
world, they may have some specific ideas about a particular topic, which
influences the way a topic is developed into a story and the story into an
item on a television news programme or an article in a newspaper.[14]
In fact, research has shown that later on in the production process, at the
stage when raw material is put together, journalists tend to focus on and
frame this material in such a way that it confirms or is adaptable to their
'basic narratives'[15] rather than re-orientate their approach substantially.

To provide an example of this drawn from the data of this study by
Gross et al, I will analyse a package on debates over the Human Rights Act
by the journalist Lucy Manning on Channel 4 *News* on 13 May 2006. In this
report Manning discusses recent political controversies about human
rights legislation, which revolved around the suggestion that the legislation and its interpretation by judges favoured the "rights of criminals" over
the right of the public to be protected. One example cited is the case of a
group of men from Afghanistan who hijacked a plane to come to Britain
and to claim asylum, who were eventually allowed to stay without being
given refugee status. Their (collective) voice enters the piece via a written
statement that they released—apparently, in reaction to the debate. The
letter, written in the first person plural, is represented as part of a graphic

---

[12] N Fairclough, *Media Discourse* (London: Arnold, 1995), 81.

[13] Cf. J. Blommaert, *Discourse* (Cambridge: Cambridge University Press, 2005), 45–48.

[14] S.E. Clayman, "Defining Moments, Presidential Debates, and the Dynamics of
Quotability" 45 *Journal of Communication*, 118.

[15] M. Nylund, "Asking questions, making sound-bites: research reports, interviews and
television news stories" 5 *Discourse Studies*, 517.

sequence that also shows mug-shots of the men and is read out by a journalist.

By analysing the story in sequence, the same way it was broadcast, I intend to highlight how a particular position for their statement within the discursive structure of the piece is developed as the package progresses. In this case this process is set in motion within in the first second of the coverage. Research has highlighted the important role a news presenter or anchor, "who frames the subject area and provides basic information and a preview of the story",[16] plays for the discursive development of a whole item during the introduction phase of a topic. It is there that discursive frames are established against which and within which the remainder of the coverage occurs. In this case, this phase consists of two sequences, a trailer at the beginning of the programme and the actual introduction to the package both presented by Channel 4 News anchor Krishnan Guru-Murthy.

During the trailer the Afghan men are not visually represented but are mentioned verbally in the anchor's voice-over. On the visual level the screen is split. One half shows the mug-shot of a man the other that of a plane in front of an airport hangar. The man, who is not identified at this point, is the convicted sex offender Anthony Rice. Rice committed murder while being released on probation. The plane presumably is the plane that the 9 Afghani men hijacked in 2000. In his commentary Channel 4 *News* presenter Krishnan Guru-Murthy starts by evoking a number of voices: "Amid rows over Afghan hijackers and criminals freed to commit murder"—but only identifies one specific voice that is involved in the rows— "the government says it needs to clarify the balance between public safety and human rights". He concludes in his own voice that is his own professional voice as the presenter of a news programme by raising the question that will presumably be answered within the coverage of the issues: "But can it be done without tearing up the European Convention?"

Later, when the programme returns to the topic, Guru-Murthy names, or rather specifies a few more voices in the introduction to the package. The voice of the government is represented through specific comments made by the then Lord Chancellor, Lord Falconer, in a radio interview given that morning that Guru-Murthy seems to be referring to and which appears to provide the reason to cover the topic on this particular day.

---

[16] J. Lewis, S. Inthorn and K. Wahl-Jorgensen *Citizens or Consumers: what the media tell us about political participation* (Maidenhead and New York: Open University Press 2005), 74.

Guru-Murthy presents the introduction seated, while a screen behind him shows an image consisting of several statues of Lady Justice. He says:

> Public safety comes first the Lord Chancellor insisted today, as he admitted the government was considering changes to the Human Rights Act. Lord Falconer said, there was real concern about how the act was working in practice and new legislation might be needed to make sure public safety wasn't endangered.

The presenter then brings in a new voice, likely to be another one of those involved in the rows mentioned in the trailer and finishes by introducing the reporter who covered the topic: "Human rights campaigners said current worries weren't the fault of the act itself—as Lucy Manning reports."

So far the audience has been introduced to three voices: the Lord Chancellor's, human rights campaigners', both of which are channelled through the third voice, the voice of the presenter. The latter voice is dominant at this point and establishes a discursive frame, assigning particular roles to the participants in the debate over balancing the Human Rights Act. On the one side is the government and on the other are 'human rights campaigners'. At stake is the safety of the public. This is actually presented as something these two sides agree on. Their disagreement appears to be over how this can be achieved. Whereas the government finds fault with the Human Rights Act and wants to change it, the 'human rights campaigners' seem to suggest that it is not the act that is the problem. The way these explicit points of agreement and disagreement are presented also imply the further point of agreement over public safety: There is a problem, public safety should come first and is indeed at risk. The risk comes from cases such as those cited by Guru-Murthy at the very beginning, "Afghan hijackers and criminals freed to commit murder". Through the labelling as hijackers as well as the close association with murderers, the Afghan men have already developed the potential to be cast as criminals, if not one of the villains in the emerging discursive structure. Their role at this point, however, is not particularly central and their voice has been set up as marginal to the discursive structure. They are merely examples of villainy, turned into an iconic sign of the potential risk to public safety that sparks of the debate around the balance of justice, which is the focus of the coverage—a focus visually highlighted by the image of blind Lady Justice.

While the initial phase of the coverage is important it does not mean following developments could not change these positionings. However, the piece by Lucy Manning echoes and further solidifies this discursive structure. It starts out with a summary of the Anthony Rice case as well as the case of the Afghan men that uses similar visual elements as those used during the trailer at the beginning of the programme. Manning says:

> Convicted sex attacker Antony Rice was freed to kill Naomi Bryant. The enquiry finding too much attention was paid to his human rights. And a judge decided the government should let 9 Afghan hijackers stay in the country as refugees, because under human rights law the men couldn't be sent home as their lives would be at risk—both cases tipping the government into doing something about the Human Rights Act.

Again the journalist, in this case Manning, becomes the filter for other, paraphrased voices—the voice of 'the enquiry' and the voice of the judge. By interpreting the government's action as a reaction to these two cases, she also establishes a certain level of equivalence between the two. The decision to free Anthony Rice and the judge's decision in the case of the Afghan men are presented as equally flawed. For flaws in the Rice case she can cite an official enquiry. Her claims for the Afghan men are less clear. She does not engage in the judge's argument herself, nor does she cite another source of criticism to back up her claim. Her only evidence seems to lie in the reaction of the government, i.e. the reaction of the government proves that the judge's decision is wrong. Since Manning does not question the government's line of argument at this point this suggests that she may be sharing it. However, again this is a question that can only be answered by looking at the further development of the discursive structure.

The next two voices brought into the web are David Cameron, the leader of the opposition Conservative Party, and Lord Falconer. Both are paraphrased. The Lord Chancellor's voice is also heard directly in an excerpt from a BBC 4 radio interview. While the excerpt is played the screen shows a graphic: a photo with the caption "Lord Falconer speaking on BBC Radio 4" is positioned in the centre of the frame on a background containing an image of a statue on the left and an photograph showing the crest on the wall at the Royal Courts of Justice building in London. The framing of the statue and the quality of the image is such that it is impossible to ascertain whether it is an image of Lady Justice again. However, considering the context and the previous use of the statue as a symbolic sign for justice within the programme, it is highly likely. This imagery of justice not only picks up on the focus of the coverage but also parallels the comparatively abstract contribution of Lord Falconer. Neither Cameron nor Falconer picks up on the specific examples that may pose a threat to public safety. Both of their voices, however, add to the argument that the Human Rights Act may be compromising public safety and suggest possible remedies, ripping it up in Cameron's case and amending it in Lord Falconer's opinion.

In difference to these comparatively abstract points about legislation and public safety, the voice immediately following the interview excerpt points more explicitly to the criminals that are a danger to the public. It is the voice of Denis MacShane, a Member of Parliament for the Labour Party, here identified as "Denis MacShane MP, Former Europe Minister". He is shown standing in front of the Houses of Parliament delivering the following statement:

> I remember when the act went through. It wasn't envisaged that the civil rights lawyers funded by taxpayers with judges would act against the will of parliament. There isn't a single MP across the road who doesn't have his constituents' safety and right to be protected from some of these people at the heart of their thinking. And it is really the judges and the civil rights— rights lawyers who got this so desperately wrong.

Two aspects I want to highlight here are: a) the deictic expression "from some of *these* people", b) the positioning of civil rights lawyers and judges as part of the problem. "*These* people" may be meant as a *general* reminder of the criminals who threaten public safety under the protection of the Human Rights Act. In the context of this coverage the general reminder finds two *specific* targets. "*These* people" are Anthony Rice and the Afghan men. Again, however, they are restricted to the part of bit-players. According to MacShane, they do pose the immediate risk, but it is the civil rights lawyers and judges who are responsible for creating the risk in the first place. This leads me to return to the start of the Manning segment. It is this line of argument that could explain her interpretation of the government's reaction. Following MacShane, the reaction is a commonsensical response to the judge's "desperately wrong" ruling in the case of the Afghan men.

Already foreshadowed by MacShane's comments about how the act has strayed from its intended path, the piece now turns to the origins of the Human Rights Act. A short sequence shows the then Home Secretary Jack Straw in October 2000, presenting the act and giving his assessment of the act in a statement. He says: "It is an important day for the rights of the citizens of this country against the state." Within the discursive structure Straw's comments represent a turning point. They are a reminder of the promise of the act. A promise that some but not everyone feels has since been compromised. It is from here that voices in favour of the act are brought into the web. It is only somewhat of a turning point, however, because the discursive structure is not abandoned or reversed. The look back has merely provided a point of entry to bring in voices pro-Human Rights Act. These voices are positioned within the existing discursive structure with little scope to challenge it.

Straight after Straw's statement the piece returns to the present (2006), to Downing Street, the official residence of the British Prime Minister, in front of which Lucy Manning is shown standing as she gives a short piece to camera:

> Well, Downing Street is obviously taking note of the public's outrage over recent court decisions that appear to protect the rights of criminals above those of the public and they are no doubt also looking at the tabloid campaign to get the Human Rights Act abolished. But while the government hasn't shirked away from criticising the decisions of judges, is the threat to introduce legislation a step too far?

Structurally, this short segment leads up directly to a statement by Shami Chakrabarti, the director of pro-human-rights organisation Liberty, who provides an implicit answer to the question posed by Manning. Before Chakrabarti can give her answer, however, the segment solidifies the discursive structure of the piece by introducing two more, anti-human-rights voices: the tabloid media and the public. Again, their voices do not appear directly but are merely referenced by Manning to provide evidence. Assessed on the basis of the piece itself, however, the evidence is rather weak. So far positions or groups supposedly holding these positions cited by Manning have at least been ascribed to specific people or have been represented by an example, e.g., Dennis MacShane as an example of the politicians in the House of Commons. In this instance, however, the alleged media campaign to abolish the Human Rights Act is summarily ascribed to the tabloid media in general. Manning provides no further specifics or examples. Nor does she question the reasons why the tabloids may be running such a campaign. In fact, combined with her claim about "the public's outrage" the tabloids' position seems to be merely reflecting the will or rather the emotional condition of the people, a condition, however, for which Manning provides no obvious evidence. It remains unclear how Manning has assessed public opinion to arrive at the conclusion that the public is outraged. It is not uncommon for journalists to cite the public in their coverage. In fact using an assumed public opinion without evidence is a standard technique in television news.[17] This can become rather problematic, because journalists regularly make inaccurate assumptions

---

[17] J. Lewis et al (2005), 21.

about public opinion. A point confirmed in their research on the representation of citizens in US and UK television news, by Lewis et al[18] who found
that "conventional journalistic wisdom may fly in the face of polling data".
This is not to say that Manning does get it wrong here, only that she provides no evidence that she got it right. Regardless of the accuracy of these
claims, they suggest an outraged populace by the incorrect application of
the Human Rights Act and a tabloid media keen on getting rid of it
altogether.

This anti-human-rights position is given further credence by the government's criticism of the judges' decision. Again, Manning does not question the appropriateness of this criticism. Suggesting that the government's
possible introduction of further legislation could be a step too far, Manning
seems to imply that all previous steps have been within the acceptable
limits. Moreover, Manning uses a question to raise the criticism rather
than a declarative statement, thus further distancing herself from its content. Now with an outraged British public, the government, the opposition, and the House of Commons against her, the stage is set for Shami
Chakrabarti, director of Liberty, to provide a response from the pro-
human-rights side and give an answer to Manning's question. Similar to
McShane she is filmed in with the Houses of Parliament in the background
when she delivers this statement:

> I completely understand why politicians of all colours don't like human
> rights. They are there to provide a check on politicians. Human rights belong
> to the people. It's up to us not to be conned by politicians on the run. It's up
> to us to decide—Do we want them to be more accountable to us or not? We
> shouldn't give in to the lies and spin about the act. The act gives us rights
> against them, including victims' rights against gross failures in public
> protection.

Chakrabarti's implicit answer to the question Manning posed seems to be
"Yes, new legislation is a step too far.", i.e., the Human Rights Act in its current form is a good thing and should not be changed. She attempts to
reposition the 'Us vs. Them' dichotomy to suggest that the Human Rights
Act actually does benefit the public. Her argument, however, is rather
generic, i.e., abstract rather than specific. She does suggest that human
rights protect victims' rights, but where and how as well as in which
instances exactly—theses questions remain unanswered. Her answer
does not explain or even refer to the specifics of the case of Anthony
Rice or the case of the Afghan men. Hence it remains questionable how

---

[18] Ibid., 22.

effective her attempt to introduce a new 'Us vs. Them'-dichotomy is. Through her use of personal pronouns she appears to try to replace 'Us' the public vs. 'Them' the criminals who threaten the public with 'Us' the people vs. 'Them' the politicians and other people in powerful positions who try to 'con' the people. This new dichotomy runs counter to the discursive development of the piece, and this change in direction is not supported by Manning. Chakrabarti's inclusion merely suggests an attempt to establish a level of journalistic balance.[19] Through the inclusion of the Liberty director, it could be argued that pro-Human Rights Act voices have their say, too, and journalistic balance has been achieved. But they only have had their say technically speaking. Manning does not develop Chakrabarti's argument; instead she counters the campaigner's statement by looking at the case of the Afghan men. It is worth reiterating here that so far the Afghan men have been cited as an example of abuses of the Human Rights Act, first by Guru-Murthy then by Manning. Thus Manning's return to the case seems to contradict directly Chakrabarti's claims, unless, of course, Manning intends to challenge the discursive web she has been drawing in the piece so far.

Straight after Chakrabarti, the piece cuts to a graphic that includes the mug-shots of the nine Afghan men. As the camera zooms in on the faces of the men, Manning says: "And now the Afghan hijackers have joined the debate about the human rights legislation which helped them. In a statement arguing that it was right they were allowed to stay, the nine hijackers said:" In this lead-up to the statement that is to follow, the discursive web remains firmly in place. Not only do the mug-shots as well as the labelling of the Afghan men as hijackers connote criminal behaviour in general the mug-shots in particular echo the visual representation of convicted murderer Anthony Rice from earlier on. Seen through the prism of the dichotomy of 'Us' the outraged people vs. 'Them' the criminals, the fact that the human rights legislation has "helped them" does not support Chakrabarti's claim that it protects "victims' rights against gross failures in public protection".

Now comes the point where the Afghan men are given space for their (collective) voice to be heard for the first and only time. It is possible that the statement which was released through the solicitor of the Afghan men was not written by them alone, but this is not the issue here. What is of concern is whether their voice carries enough agency to actually

---

[19] cf. J. Lewis, *The Ideological Octopus: an exploration of television and its audience* (London and New York: Routledge, 1991), 124.

challenge the discursive web established in and through the piece overall. Before they have said anything they have been put on the defensive. They stand accused of not only being a threat to public safety but of being an example of the failure of the Human Rights Act.

From the mug-shots the graphic then switches to one with a plane in the background and the text of a statement released by the Afghan men in the foreground, which besides being on screen is also read out by an unidentified male, presumably a member of the Channel 4 *News* staff:

> We do realise, for the other people on that plane, the hijack was terrifying and we regret causing such fear in the hearts of others. But we did it because we were desperate, and we did not believe we could all get away safely in any other way" Manning interrupts to say: "They added." The male voice then continues: "We face being accused of sponging and living off the state, when it is the last thing we wish or need to do.

Their statement does not engage explicitly with the Human Rights Act. Rather its content suggests an attempt to personalise their experience in order to excuse their actions. In the context of the discursive structure of the piece, however, it does not challenge their association with criminality. No further context is provided that could elaborate on their claims that they acted under duress and out of desperation. The second part of their statement seems almost irrelevant in the context of this piece but was used. The question of whether they are sponging is not one that has an immediate relevance to the rows regarding public safety and human rights—the focus of this piece. Even more so than the statement by the director of Liberty, this statement is marginalised in the discursive web established through the package. Chakrabarti's statement at least engages directly with the specific issue of the day. The statement by the Afghan men does so only partially and seems oddly out of place as a consequence. This becomes even clearer when looking at the concluding segment of the piece.

Immediately after the statement Manning finishes off by saying: "Downing Street knows it will be judged in the polls if criminals keep benefiting from the Human Rights Act. This is Number 10 stepping up the pressure on the judiciary." Her commentary is accompanied by a panning shot of Downing Street starting on a sign that reads "Judges Parking". Manning does not engage in the content of the statement of the Afghan men at all. She appears to suggest that the Afghan men are criminals without engaging in the details of the case, which involved the quashing of their criminal convictions on appeal. The proximity of their statement, their overall positioning within the discursive web of voices—all these aspects suggest that it is the Afghan men who must be some of those "criminals who keep benefiting from the Human Rights Act". Through her commentary Manning appears to dismiss and re-contextualises it as the empty pleading of the guilty. This is how they were defined at the beginning of the piece and this is how they are defined at the end of it in spite of the inclusion of their voice. Their voice has not made a difference.[20]

CONCLUSION

The above analysis raises important questions about the condition of news access and highlights the *potential* for re-and entextualisation, the *(re)packaging of voices*: Voice is given space to provide content. The content is accurate in terms of what was said. In terms of standard journalistic practice, there is nothing that could be called into question. Still, packaging the voice of the Afghan men in the ways noted above have moved its meaning beyond their control. It is shaped by context and the voice's position within the discursive web of voices. Simply getting on the news does not seem to be enough, as the how one is then represented still remains open.

Clearly, this situation is the same for all voices heard on the news. As Harrison points out in this volume, User Generated Content by members of the (mainstream) public are also filtered according to a journalist's 'common sense' understanding and may be appropriated by and adapted to journalistic needs; moreover, intervening with journalistic practice through legislation may result in an unjustifiable curtailment of the freedom of the press. However, considering how refugees and asylum seekers

---

[20] It is interesting to note that the package is followed by a studio interview conducted by Guru-Murthy with Lord Lester, a Liberal Democrat peer and human rights lawyer. In the interview Lord Lester supports the Human Rights Act. He takes issue with the connections made by politicians between public safety and the act and explains in some detail points about the motivation behind the tabloid campaign as well as the case of Afghan men. In his defence of the Human Rights Act on principle Lord Lester echoes Chakrabarti's stance on the issue. When pressed on the issue of the hijack by Guru-Murthy, for instance, Lord Lester says:

"Now that's a very difficult thing when they [Afghan hijackers] have taken the law into their own hands and it's very hard to justify to public opinion. I agree with that. But what is wrong is not the Human Rights Act—as I say—it's explaining to everyone why it is in all out interest that all our rights and freedoms are protected by a law that gives us a direct remedy instead of having to go to Europe."

What becomes clear is that Lord Lester defends principles of law, not the actions of the Afghan men. His voice challenges the position of the Human Rights Act within the discursive web proposed by Manning's piece, not that of the Afghan men.

are often represented in parts of the British media, how rarely they are given space to be heard in their own voices and how legislation on minority news access does not necessarily apply, it is worth examining the issue of the significance of *packaging voices* and how they are assembled and presented by the news media as well as the consequences of this for our understanding of, in this case, the minority voice(s) of the asylum seeker.

THE COUNCIL OF EUROPE'S STANDARDS ON ACCESS TO THE MEDIA FOR MINORITIES: A TALE OF NEAR MISSES AND STAGGERED SUCCESSES

Tarlach McGonagle

INTRODUCTION[1]

The primary object of the type of access under discussion in this chapter is the media, although access to other types of expressive opportunities and fora will also be considered at relevant junctures. The reasons for giving pride of place to the media are manifold. The societal presence of the media is virtually ubiquitous and they have properly been described by Roger Silverstone as constituting "an essential dimension of contemporary experience".[2] Ed Baker has called the media "the central *institution* of a democratic public sphere".[3] It is easy to understand the premises on which these observations have been made. In practice, information and ideas are circulated and debate is conducted primarily in the media. By virtue of their reach, speed, influence and impact, more often than not, the media are the most effective means of receiving, imparting and seeking information and ideas.

These factors—and others—explain why the media can also be important vectors of culture, (cultural) identity and language. Insofar as minority cultures, identities and languages are often marginalised, disadvantaged or discriminated against, corrective measures are required in order to ensure their preservation, transmission and development. It has also been noted that minority cultures, identities and languages undergo "public validation" when they feature in (mainstream) media.[4] In light of

---

[1] The author would like to thank the editors of this volume for their very helpful comments on a draft version of this chapter.

[2] Roger Silverstone, *Why Study the Media?* (London/Thousand Oaks, CA/New Delhi, SAGE Publications, 1999), 1. See also, Peter Dahlgren, *Television and the Public Sphere: Citizenship, Democracy and the Media* (London: SAGE Publications, 1995), 155.

[3] (emphasis per original). C. Edwin Baker, "Viewpoint Diversity and Media Ownership", 60 *Federal Communications Law Journal* (No. 3, 2009), 651–671, at 654.

[4] Stephen Harold Riggins, "The Promise and Limits of Ethnic Minority Media", in Stephen Harold Riggins, ed., *Ethnic Minority Media: An International Perspective* (USA: SAGE Publications, 1992), 276–287, at 283.

the foregoing, it is clear that the media have the potential to pursue such goals. Considerations of representation and participation are crucial in this connection.

Any discussion of issues concerning minorities' access to the media or their representation in the media must carefully navigate several definitional reefs. Key terms and concepts are capable of having multiple—and sometimes divergent—interpretations. This chapter will begin with an attempt to smooth the jagged definitional edges of these terms and concepts and explain (the significance of) the various meanings that can be ascribed to them.

The Council of Europe's normative efforts to create, consolidate and advance rights of access of minorities to the media will then be examined. As such, relevant provisions of its three most salient treaties in this connection, i.e., the European Convention on Human Rights (ECHR), the Framework Convention for the Protection of National Minorities (FCNM) and the European Charter for Regional or Minority Languages (ECRML), will be analysed. Notwithstanding the *prima facie* differences between the treaties in terms of their respective focuses and objectives, they also usefully complement each other in various ways. The present analysis will briefly show how each of the three treaties has contributed to the goal of ensuring representation in/access to the media for minorities. Put succinctly, the ECHR has provided a basis for the elaboration of important principles concerning minority participation in pluralist democratic society and in public debate, including via the media. Relevant case-law of the European Court of Human Rights also underscores the general importance for democracy of effective access to the media and other expressive fora. For its part, the FCNM provides a minority-specific perspective on rights and issues that are relevant to all sections of society, e.g., freedom of expression, media access, participatory and cultural rights. The ECRML, in turn, foregrounds the linguistic dimension to questions of media access and functions.

DEFINITIONAL DILEMMAS

A cluster of related terms and concepts will feature recurrently in the present discussion. In this section, "minority", and the closely congruent terms, "representation" and "access", have been selected as meriting particular scrutiny.

(i) *Minority*

There is no authoritative, binding and universally-accepted definition of "minority" in international human rights law.[5] Attempts to define the term for legal purposes tend to generate highly-charged political discussions. Nevertheless, an approximation of a definition of "minority", developed in the context of the International Covenant on Civil and Political Rights (ICCPR),[6] has become a standard reference point for relevant discussions. It reads as follows:

> [A] group numerically inferior to the rest of the population of a State, in a non-dominant position, whose members—being nationals of the State— possess ethnic, religious or linguistic characteristics differing from those of the rest of the population and show, if only implicitly, a sense of solidarity, directed towards preserving their culture, traditions, religion or language.[7]

It is clear from this definition that a considerable hiatus exists between the meaning of "minority" in everyday language and the meaning it has come to acquire under international human rights law. Whereas the former is concerned above all with the status of numerical inferiority, the latter is additionally and expressly concerned with a number of distinctive features that are taken to be characteristic of a minority group, e.g. a shared language, religion, culture or ethnicity. As a result of the definitional focuses on nationality, a limited number of constitutive group characteristics, and a sense of purposive solidarity among group members, the term, "minority", acquires a complexity that it lacks in its ordinary usage. Not all minorities (loosely defined) meet the more specific cumulative criteria of international human rights law. In consequence, not all minorities are entitled to enjoy the *specific* benefits of the international regime for

---

[5] See generally, John Packer, "Problems in Defining Minorities", in Deirdre Fottrell and Bill Bowring, eds., *Minority and Group Rights in the New Millennium* (The Hague, etc.: Martinus Nijhoff Publishing, 1999), 223–273.

[6] Article 27, ICCPR, deals with the rights of persons belonging to minorities. It reads: "In those States in which ethnic, religious or linguistic minorities exist, persons belonging to such minorities shall not be denied the right, in community with the other members of their group, to enjoy their own culture, to profess and practise their own religion, or to use their own language."

[7] This definition was first put forward by Francesco Capotorti, then Special Rapporteur for the UN Sub-Commission on Prevention of Discrimination and Protection of Minorities, in 1979. Francesco Capotorti, *Study on the rights of persons belonging to ethnic, religious and linguistic minorities* (E/CN.4/Sub.2/384/Rev.1) (New York: United Nations, 1979), esp. p. 96, para. 568.

minority rights protection. In a European context, the term "national minority" is commonly used, bringing with it a host of extra definitional complexities (the details of which are beyond the scope of this paper)[8] and circumscribing the applicability of relevant legal norms accordingly.

The foregoing observations should be borne in mind when considering the FCNM and ECRML, which are discussed below as examples of treaties with detailed provisions concerning minorities' access to the media. The range of programmatic measures set out in the FCNM and ECRML only apply to certain types of minorities, *viz.*, national and linguistic minorities, respectively. However, the limited scope of application of those treaties does not preclude States from adopting measures to facilitate access to the media for a broader range of minorities, including in ways other than those contemplated by the two treaties. As will be explained in more detail below, the protection afforded minorities by the ECHR is not limited to national or linguistic minorities.[9]

(ii) *Representation*

The term, "representation", requires further analysis and (at least) two questions must be answered:

(1) Does the term imply the direct representation of groups (in this case, minorities) or merely the representation of their interests and views by intermediaries?

(2) Does the term refer only to programming and content/output, or does it also include representation in editorial, production and managerial structures and processes?

The answers to these questions can have far-reaching implications for media law, policy and practice alike. They are also very relevant for any assessment of the effectiveness of measures adopted to promote minority representation in the media. Direct, active, multi-level representation obviously makes for (but does not necessarily guarantee) high quality participation by minorities in media activities. Such participation can be

---

[8] For relevant discussion, see: Geoff Gilbert, "The Council of Europe and Minority Rights", 18 *Human Rights Quarterly* (1996) 160–189, at 169; Heinrich Klebes, "The Council of Europe's Framework Convention for the Protection of National Minorities", 16 *Human Rights Law Journal* (No. 1–3, 1995) 92–98, at 93; Rosalyn Higgins, "Minority Rights: Discrepancies and Divergencies Between the International Covenant and the Council of Europe System", in Rick Lawson & Matthijs de Blois, eds., *The Dynamics of the Protection of Human Rights in Europe: Essays in Honour of Henry G. Schermers (Vol. III)* (Dordrecht: Martinus Nijhoff Publishers, 1994), 195–209, at 202.

[9] This point is illustrated by the case of *Khurshid Mustafa & Tarzibachi v. Sweden*, which is discussed in detail below.

an important source of empowerment for minorities insofar as it allows them to influence and challenge perceptions of their groups generated and held by dominant sections of society.[10] It enables them to portray themselves on their own terms. An appreciation of the importance of this kind of empowerment for minorities is evident in Lee C. Bollinger's claim that "free speech is a means by which the society, or the State, continually articulates its positions about the 'goodness' or 'badness' of particular minorities".[11]

However, the benefits of effective representation and participation of minorities in media activities are by no means limited to the members of minority groups. Effective participation by minorities in media activities is likely to have the net effect of enhancing the diversity of information and opinions circulated by the media and of thereby enriching public debate. Another plausible result of increased and more effective participation by minorities in media activities is that different groups in society would be more readily exposed to the views and values of others: an important first step towards greater mutual awareness, communication, understanding and tolerance among different groups in society. This majority-minority dialectic is a crucial, but sometimes understated dimension to minority rights protection.

Conversely, however, indirect representation of minorities or their interests can lead to the production of content *for* minorities rather than *by and for* minorities. This, in turn, can result in an unfortunate mismatch between the content offered to minorities and their actual expressive and informational needs. For instance, it has been noted that problematic practices concerning the presentation and representation of minorities can include: "tokenism; negative stereotyping; unrealistic and simplistic portrayals of their community; negative or non-existent images of their countries or areas of origin".[12]

---

[10] See further: Roger Silverstone & Myria Georgiou, "Editorial Introduction: Media and Minorities in Multicultural Europe", 31 *Journal of Ethnic and Migration Studies* (No. 3, May 2005), 433–441, at 434; Myria Georgiou, *Diaspora, Identity and the Media: Diasporic Transnationalism and Mediated Spatialities* (Cresskill, New Jersey, Hampton Press, Inc., 2006), 28–29; David Morley & Kevin Robins, *Spaces of Identity: Global Media, Electronic Landscapes and Cultural Boundaries* (London: Routledge, 1995).

[11] Lee C. Bollinger, "Notes Toward an Idea: Freedom of Speech and Minorities in the United States", in Yoram Dinstein & Mala Tabory, eds., *The Protection of Minorities and Human Rights* (Dordrecht: Martinus Nijhoff Publishers, 1992), 171–185, at 179.

[12] Andrea Millwood Hargrave, ed., *Multicultural Broadcasting: concept and reality*, Report for the British Broadcasting Corporation, Broadcasting Standards Commission, Independent Television Commission and Radio Authority, November 2002, 2.

(iii) *Access Issues*

The "media" can be described as a convenient, amalgamated concept that comprises content, structures and processes alike.[13] Access to each of those components of the media is assured in different ways, which makes it useful to frame the broader discussion of access in terms of a "taxonomy of access".[14] Karol Jakubowicz's distinction between "a number of levels and forms of access and participation: at the level of (i) programming, (ii) work-force, (iii) editorial control and management, (v) [*sic*] ownership of media, (vi) regulation and oversight of the media, (vii) legislation, etc.", is very useful for analytical purposes.[15] Moreover, the usefulness of this distinction can also be measured in evaluative terms. As Jakubowicz further suggests, the grading of these "different forms of access in terms of the benefits they bring to minorities" could enhance the effectiveness of relevant international standards in which the term "access" is used (see further, the analysis of the FCNM, below).[16]

Conceptual disaggregation is also particularly useful in light of the rapidly changing nature of the media, which are generally becoming increasingly instantaneous, international and interactive.[17] As a result of these changes—the drivers of which are technological, social and cultural in

---

[13] For discussion of "the various structures, contexts and dynamics that inform and shape media representations", see Simon Cottle, "Introduction—Media Research and Ethnic Minorities: Mapping the Field", in Simon Cottle, ed., *Ethnic Minorities and the Media: Changing Cultural Boundaries* (Buckingham & Philadelphia: Open University Press, 2000), 1–30, at 16–18.

[14] Monroe E. Price, *Television The Public Sphere and National Identity* (New York, Clarendon Press, 1995), 194. See also: Monroe E. Price, "An Access Taxonomy", in Andras Sajo, ed., *Rights of Access to the Media* (The Hague, Kluwer Law International, 1996), 1–28.

[15] Karol Jakubowicz, "Report: A critical evaluation of the first results of the monitoring of the Framework Convention on the issue of persons belonging to national minorities and the media (1998–2003)" in *Filling the Frame: Five years of monitoring the Framework Convention for the Protection of National Minorities* (Strasbourg: Council of Europe Publishing, 2004), 113–138, at 116; Karol Jakubowicz, "Persons Belonging to National Minorities and the Media", 10 *International Journal on Minority and Group Rights* (2004), 291–314, at 294–295; Karol Jakubowicz, "Minority Media Rights: A Brief Overview", in George Jones, Sally Holt & John Packer, eds., 8 *Mercator Media Forum* (2005), 100–113, at 104–5.

[16] Karol Jakubowicz, "Report: A critical evaluation of the first results of the monitoring of the Framework Convention on the issue of persons belonging to national minorities and the media (1998-2003)", Op. cit., at 130, and followed by John Packer & Sally Holt, 'ARTICLE 9', in Marc Weller, ed., *The Rights of Minorities in Europe: A Commentary on the European Framework Convention for the Protection of National Minorities* (Oxford and New York: Oxford University Press, 2005), 263–300, at 300.

[17] See generally, Karol Jakubowicz, *A new notion of media?: Media and media-like content and activities on new communications services* (Strasbourg, Council of Europe, April 2009).

nature[18]—the current media offer is more plentiful, quantitatively and qualitatively, than at any point in history. There is a greater range of media at our disposal, offering wider and more diversified functionalities/capabilities and greater differentiation in types of access.[19] A failure to engage with the constantly increasing functional differences of the media will inevitably result in blunt analysis of questions of access to the media. A first step towards a proper appreciation of the divergent functionalities on offer involves prising open the notion of "new media", for instance along the lines of Karol Jakubowicz's comprehensive study, *A new notion of media?* He distinguishes three new notions of media: (i) new-media-to-be;[20] (ii) forms of media created by new actors, and (iii) media or media-like activities performed by non-media actors.[21] The emergence of this third category (or more specifically, new actors making important contributions to public debate) has already been reflected in the case-law of the European Court of Human Rights.[22] This trend is developing rapidly and is flagged here as one that will become increasingly prevalent in the future.

Circumspection is required when describing access to the media as a right. International law has traditionally been reluctant to recognise an individual or group right of access to a *particular* medium or a *particular* type of content. The tendency has rather been to recognise "contingent" rights of access, otherwise—the pragmatic argument runs—the way would be open "for such overload and chaos as to constitute a virtual reductio ad absurdum".[23] Although "access" can hardly be described as a human right in itself, it can be a crucial factor in rendering the human right to freedom of expression effective in practice. If an individual does not have access to a forum or channel in or via which s/he can receive and

---

[18] Ibid., 3; 5–7, and Karol Jakubowicz, "A New Notion of Media", Keynote speech at the 1st Council of Europe Conference of Ministers Responsible for Media and New Communication Services, Reykjavik, 28–29 May 2009.

[19] See further, Recommendation CM/Rec(2011)7 of the Council of Europe's Committee of Ministers to member states on a new notion of media, 21 September 2011.

[20] Whereas the other two new notions of media are self-explanatory, this one may require additional explanation. As Jakubowicz himself writes: "With the digitisation of all media, they may all be transformed into convergent media distributed on broadband networks. Older media will not be substituted for and disappear, but may re-emerge in changed form, as another source of content available on broadband Internet and other broadband networks", Op. cit., 19.

[21] Op. cit., 19 *et seq.*

[22] See, for example, *Steel & Morris v. the United Kingdom*, discussed below. See also, *Társaság a Szabadságjogokért v. Hungary*, Judgment of the European Court of Human Rights (Second Section) of 14 April 2009, para. 36.

[23] Judith Lichtenberg, "Introduction", in Judith Lichtenberg, ed., *Democracy and the mass media* (Cambridge, etc., Cambridge University Press, 1990), 1–20, at 17.

impart information and ideas, then his/her expressive opportunities are curtailed and consequently, his/her right to freedom of expression clearly is not effective in practice. Viewed from this perspective, access to the media is of great instrumental importance for the realisation of the right to freedom of expression in practice. A guiding principle of the European Court of Human Rights is that the ECHR seeks to "guarantee not rights that are theoretical or illusory but rights that are practical and effective".[24]

The European Convention on Human Rights (ECHR)

(i) *Scope and General Observations*

Relevant Council of Europe treaty-based and other normative standards aim to give meaningful and *effective* application to the right to freedom of expression.[25] They seek to ensure the "translation" of *principles* relating to freedom of expression into *law, policy* and *practice*. This translation exercise involves a variety of strategies and mechanisms, ranging from the legal and political to the socio-cultural and educational. Although first principles inform, and are articulated in, Article 10, ECHR, they are not self-executing. The substance and scope of the principles need to be—and in practice are—further developed by the European Court of Human Rights in its case-law.

The right to freedom of expression, as safeguarded by Article 10, comprises three main elements: the right to hold opinions; the right to receive information and ideas and the right to impart information and ideas.[26] The practical application of each of the component elements of Article 10 will be discussed below.

---

[24] See, inter alia, Airey v. Ireland, Judgment of the European Court of Human Rights of 9 October 1979, Series A, no. 32, para. 24.

[25] See generally in this connection, Declaration of the Committee of Ministers of the Council of Europe on measures to promote the respect of Article 10 of the European Convention on Human Rights, 13 January 2010, discussed in detail below.

[26] The full text of Article 10, ECHR, is available in the Appendix to this volume. For general commentary, see: Harris, O'Boyle & Warbrick, *Law of the European Convention on Human Rights* (Second edition) (Oxford: Oxford University Press, 2009), 443–513; Mario Oetheimer, ed., *Freedom of Expression in Europe: Case-law concerning Article 10 of the European Convention on Human Rights*, Human rights files, No. 18 (Strasbourg, Council of Europe, 2007); Pieter van Dijk, Fried van Hoof, Arjen van Rijn & Leo Zwaak, eds., *Theory and Practice of the European Convention on Human Rights* (Fourth Edition) (Antwerp/Oxford, Intersentia, 2006), 773–816.

By way of historical aside, it is interesting to note that minority interests have informed debates about the development of Article 10, ECHR. In the early/mid- 1990s, the Council of Europe gave formal consideration to the desirability of revising Article 10, ECHR, "with a view to adding journalistic and editorial freedom, access by various groups in society to the media, and copyright". Ultimately, the Bureau of the Council of Europe's Steering Committee on Human Rights (under whose auspices the discussion was conducted) concluded[27] that it was not appropriate at that time to redraft Article 10 because, as a specially commissioned study found, "[T]he indefiniteness and open character of the formulation and construction of the Article leads to an ever developing, dynamic and expanding influence of it".[28] In other words, the "living instrument" doctrine[29] would likely ensure that issues such as "access by various groups in society to the media" would (continue to) be adequately safeguarded under Article 10.

The ECHR does not provide explicitly for the protection or promotion of minority rights. Article 14, ECHR, states that the rights and freedoms set forth in the Convention shall be enjoyed without discrimination on a number of grounds. One of those impermissible grounds of discrimination is "association with a national minority". This formula is also used in Protocol No. 12 to the ECHR, which extends the right to non-discrimination beyond the rights set forth in the Convention to "any right set forth by law". In those States which have ratified Protocol No. 12, the right to non-discrimination no longer has to be invoked in conjunction with another Convention right.

The omission of a specific provision on minority rights from the ECHR was by no means an oversight on the part of the drafters of the Convention. The formal record of the drafting process shows that there was a clear sense of the importance of minority rights protection. Nevertheless,

---

[27] Steering Committee on the Mass Media (CDMM), Secretariat Memorandum prepared by the Directorate of Human Rights, 11 May 1994, Doc. No. CDMM (94) 31. This document contains an excerpt from the Report of the 42nd Meeting of the Bureau of the Steering Committee on Human Rights.

[28] Dirk Voorhoof, *Critical perspectives on the scope and interpretation of Article 10 of the European Convention on Human Rights*, Doc. No. CDMM (93) 36 (October 1993), 65.

[29] According to this doctrine, initially enunciated in *Tyrer v. UK*, the ECHR is taken to be a "living instrument" which "must be interpreted in the light of present-day conditions": *Tyrer v. the United Kingdom*, Judgment of the European Court of Human Rights of 25 April 1978, Series A, no. 26, para. 31. For an overview of the historical development of the "living instrument" doctrine by the European Court of Human Rights, see: Alastair Mowbray, "The Creativity of the European Court of Human Rights", *Human Rights Law Review* 5:1 (2005), 57–79.

instead of including minority rights in "an immediate international guarantee", it was decided that the question should be examined subsequently, "with a view to defining more exactly the rights of national minorities".[30] That was the drafters' preferred *general* approach to the protection of minority rights. Interestingly, though, a couple of proposals focused *specifically* on the expressive rights of minorities. The first proposed that various rights, including "freedom of speech and expression of opinion generally", be secured for all citizens, "and particularly for any minority [...]".[31] The second proposed that national minorities should not be restricted from giving "expression to their aspirations by democratic means".[32] These brief examples drawn from the drafting history of the ECHR are portentous insofar as they anticipated issues which were to arise later in the case-law of the European Court of Human Rights.[33]

Notwithstanding the textual limitations of the ECHR, the European Court of Human Rights has managed to develop a "burgeoning",[34] if "equivocal",[35] body of case-law concerning minority rights.[36] It has done so by exploring the *minority-specific* dimension to selected rights safeguarded by the Convention and enjoyed by everyone. Examples include non-discrimination/equality, enjoyment of a particular way of life, association, religion, education and expression. It is worthy of note that the Court's recognition of minority rights is not predicated on the somewhat restrictive understandings of "minority" and "national minority" which generally inform international and European human rights law.

[30] A.H. Robertson, ed., *Collected Edition of the Travaux Préparatoires of the European Convention on Human Rights* (The Hague, Martinus Nijhoff Publishers, 1975), Vol. I, 200 and 222.

[31] Ibid., 104.

[32] Ibid., Vol. V, 60.

[33] For further commentary, see: Tarlach McGonagle, *Minority Rights, Freedom of Expression and of the Media: Dynamics and Dilemmas*, Vol. 44, School of Human Rights Research Series, (Antwerp, etc.: Intersentia, 2011), 177–181.

[34] Geoff Gilbert, "The Burgeoning Minority Rights Jurisprudence of the European Court of Human Rights" *Human Rights Quarterly* 24 (2002) 736–780.

[35] Patrick Thornberry, "Treatment of Minority and Indigenous Issues in the European Convention on Human Rights" in Gudmundur Alfredsson & Maria Stavropoulou, eds., *Justice Pending: Indigenous Peoples and Other Good Causes* (The Hague: Martinus Nijhoff Publishers, 2002), 137–167, at 167.

[36] For an overview of relevant case-law of the European Court of Human Rights, see: Patrick Thornberry & María Amor Martín Estébanez, *Minority Rights in Europe* (Strasbourg, Council of Europe, 2004), 39–87; Kristin Henrard, "A patchwork of 'successful' and 'missed' synergies in the jurisprudence of the ECHR", in Kristin Henrard & Robert Dunbar, eds., *Synergies in Minority Protection: European and International Law Perspectives* (Cambridge, Cambridge University Press, 2008), 314–364.

(ii) *Selected Principles and their Application*

The jurisprudential trend to develop minority rights is consistent with the Court's vision of democratic society, in which the safeguarding of pluralism, diversity and tolerance are central objectives. A number of general principles from its case-law emphasise that pluralism demands a certain balancing of majority/minority interests and the democratic accommodation of the latter. The Court has, for instance, repeatedly found that:

> Although individual interests must on occasion be subordinated to those of a group, democracy does not simply mean that the views of a majority must always prevail: a balance must be achieved which ensures the fair and proper treatment of minorities and avoids any abuse of a dominant position.[37]

This finding is firmly anchored in the principle of pluralism, for which freedom of expression is a prerequisite.[38] According to the Court:

> [...] pluralism is also built on the genuine recognition of, and respect for, diversity and the dynamics of cultural traditions, ethnic and cultural identities, religious beliefs, artistic, literary and socio-economic ideas and concepts. The harmonious interaction of persons and groups with varied identities is essential for achieving social cohesion.[39]

This *general* approach to the interests of minorities has been followed by the Court *specifically* in respect of the expressive and informational interests of minorities and groups espousing minority viewpoints.

For instance, in *Steel & Morris v. the United Kingdom*, it held that:

> in a democratic society even small and informal campaign groups [...] must be able to carry on their activities effectively and [...] there exists a strong public interest in enabling such groups and individuals outside the mainstream to contribute to the public debate by disseminating information and ideas on matters of general public interest [...].[40]

In the *Steel & Morris* case (popularly known as the *McLibel* case), members of a small environmental organisation had distributed leaflets

---

[37] *Young, James & Webster v. United Kingdom*, Judgment of the European Court of Human Rights of 13 August 1981, Series A No. 44 p. 25, para. 63; *Chassagnou & Others v. France*, Judgment of the European Court of Human Rights of 29 April 1999, para. 112; *Gorzelik & Others v. Poland*, Judgment of the European Court of Human Rights (Grand Chamber) of 17 February 2004, para. 90.

[38] *Gorzelik & Others v. Poland*, Op. cit., para. 91.

[39] Ibid., para. 92.

[40] *Steel & Morris v. United Kingdom*, Judgment of the European Court of Human Rights (Fourth Section) of 15 February 2005, para. 89.

criticising McDonald's. The leaflets contained serious allegations about McDonald's, which were presented as statements of fact rather than as opinions. Steel and Morris were convicted of defamation by the UK courts. In its finding of a violation of Steel and Morris' right to freedom of expression under Article 10, the European Court of Human Rights attached greater importance to the public interest in the topic under discussion and in the need for procedural fairness in defamation proceedings than to the need for complete accuracy of specific details published in the leaflets.

In the *Appleby* case, the applicants argued that a shopping centre, to which they sought to gain access in order to collect signatures for a petition, should be regarded as a "quasi-public" space because it was *de facto* a forum for communication.[41] The case is relevant to the present discussion—despite not having a specific "minority" component—because the Court's judgment in the case appreciates that expressive fora other than the media can also be important for participation in public debate. The Court held that:

> [Article 10, ECHR], notwithstanding the acknowledged importance of freedom of expression, does not bestow any freedom of forum for the exercise of that right. While it is true that demographic, social, economic and technological developments are changing the ways in which people move around and come into contact with each other, the Court is not persuaded that this requires the automatic creation of rights of entry to private property, or even, necessarily, to all publicly-owned property (Government offices and ministries, for instance). *Where however the bar on access to property has the effect of preventing any effective exercise of freedom of expression or it can be said that the essence of the right has been destroyed, the Court would not exclude that a positive obligation could arise for the State to protect the enjoyment of Convention rights by regulating property rights.*[42]

Whereas the aforementioned cases involved the distribution of pamphlets and access to a particular physical space, a case directly relevant to issues and principles in respect of the broadcast media is *Khurshid Mustafa & Tarzibachi v. Sweden*.[43] The case deals with relevant issues and principles overtly in respect of the broadcast media. The applicants—Iraqi immigrants living in Sweden—were effectively prevented from

---

[41] *Appleby and Others v. the United Kingdom*, Judgment of the European Court of Human Rights (Fourth Section) of 6 May 2003.

[42] (emphasis added) Ibid., para. 47.

[43] Judgment of the European Court of Human Rights (Third Section) of 16 December 2008. For a short case-note, see: "Eviction: Satellite Dish", E.H.R.L.R. 2009, 2, 268–270.

receiving television programmes in Arabic and Farsi transmitted by satellite from their native country or region. A clause in the applicants' tenancy agreement prohibited, *inter alia*, the installation of "outdoor antennae and the like". The applicants had been making use of a satellite dish which had been installed prior to their tenancy of the flat. The landlord demanded that the dish be dismantled and when the applicants did not comply, notice of termination of their tenancy agreement was served on them. The dispute culminated in the landlord taking legal action against the applicants and ultimately securing an eviction order against them.

The European Court of Human Rights acknowledged that it was of "particular importance" for the applicants, as an immigrant family with children, to be able to receive a wide range of information (i.e., not just political and social news, but also "cultural expressions and pure entertainment") from their country of origin in order to be able to maintain contact with their native culture and language.[44] The significance of this acknowledgement is that it interprets general freedom of expression principles in a minority-specific and minority-sensitive way. It is also consistent with the former European Commission of Human Rights' suggestion that a problem would arise under Article 10 if a refusal to grant a broadcasting licence "resulted directly in a considerable proportion of the inhabitants of the area concerned being deprived of broadcasts in their mother tongue".[45]

The *Khurshid Mustafa & Tarzibachi* judgment is also noteworthy for the Court's readiness to focus not only on "the substance of the ideas and information expressed, but also the form in which they are conveyed".[46] It found that the applicants:

> might have been able to obtain certain news through foreign newspapers and radio programmes, but these sources of information only cover parts of what is available via television broadcasts and cannot in any way be equated with the latter.[47]

As such, the Court recognises that media functionality is an important factor for assessing whether particular expressive or informational

---

[44] Ibid., para. 44.

[45] *Verein Alternatives Lokalradio Bern & Verein Radio Dreyeckland Basel v. Switzerland*, Inadmissibility decision of the European Commission of Human Rights of 16 October 1986 (Appn. No. 10746/84), 49 DR 126, at 141.

[46] See, *inter alia*, *Oberschlick v. Austria*, Judgment of the European Court of Human Rights of 23 May 1991, Series A no. 204, para. 57; *Jersild v. Denmark*, Judgment of the European Court of Human Rights of 23 September 1994, Series A no. 298, para. 31.

[47] *Khurshid Mustafa & Tarzibachi v. Sweden*, Op. cit., para. 45.

opportunities are effective for particular groups. The mere existence of other expressive or informational opportunities is not sufficient: they must also be viable opportunities in the sense that they are suited to the expressive or informational purpose of the individual or group concerned. In other words, functional equivalence between media cannot simply be assumed.

Whereas in *Appleby* and *Steel & Morris*, the effectiveness of the right to *impart* information and ideas was under consideration, in *Khurshid Mustafa & Tarzibachi*, the effectiveness of the right to *receive* information and ideas rather than the right to impart information was central. This usefully demonstrates that access to the media can be crucial in different ways, depending on which component part of the right to freedom of expression is at issue in given circumstances.

(iii) *Selected Principles and their Implications*

Four main points emerge from the foregoing selection of principles from the European Court of Human Rights' case-law concerning Article 10, ECHR. First, participation by minorities (broadly defined) in public debate is regarded as a prerequisite for a healthy, pluralistic democratic society.

Second, the ability to participate in public debate is shaped in large measure by the ability to gain access to the channels via which information and ideas are disseminated and the fora in which debate is conducted. As noted, above the media are predominant in this regard. The quality and extent of access to expressive fora and the media tend to be determined by a range of factors, eg. "demographic, social, economic and technological". These factors—and their impact on communicative practices and patterns—are dynamic; the Court needs to bear this in mind when interpreting Article 10, ECHR.

Third, the positive obligations on States arising from Article 10 and its interplay with other rights could conceivably include the regulation of property rights when the denial of access to privately-owned property would otherwise prevent "any effective exercise of the right to freedom of expression" or destroy the essence of the right. The recognition of certain rights of access to private property for communicative purposes could therefore be of potential analogous relevance for privately-owned media. It is likely that this kind of question will arise increasingly in the future in respect of media with an online presence.

Fourth, the functionality of different media should be examined from the perspective of the users, especially when the users are members of minority communities. Particular media which one section of society may regard as functional or effective for its expressive and informational needs may be regarded as unsuitable or ineffective by others.

For example, if a minority group speaks a language that is traditionally and primarily oral in character, the existence of a newspaper in that language may be of little functional value for many members of the minority. That could be the case when there are low levels of literacy within a particular group, or when reading habits are underdeveloped. Similarly, a local radio station broadcasting programmes intended for a particular minority group may not be effective if the group is dispersed throughout the State, or nomadic, and a majority of its members is therefore unable to receive the broadcasts. Internet-based broadcasting might appear to be a creative solution, but it would not necessarily resolve the problem because the technological means of distribution must also be suitable for the target audience. Digital television, for instance, may well prove unsuitable for economically disadvantaged minority groups (at least in the short-term) due to the prohibitive expense involved in acquiring the technology needed to be able to receive content. Levels of Internet penetration, general uptake of new communicative technologies and (multi-)media literacy are relevant variables here.[48]

At the beginning of this section, the importance of ensuring an *effective* right to freedom of expression was stressed. Prompted by concerns about the effectiveness of the implementation of Article 10 of the European Convention on Human Rights, the Council of Europe's Committee of Ministers (CM) adopted a Declaration on measures to promote the respect of Article 10 on 13 January 2010.[49]

The Declaration recognises, amongst other things, the importance of strengthening the implementation of relevant standards in "law and practice" at the national level, a task which requires "the active support, engagement and co-operation" of all Member States. In the Declaration, the CM "welcomes the proposals" made by the Council of Europe's Steering Committee on the Media and New Communication Services (CDMC)

---

[48] These are merely examples—not generalisations; as was correctly suggested to me by the editors of this volume, levels of uptake of new technologies can vary considerably and surprisingly. In some countries, lower-income households have been quicker to switch to digital television than their middle-income counterparts. Moreover, some minority groups (especially diasporic minorities) often rely extensively on Internet-based media and other forms of communication.

[49] Declaration of the Committee of Ministers on measures to promote the respect of Article 10 of the European Convention on Human Rights, 13 January 2010.

aimed at improving the promotion, by various organs of the Council of Europe, of respect of Article 10 in Member States. The Declaration, however, only provides summary details of the CDMC's proposals and fails to indicate that the proposals are described more expansively in Appendix IV of the CDMC's 11th Meeting Report.[50] The main proposals are listed in the Meeting Report as follows: enhanced information collection; enhanced coordination; enhanced technical follow-up (expert assistance); enhanced political follow-up, and evaluation (by the Secretary General of the Council of Europe).

The Declaration's call for "improved collection and sharing of information and enhanced co-ordination" across the Council of Europe is prefaced by a roll-call of the various "bodies and institutions" which "are able, within their respective mandates, to contribute to the protection and promotion of freedom of expression and information and of freedom of the media". It names the Committee of Ministers, the Parliamentary Assembly, the Secretary General, the Commissioner for Human Rights and "other bodies" as all being "active in this area". Explicit references to the Advisory Committee on the FCNM and the Committee of Experts on the ECRML, for example, are conspicuous by their absence. This omission is both puzzling and disappointing, given the significant levels of activity of both committees "in this area".[51]

OTHER COUNCIL OF EUROPE TREATIES: FRAMEWORK CONVENTION FOR THE PROTECTION OF NATIONAL MINORITIES (FCNM) AND EUROPEAN CHARTER FOR REGIONAL OR MINORITY LANGUAGES (ECRML)

General Considerations

Aside from the ECHR, other Council of Europe treaties, such as the FCNM and ECRML, develop specific aspects of general freedom of expression principles in accordance with their own thematic priorities and emphases. In other words, they pursue discrete national minority and linguistic agendas in respect of freedom of expression. The specificity of their

---

[50] Steering Committee on the Media and New Communication Services, 11th Meeting (20–23 October 2009) report, 16 November 2009, Doc. No. CDMC(2009)025.

[51] For a comprehensive analysis of relevant Council of Europe treaty-based approaches to issues relating to new media, see: Tom Moring, "New Media and the Implementation of Instruments in Support of Minority Rights Related to Media", 6 *European Yearbook of Minority Issues* (2006–7), 19–50.

approaches facilitates consideration of, and engagement with, the precise expressive and informational needs and interests of minorities. This, in turn, helps to make the right to freedom of expression of persons belonging to minorities effective in practice.

The implementation of both the FCNM and the ECRML is assured by systems of State reporting which are subject to independent expert monitoring. Both monitoring systems allow for scrutiny of the laws, policies and practice in States Parties to the two treaties, an exercise which necessarily enquires into the effectiveness of adopted measures for the operationalisation of relevant first principles.

Framework Convention for the Protection of National Minorities

The FCNM sets out a range of rights to be enjoyed by persons belonging to national minorities, including: equality and non-discrimination (Article 4); culture, identity and non-assimilation (Article 5); freedom of religion or belief (Article 8); freedom of expression (Article 9); use of own language in public and in private and (in certain circumstances) in dealings with administrative authorities (Article 10); use of names (personal and geographical) in own language (Article 11); education (Articles 12 and 13); language learning (Article 14); effective participation in cultural, social and economic life and in public affairs (Article 15).[52]

The FCNM is, as its title suggests, a framework treaty. Its combination of principles and programmatic measures serves to provide States Parties with a legal framework within which to protect the rights of persons belonging to national minorities. Key to this conception of the FCNM as a *framework* treaty is the leeway accorded States Parties in their honouring of the commitments entered into under the Convention. States may implement the programmatic provisions of the Convention in such a way as to reflect relevant national/local cultural and other particularities.[53] Under the FCNM, the rights that the treaty purports to safeguard are not

---

[52] See, by way of overview, Heinrich Klebes, "The Council of Europe's Framework Convention for the Protection of National Minorities", Op. cit., and more recently, Asbjorn Eide, "The Council of Europe's Framework Convention for the Protection of National Minorities", in Kristin Henrard & Robert Dunbar, eds., *Synergies in Minority Protection: European and International Law Perspectives*, Op. cit., 119–154.

[53] According to the Explanatory Report to the FCNM, because the Convention's provisions are not directly applicable, States are left with "a measure of discretion in the implementation of the objectives which they have undertaken to achieve, thus enabling them to take particular circumstances into account": para. 11.

subject to determination or enforcement by an international court. Rather, the implementation of the FCNM at national level is assessed in the context of a system of State-reporting. Ultimate control and responsibility for monitoring the implementation of the FCNM rests with the Committee of Ministers of the Council of Europe and a purpose-created Advisory Committee (AC) assists it in this regard. The AC does the lion's share of the work, even though its role is formally described as one of "assistance" to the Committee of Ministers.

As far as the right to freedom of expression is concerned, the most important provision is Article 9, FCNM.[54] It reads:

1 The Parties undertake to recognise that the right to freedom of expression of every person belonging to a national minority includes freedom to hold opinions and to receive and impart information and ideas in the minority language, without interference by public authorities and regardless of frontiers. The Parties shall ensure, within the framework of their legal systems, that persons belonging to a national minority are not discriminated against in their access to the media.

2 Paragraph 1 shall not prevent Parties from requiring the licensing, without discrimination and based on objective criteria, of sound radio and television broadcasting, or cinema enterprises.

3 The Parties shall not hinder the creation and the use of printed media by persons belonging to national minorities. In the legal framework of sound radio and television broadcasting, they shall ensure, as far as possible, and taking into account the provisions of paragraph 1, that persons belonging to national minorities are granted the possibility of creating and using their own media.

4 In the framework of their legal systems, the Parties shall adopt adequate measures in order to facilitate access to the media for persons belonging to national minorities and in order to promote tolerance and permit cultural pluralism.

It is modelled closely on Article 10, ECHR and represents a modest extension of scope of the former. The foregrounding, in Article 9(1), FCNM, of non-discriminatory access to the media, is a good example of how it goes beyond the actual wording of Article 10, ECHR, in a way that is informed by: (i) needs and interests of national minorities, and (ii) principles relating to the right to freedom of expression, as developed in the case-law of the European Court of Human Rights. Next to the principles already discussed above, the Court's finding that the State is the "ultimate guarantor" of pluralism, especially "in relation to audio-visual media, whose

---

54 For commentary, see: John Packer & Sally Holt, 'ARTICLE 9', in Marc Weller, ed., *The Rights of Minorities in Europe: A Commentary on the European Framework Convention for the Protection of National Minorities*, Op. cit.

programmes are often broadcast very widely", is also important here.[55] This finding places the State under a positive obligation to uphold pluralism, in particular in the broadcasting sector. The facilitation of access to the media for persons belonging to national minorities could also reasonably be regarded as a logical outcrop of the Court's case-law on freedom of expression, but its explicit inclusion in Article 9(4) helps to underscore its importance, not least symbolically.

Article 9(3), however, is disappointing: it is no more than a passive reformulation of basic non-discrimination principles in the context of media outlets. The tame wording of Article 9(3) is the outcome of another missed opportunity in the drafting process. At one stage, there was a proposal on the table which read that persons "belonging to ethnic groups" "shall have the right to equal access to the State's or to other public mass media, as well as the right to their own means of communication and adequate public subsidies for this purpose".[56] Ultimately, no explicit provision along these lines was retained in the final text of Article 9(3) specifically (or in any other part of Article 9 either). According to the Explanatory Report to the FCNM, "No express reference has been made to the right of persons belonging to a national minority to seek funds for the establishment of media, as this right was considered self-evident".[57] This explanation is somewhat inadequate, however. There is a considerable gap between guaranteeing that adequate public subsidies are available (or a provision to that effect) and merely allowing minorities to *seek* funds.

Welcome and relevant as they are, the references to "access to the media" in Article 9(1) and (3) have given rise to some interpretive difficulties. As already explained at the start of this chapter, the term "access" is vague and encompasses many different modalities of access (to the media). The AC now distinguishes between active and passive access, a distinction corresponding roughly to the right to impart and receive information and ideas (via the media).[58] The usefulness of this new terminological departure can be appreciated when assessing the effectiveness of State measures to assure access to the media. In this connection, it is

---

[55] *Informationsverein Lentia & Others v. Austria*, Judgment of the European Court of Human Rights of 28 October 1993, para. 38.

[56] Fundamental Rights of Persons Belonging to Ethnic Groups in Europe, Draft for an Additional Protocol to the ECHR (Revised FUEN Draft), 1994, Article 10(2).

[57] Explanatory Report to the FCNM, para. 61.

[58] For analysis, see: Karol Jakubowicz, "Report: A critical evaluation of the first results of the monitoring of the Framework Convention on the issue of persons belonging to national minorities and the media (1998–2003)", Op. cit., at 129–130 and 133–134 (and followed by: Tarlach McGonagle, "Commentary: Access to the media of persons belonging to national minorities", Op. cit., at 156).

useful to recall this chapter's earlier observation that distinctions between various levels and forms of access and participation make for targeted, meaningful analysis and evaluation.

The text of the FCNM enables States Parties to give due consideration to relevant national (or sub-national) sensibilities and needs when adopting and implementing measures facilitating access to the media for persons belonging to national minorities. By the same token, the treaty's monitoring system enables the AC to consider the adequacy/efficiency of State measures in light of relevant "particular circumstances" obtaining in the State, in any region of the State, or in respect of any minority group in the State. This results in a dialogue which facilitates the identification of issues governing the effectiveness of access to the media for persons belonging to national minorities and, by extension, the effectiveness of their right to freedom of expression. It also facilitates the compilation of relevant best practices.

In the context of its monitoring work, the AC has frequently focused on the impact of geographical, technological and market-related factors on the effectiveness of national minorities' access to the media. Such focuses would, for example, invite consideration of whether the geographical reach of particular media targeting a particular minority group matches the actual demographic concentration of that minority. Useful distinctions in this regard include: sub-national (i.e., local and regional), national and transfrontier reach. Another relevant line of enquiry is the suitability of the means of distribution for media content. In other words, is the distribution platform in question accessible to, and widely used by, members of the target minority group (or groups)? Finally, as regards market-related factors: media output catering for the interests of national minorities or in their languages is often less lucrative than mainstream equivalents. This fact can make it difficult for (minority) media to secure investment capital and advertising, which in turn makes it difficult for them to operate independently and efficiently. Such difficulties militate against the growth of minority (language) media, thereby maintaining access opportunities at a low level.[59]

The AC also tends to distinguish between access to different types of media, eg. public-service, community and commercial, each of which can serve the expressive and informational needs and interests of persons belonging to national minorities in different ways. Given that the media comprise content, structures and processes, regulation tends to be both

---

[59] See generally: Mike Cormack & Niamh Hourigan, eds., *Minority Language Media: Concepts, Critiques and Case Studies* (Clevedon: Multilingual Matters Ltd., 2007).

behavioural and structural. The Advisory Committee therefore monitors the calibration of prescriptions (eg. broadcasting quota and percentages of programming budgets) of particular types of content, such as that produced by or for minorities, including in their own languages. It also monitors the allocation of time-slots for the same with a view to determining whether they are long enough, frequent enough and scheduled at appropriate times. Subtitling and dubbing practices are also routinely monitored on account of their potential for making content accessible to a wider audience comprising varied linguistic backgrounds. The need for broadcast licensing processes to recognise and accommodate the needs, interests and situational specificities of national minorities, is another recurrent priority theme. The general question of the official recognition of national minorities and their languages (to the extent that the applicability of media laws and policies is conditional on the enjoyment of official status) is often addressed as well.

The foregoing paragraphs have: (i) emphasised the need for conceptual and linguistic precision in the ongoing exercise of "filling in the frame" of Article 9, FCNM; (ii) pointed towards the desirability of compiling relevant best practices, and (iii) given a brief inventory of issues dealt with by the AC in the context of Article 9, FCNM. These three focuses jointly prompt a further—and broader—conclusion: there is a need for the AC to systematically seek to ensure interpretive refinement in its engagement with relevant terms and concepts and to derive general principles from specific country situations. As I have argued elsewhere:

> What is required for each substantive issue addressed [under Article 9, FCNM] is the elaboration of a strong formula with maximum reach and for it to be consistently applied across different country situations. Such an approach would have the merit of enhancing predictability and elevating country-specific analysis to a higher, more general plane on which it would achieve greater impact. Of course, the obvious subtext here is that the quest for consistency, predictability and generality should not be allowed to ride roughshod over the subtleties and sensitivities of specific country-situations. Like in the jurisprudence of Article 10, ECHR, the challenge here is to strike a careful balance between lofty ideals and the hard political and social realities of individual cases. If met squarely, this challenge could lead to immensely instructive and immensely rewarding results, not least for the future monitoring of the FCNM.[60]

---

[60] Tarlach McGonagle, "Commentary: Access to the media of persons belonging to national minorities", Op. cit., at 155. See also, Ibid., 159 and Karol Jakubowicz, "Report: A critical evaluation of the first results of the monitoring of the Framework Convention on the issue of persons belonging to national minorities and the media (1998–2003)", Op. cit., at 135.

The AC has begun to conduct thematic work on specific articles of the FCNM. At the time of writing, it had elaborated two commentaries on the rights to education and effective participation of persons belonging to national minorities.[61] Given the accumulated experience of the monitoring process to date and the ongoing fundamental changes to the nature of the media, the time is now ripe for the preparation of a similar commentary on freedom of expression and the media. Such an initiative could include among its objectives: the clarification of key terminology; the distillation of good/best practices, and the development of appropriate bench-markers for future monitoring work. As such, it would help to meet one of the challenges facing the AC, as identified by its former President, Rainer Hofmann, *viz.*, to "develop clear criteria which could be used in order to determine issues, such as 'insufficient' access to, or 'insufficient' coverage by, public media or 'insufficient' financial funding of private radio and television programmes run by national minorities".[62] In the absence of suitable explanatory or evaluative criteria, it is easy to be sceptical about the practical worth of such well-meaning, but ultimately ineffective terms. As noted by one commentator in a different context, "Terms such as "reasonable" or "substantial" amounts of informational programming are mushy [... and quoting a former Chairman of the US Federal Communications Commission], 'These are, in the vernacular, 'marshmallow' phrases—they mean almost nothing in and of themselves or, conversely, almost anything that one wants them to mean.'".[63]

The timeliness of such a thematic venture is further underscored by the fact that the Committee of Experts on Issues Relating to the Protection of National Minorities (DH-MIN),[64] which operates in the penumbra of the

---

[61] Advisory Committee on the Framework Convention for the Protection of National Minorities, Commentary on Education under the Framework Convention for the Protection of National Minorities, 2 March 2006, Doc. ACFC/25DOC(2006)002; Advisory Committee on the Framework Convention for the Protection of National Minorities, Commentary on the Effective Participation of Persons Belonging to National Minorities in Cultural, Social and Economic Life and in Public Affairs, 5 May 2008, Doc. ACFC/31DOC(2008)001.

[62] Rainer Hofmann, 'Implementation of the FCNM: Substantive Challenges', in Annelies Verstichel, Andre Alen, Bruno De Witte & Paul Lemmens, eds., *The Framework Convention for the Protection of National Minorities: A Useful Pan-European Instrument?* (Antwerp/Oxford/Portland: Intersentia, 2008), 159–185, at 170.

[63] Henry Geller, "Mass communications policy: where we are and where we should be going", in Judith Lichtenberg, ed., *Democracy and the mass media*, Op. cit., 290–330, at 306.

[64] An intergovernmental committee acting under the aegis of the Council of Europe; see further: http://www.coe.int/t/dghl/monitoring/minorities/5_IntergovWork/DH-MIN_Intro_en.asp (last visited on 8 February 2010).

FCNM, has already devoted significant attention to issues concerning the access of national minorities to the (new) media.[65]

European Charter for Regional or Minority Languages[66]

The central purpose of the ECRML is to protect and promote regional or minority languages in Europe. Its conceptual point of departure is that regional or minority languages are a "threatened aspect of Europe's cultural heritage" and therefore merit protection and promotion.[67] The Charter's dual strategy is to focus on (i) non-discrimination as regards the use of regional or minority languages, and (ii) measures offering active support for such languages.[68] The promotional measures set out in the Charter concentrate on the use of regional or minority languages in specific spheres of public life: education (Article 8), judicial authorities (Article 9), administrative authorities and public services (Article 10), media (Article 11), cultural activities and facilities (Article 12), economic and social life (Article 13), transfrontier exchanges (Article 14). The contemplated promotional measures—in a range of pertinent contexts—are seen as a means through which regional or minority languages may be "compensated, where necessary, for unfavourable conditions in the past and preserved and developed as a living facet of Europe's cultural identity".[69] As such, the objective of sustaining cultural and linguistic diversity also informs the Charter's approach.[70]

---

[65] Tom Moring, "Access of National Minorities to the Media: New Challenges", Doc. No. DH-MIN(2006)015, and accompanying "Comments" by Tarlach McGonagle, Doc. No. DH-MIN(2006)016 and Karol Jakubowicz, Doc. No. DH-MIN(2006)017, all dated 20 November 2006; Tom Moring & Tarlach McGonagle, "Analysis of Information provided by DH-MIN members on the Questionnaire on the access of national minorities to new media in the information society", Doc. No. DH-MIN(2009)003, 9 March 2009; all available at: http://www.coe.int/t/dghl/monitoring/minorities/5_IntergovWork/DH-MIN_Working Documents_en.asp (last visited on 8 February 2010).

[66] See further: Patrick Thornberry & María Amor Martín Estébanez, Minority Rights in Europe, Op. cit., 137–168; Jean-Marie Woehrling, The European Charter for Regional or Minority Languages: A critical commentary (Strasbourg, Council of Europe Publishing, 2005); Robert Dunbar, Gwynedd Parry & Simone Klinge, eds., The European Charter or Regional or Minority Languages: Legal Challenges and Opportunities (Regional or Minority Languages, No. 5) (Strasbourg: Council of Europe Publishing, 2008); Robert Dunbar, "The Council of Europe's European Charter for Regional or Minority Languages", in Kristin Henrard & Robert Dunbar, eds., Synergies in Minority Protection: European and International Law Perspectives, Op. cit., 155–186.

[67] Explanatory Report to the ECRML, para. 10.

[68] Ibid.

[69] Ibid.

[70] Ibid., para. 11.

The Charter is concerned first and foremost with regional or minority languages and not with the users of those languages *per se*.[71] As a result, it is often considered to be an interloper among human rights or minority rights treaties.[72] Whereas it requires contracting States to undertake various legal obligations, it does not set out to create rights for either individuals or groups, as such.[73] Nevertheless, this does not mean that State obligations under the Charter cannot have the effect of strengthening individual or group linguistic rights in practice.[74] The extent to which rights for individuals or groups flow from, or are affirmed by, State obligations can therefore be regarded as incidental to the central purpose of the Charter.

In terms of scope, the Charter covers "regional or minority languages", which are defined as languages: "(i) traditionally used within a given territory of a State by nationals of that State who form a group numerically smaller than the rest of the State's population; and (ii) different from the official language(s) of that State".[75] Furthermore, "dialects of the official language(s) of the State or the languages of migrants" are not included in the definition of regional or minority languages.[76] These definitional stipulations are another good indication of the tension between literal and legal notions of minorities and minority languages. The main practical consequence of this definitional approach is that the languages of so-called new minorities and migrants are *presumptively* excluded from the protection and promotion generally offered by the Charter's provisions. However, as noted by Robert Dunbar, there may be "some room for flexibility" in this connection.[77] He argues that "where newcomers speak a language that is already constituted as a regional or minority language because of its long presence on the territory of the state, there seems little basis for excluding such newcomers from the benefits of the Charter's protection".[78]

---

[71] Ibid.

[72] See further, Robert Dunbar, "The Council of Europe's European Charter for Regional or Minority Languages", Op. cit., at 155–156.

[73] Explanatory Report to the ECRML, Op. cit., para. 11.

[74] Ibid.

[75] Article 1(a), ECRML.

[76] Ibid. For further explanation, see the Explanatory Report to the ECRML, Op. cit., paras. 30–33.

[77] Robert Dunbar, "The Council of Europe's European Charter for Regional or Minority Languages", Op. cit., at 164 and generally 163–166. He supports his argument with references to the monitoring of the Charter.

[78] Ibid.

In terms of structure, the Charter has a number of idiosyncratic design features. States Parties to the ECRML enjoy a large measure of discretion in determining their commitments under the Charter.[79] Part II of the ECRML, comprising one single article (Article 7), sets out the central objectives and principles of the Charter. It is applicable to all regional or minority languages spoken in a State. Part III, comprising Articles 8–14, is to be applied by States to each language specified by States upon ratification of the Charter. If it so wishes, a State Party may undertake different commitments for each of the regional or minority languages it has specified. The Charter's approach to undertakings by its States Parties has been aptly described as "resembling a *table d'hôte* menu, where one is expected to chose something from each course".[80] There is a clear scale of onerousness present in the range of commitments offered within Articles 8–13 of the Charter. As long as States comply with the requirements set out in Article 2(2), they are free to choose the level of onerousness of the commitments they enter into.

The ECRML's unusually flexible approach was designed to make the Charter attractive to States and encourage its wide ratification. Dónall Ó Riagáin has argued that "A less flexible formula would not work because of the greatly differing language situations obtaining in Europe".[81] However, it is debatable whether this strategy has been successful: to date, only 25 of the Council of Europe's 47 Member States have ratified the Charter since its adoption in 1992.[82] In practice, the success of the ECRML depends in the first place on the *bona fide* engagement of States and their

---

[79] Article 2, ECRML, which is entitled 'Undertakings', sets out the relevant requirements. It reads:

> "1. Each Party undertakes to apply the provisions of Part II to all the regional or minority languages spoken within its territory and which comply with the definition in Article 1.
> 2. In respect of each language specified at the time of ratification, acceptance or approval, in accordance with Article 3, each Party undertakes to apply a minimum of thirty-five paragraphs or sub-paragraphs chosen from among the provisions of Part III of the Charter, including at least three chosen from each of the Articles 8 and 12 and one from each of the Articles 9, 10, 11 and 13."

[80] Dónall Ó Riagáin, "The Charter: An Overview", in François Grin, *Language policy evaluation and the European Charter for Regional or Minority Languages* (New York: Palgrave Macmillan, 2003) 55–68, at 64.

[81] Ibid.

[82] In total, 33 States have signed the Charter (source: Council of Europe Treaty Office Website, 2 May 2012). By way of comparison/contrast: the FCNM has been ratified by 39 Member States of the Council of Europe and signed/acceded to by a total of 43 States.

willingness to commit themselves to the more far-reaching options available and not just the lowest common denominator.[83]

Article 11 is the Charter's principal article concerning the right to freedom of expression and the media.[84] Like Article 9, FCNM, its wording also borrows from that of Article 10, ECHR.[85] It opens with an acknowledgement that national public authorities have varying levels of competence in respect of media regulation and oversight and a call for the principle of "the independence and autonomy of the media" to be respected (Article 11(1)). The main substantive focuses of the Article are:

- public service radio and television (Article 11(1)(a));
- radio and television generally (Article 11(1)(b) and (c), respectively);
- production and distribution of audio and audiovisual works (Article 11(1)(d));
- newspapers (Article 11(1)(e));
- funding for the media/audiovisual production (Article 11(1)(f));
- support for the training of journalists and media professionals (Article 11(1)(g));
- freedom of direct reception and non-opposition of retransmission of radio and television broadcasts from neighbouring countries (Article 11(2));
- non-restriction of free circulation of information in the written press (Article 11(2)), and
- representation/taking into account of interests of regional or minority language speakers within bodies with "responsibility for guaranteeing the freedom and pluralism of the media" (Article 11(3)).[86]

States Parties are required to choose and apply at least one paragraph or sub-paragraph from Article 11. Most of the paragraphs and sub-paragraphs contain internal choices between commitments of varying degrees of onerousness. The extent of the available choice is widened further

---

[83] See further in this connection, Robert Dunbar, "Minority Language Rights in International Law", 50 ICLQ (2001) 90–120, at 113.
[84] See further, Jean-Marie Woehrling, *The European Charter for Regional or Minority Languages: A critical commentary*, Op. cit., 200–214, and very comprehensively, Tom Moring & Robert Dunbar, *The European Charter for Regional or Minority Languages and the media* (Strasbourg: Council of Europe Publishing, 2008).
[85] For an acknowledgement of the textual similarities, see the Explanatory Report to the ECRML, Op. cit., paras. 107–113, esp. para. 112.
[86] It should be noted that each of these focuses pertains specifically to regional or minority languages.

by recurrent reliance on the formula, "to encourage and/or facilitate" [particular measures]. For instance, Article 11(1)(a) offers States a choice between the following options in respect of their public service broadcasting systems:

    i to ensure the creation of at least one radio station and one television channel in the regional or minority languages; or
    ii to encourage and/or facilitate the creation of at least one radio station and one television channel in the regional or minority languages; or
    iii to make adequate provision so that broadcasters offer programmes in the regional or minority languages;

The ability to make internal choices within paragraphs therefore clearly offers States a lot of flexibility to determine the precise focus and extent of their commitments in respect of the media.

Furthermore, the State obligations are mainly obligations of conduct, not of result because for most of the obligations, States are not even required to assure the targeted outcome: they merely have to encourage and/or facilitate it. It has been observed that these formulae show due deference to constitutional and/or legislative provisions in some States which prevent direct governmental involvement in the media.[87] This is a plausible (but partial[88]) explanation for the choice of wording: Article 11(1) also acknowledges differences in relevant governmental competences at the national level.[89]

Notwithstanding the textual ambiguities and weaknesses of the ECRML, its monitoring system has provided a number of principles and insights in respect of the media which are of wider interest and relevance than merely to the particular State to which they are addressed. The monitoring system involves the periodic submission of States Reports to the Secretary General of the Council of Europe. These reports are examined by the Charter's specially-constituted Committee of Experts, which reports to the Committee of Ministers of the Council of Europe. The Committee of Ministers then draws up country-specific recommendations and the Secretary General of the Council of Europe makes two-yearly reports on the application of the Charter to the Parliamentary Assembly of the Council of Europe.[90]

---

[87] Dónall Ó Riagáin, "The Charter: An Overview", Op. cit., at 65.
[88] Another plausible partial explanation could be the *realpolitik* involved: the less onerous an obligation, the greater the chances of its uptake by States.
[89] See also: Explanatory Report to the ECRML, Op. cit., para. 109.
[90] See generally, Articles 15–17, ECRML.

Many of the key issues identified by the Advisory Committee on the FCNM are also regularly flagged by the Charter's Committee of Experts. Engagement with these issues is similar to the engagement under the FCNM, but predictably with extra scrutiny for their linguistic dimension.[91] Also, as one would expect, there is systematic attention for the impact of general language policy on media activities in regional or minority languages. The impact of the media on the public profile, prominence and prestige enjoyed by regional or minority languages is also a recurrent issue. Arising from Article 11(3), ECRML, the representation of interests of speakers of regional or minority languages in media regulatory/monitoring authorities is frequently addressed. Article 11(3) addresses an additional dimension to the questions of representation and participation in the media, discussed at the beginning of this chapter. To ensure that the interests of the users of regional or minority languages are taken into account in bodies charged with guaranteeing freedom and pluralism of the media is a very important and potentially far-reaching policy goal. It strives for the institutional incorporation of minority interests in bodies which often have considerable influence on law and policy-making. Such policies can be regarded as outgrowths of more general democratic principles and they greatly enhance the likelihood that future regulation and policy will reflect and cater for the needs and interests of linguistic minorities.[92]

As noted by Robert Dunbar, the ECRML is "generally much more detailed, precise and comprehensive in its provisions [...] than other treaties and other international legal instruments of relevance to linguistic minorities".[93] The individualised and specific nature of the commitments entered into by States under the Charter is conducive to eliciting specific comments from the Committee of Experts on the Charter. It enables the Committee to engage with "each paragraph and subparagraph of each

---

[91] See further: Tom Moring & Robert Dunbar, *The European Charter for Regional or Minority Languages and the media*, Op. cit.

[92] See further, Tarlach McGonagle, "Introduction to and Summary of the Survey of State Practice: 'Minority-Language Related Broadcasting and Legislation in the OSCE'", in George Jones, Sally Holt & John Packer, eds., 8 *Mercator Media Forum* (2005), 84–99, at 95. For an analysis of the practical shortcomings of Article 11(3), ECRML, see: Robert Dunbar, "Definitively interpreting the European Charter for Regional or Minority Languages: the legal challenges", in Robert Dunbar, Gwynedd Parry & Simone Klinge, eds., *The European Charter or Regional or Minority Languages: Legal Challenges and Opportunities*, Op. cit., 37–61, at 50–51.

[93] Robert Dunbar, "Definitively interpreting the European Charter for Regional or Minority Languages: the legal challenges", Op. cit., at 38.

article".[94] Moreover, in its specific comments, the Committee tends to find that provisions have been "'fulfilled', 'generally fulfilled', 'partially fulfilled', 'formally fulfilled', or 'not fulfilled'".[95] This kind of evaluative differentiation helps to sharpen the monitoring process and better ascertain not only *whether* State obligations are being honoured in practice, but also *to what extent* they are being honoured.

CONCLUSION

All three of the Council of Europe treaties surveyed in this chapter make valuable contributions to the process of translating general freedom of expression principles into a right that is practical and effective for persons belonging to minorities. The angles of approach of the ECHR, FCNM and ECRML follow their primary aims: the protection of human rights and fundamental freedoms; the protection of national minorities and the protection and promotion of the regional and minority languages of Europe, respectively. Each of the three treaties recognises that effective modalities of access to the media are key to the operationalisation of the right to freedom of expression generally and for persons belonging to minorities in particular. Their combined approach ensures that there is follow-through from statements of principle about the importance of media access questions to the examination and evaluation of (programmatic) measures designed to promote the same. Although it is not formally coordinated, this combined approach is, in practice, largely coherent. This is partly because Article 9, FCNM and Article 11, ECRML, can be regarded as the progeny of Article 10, ECHR. In terms of both substance and style, the general, judicial approach of the ECHR is usefully complemented by the thematically-specific, monitoring-based approaches of the FCNM and ECRML.

As suggested by the sub-title of this chapter, and confirmed by the foregoing analysis, the Council of Europe's record in developing standards on access to the media for minorities is characterised by a string of near-misses and staggered successes. The near-misses are, on the one hand, failed attempts to have explicit, robust formulae included in relevant treaties and, on the other hand, the ultimate inclusion of compromise(d)

---

[94] Robert Dunbar, "The Council of Europe's European Charter for Regional or Minority Languages", Op. cit., at 176.
[95] Ibid., following Patrick Thornberry & María Amor Martín Estébanez, *Minority Rights in Europe*, Op. cit., at 157.

formulae instead. The staggered successes have been achieved, despite the treaties' textual, substantive and procedural deficiencies, through: (i) the gradual emergence of important principles from the case-law of the European Court of Human Rights and the monitoring mechanisms for the FCNM and ECRML, and (ii) ongoing attempts to consolidate and apply those principles in practice. Progress continues to be made, but much remains to be done before the successes can be considered "staggering" instead of "staggered".

USER GENERATED CONTENT: FREEDOM OF EXPRESSION AND THE ROLE OF THE MEDIA IN A DIGITAL AGE

Lorna Woods

Introduction

The chapters so far have focused on media institutions and the special obligations put on broadcasters due to the reach and impact of the content.[1] There has been a shift in the last decade, however, in the roles of the individual and media organisation in the dissemination of information. The individual is no longer just part of the audience, but can also participate. Consequently, it is not only media institutions which can reach out to mass audiences. The content provided through this process, user generated content (UGC), opens up the possibility of a wider range of material, or different perspectives on the material, than that traditionally available. The integration of UGC can thus add to diversity of subject matter and perspectives, both in traditional programmes and on websites, whilst engagement with the professional media can provide access to a wide audience for those providing UGC which might otherwise get lost in a blizzard of content. Thus, there is a possible relationship between the media and UGC which is to the benefit of both, and to the audience.

The relationship is not straightforward, however, particularly insofar as different standards, ethics or expectations might be seen as applying to professionally produced content and UGC. The professional media might be seen as specially favoured or subject to special obligations; certainly the professional media—or their role—have received special consideration in human rights jurisprudence; do these rights extend to UGC? Conversely, and perhaps more significantly, professional journalistic ethics and the constraints of regulation may result in the professional media limiting UGC. In this chapter, we will consider the meaning of UGC and then briefly review some issues pertaining to freedom of expression in the context of UGC. We will then outline the possible areas of law which could be

---

[1] Recital 59 Codified Version of Audiovisual Media Services Directive (COM/2009/0185 final—COD 2009/0056) (AVMSD); Case C-89/04 *Mediakabel BV* v. *Commissariaat voor de Media* [2005] ECR I-4891.

of concern in terms of freedom of expression for those providing UGC, before concluding with some areas in which further consideration might be needed. This chapter will not consider the jurisdictional issues arising from the transnational nature of the internet,[2] which may to some extent be overstated,[3] or the fact that a 'single publication' or upload rule has not been adopted.[4]

WHAT IS UGC?

UGC is a term of art, much used if not much liked. There is little clarity as to what is meant by this term and what we might suggest are synonyms (such as 'citizen-journalism', 'participatory media') do not take us much further; indeed they may refer to different types or subsets of activity.[5] A 2007 OECD report[6] suggested that there was no widely accepted definition of UGC. Whilst there may be a clear central or core activity, there are penumbral activities that, depending on your view, may or may not be UGC.

Four limiting factors can be identified: amateur versus professional;[7] technology-based (is UGC limited to material on the internet?); form (text; photos; video; audio-visual); and public versus private. One report took a broad view, involving three of these elements: the content is produced by

---

[2] For a general discussion see Hayashi, M., "The Information Revolution and the Rules of Jurisdiction in Public International Law" in Dunn, Krishna-Hensel and Mauer (eds.) *The Resurgence of the State: Trends and Processes in Cyberspace Governance* (Ashgate: Hampshire, 2007). The position on defamation and privacy actions in relation to the Rome II Regulation (Regulation 864/2007) has been the subject of some debate; the Commission has—following a comparative study (Mainstrat Study)—identified multi-jurisdictional publication as an issue. See also Wallis D., WORKING DOCUMENT <Titre>on the amendment of Regulation (EC) No 864/2007 on the law applicable to non-contractual obligations (Rome II) European Parliament, 23rd June 2010. On conflicts and the Brussels I Regulation (Regulation 44/2001/EC [2001] OJ L12/1) see e.g. Gillies, L., "A Review of the New Jurisdiction Rules for Electronic Consumer Contracts within the European Union" [2001] 1 JILT, available at www2.warwick.ac.uk/fac/soc/law/elj/jilt/2001_1/gillies/.

[3] Goldsmith and Wu *Who Controls the Internet*? (OUP: Oxford, 2006).

[4] See Ministry of Justice consultation on Defamation and the Internet: Multiple Publication Rule, available at: http://www.justice.gov.uk/consultations/defamation-internet-consultation-paper.htm, and Lord Lester's Defamation Bill, session 2010–11 and the Draft Defamation Bill 2012–13.

[5] See distinction noted by Harrison, chapter 8.

[6] OECD, *Participative Web and User Created Content: Web 2.0, Wikis and Social Networking*, 2007.

[7] This could be seen as reflecting the boundaries in the Audiovisual Media Services Directive, *supra* n. 1, the scope of which is limited to services provided for remuneration.

audiences rather than broadcasters or production companies;[8] that any media can be used in the process; and the content is published, whether by traditional or non-traditional media (and via an intermediary or not). Whilst much contributed is amateur, the boundaries of audience blur where some contributors use the medium to further professional careers, or where contributors comprise professionals in 'off-duty' moments. On one level, viewers and listeners as well as readers, have always contributed to the professional media using opportunities such as letters to the editor, radio phone-ins and television programmes featuring home videos. Even within the traditional media environment, some forms of UGC are not unknown. For many people, however, UGC is linked to the Internet—this was the approach taken by the 2007 OECD report. Material on the Internet can take a variety of forms: text, photo, video and audiovisual. Some commentators refer only to online video, though it would seem that UGC is not usually seen so narrowly. Without determining the scope of UGC definitively, this chapter will adopt a broad approach to the meaning of UGC.

The other distinction to note is that between public material and material which is private or confidential. Privacy and confidentiality are significant counter-balances to freedom of expression. This tension is particularly relevant when we consider material included in social network sites (SNS), such as Facebook and Bebo. These sites raise larger questions about public and private space in a digital age and whether content by private individuals, produced or publicised without the intention that it should be widely disseminated, should be used by the professional media.[9] The Council of Europe has started an investigation into the nature of the media so as to distinguish between media-like communications and new forms of personal communication.[10] This distinction was raised in the context of understanding the limits of media regulation, but it seems also to have relevance in this context. The status of 'private' communications on the internet is discussed below.

---

[8] This seems to be the key criterion as far as the BBC is concerned: http://www.bbc.co.uk/terms/faq.shtml, accessed 27 May 2010.

[9] In the BBC's definition, they state that UGC is material "which is submitted to or shared with the BBC either directly or indirectly." While the idea of submission suggests intent, the possibility of sharing indirectly weakens that interpretation. See http://www.bbc.co.uk/terms/faq.shtml, accessed 27 May 2010.

[10] Council of Europe, Contribution of the Council of Europe (Media and Information Society Division, Directorate General of Human Rights and Legal Affairs) for the 2009 Internet Governance Forum, DG-HL(2009) 18, 2.

APPROACH TO FREEDOM OF EXPRESSION AND THE WEIGHTING GIVEN TO THE JOURNALISTIC CAUSE

In general terms, the arguments about freedom of expression and the mass media are well rehearsed,[11] even if disagreement as to the appropriate level of protection or regulation remains. Freedom of expression in relation to individuals has been justified on three main grounds: the search for truth, upholding democracy and personal development.[12] While the last of these cannot apply to media institutions, the other two justifications apply just as well to the expression of media institutions as to personal expression. Of course, limitations on expression may not affect each of these three functions or justifications for freedom of expression equally, and our view of what is acceptable may then reflect our understanding of why freedom of expression is important. Here we will highlight those aspects which have particular relevance for the democratic function of the media and which may link in to difficulties for the professional media in practice.

Individual speech may contribute to the functioning of democracy and, to the extent that we accept the suggestion that free speech leads to truth,[13] to that goal also. While there seems to be consensus that a free media is a valuable asset in a democracy, this viewpoint tends to be justified by instrumentally.[14] While all speech is protected (in the sense that all individual have the right to speak on subjects of their choice),[15] political

---

[11] See e.g. Barendt, E., *Freedom of Speech* (2nd ed) (OUP: Oxford, 2007), 18 and chapter 1.

[12] *R v Secretary of State for the Home Department*, Ex p *Simms* [2000] 2 AC 115.

[13] For a general review of the issues see Barendt, E., *Freedom of Speech, supra* n. 11, 7–13; for a discussion of the American view that sees this argument as a version of the 'market place of ideas' Schauer, F., *Free Speech: A Philosophical Enquiry* (Cambridge University Press: Cambridge, 1982), 16 and this volume, p. 4.

[14] Barendt, *supra* n. 11, 18–21 and a linked argument based on suspicion of government, 21–23.

[15] On types of speech protected see e.g. *Handyside* v. *UK* (1976) 1 EHRR 737, para. 49: ideas which shock or offend; *Barthold* v. *Germany* (1985) 7 EHRR 383, para. 42: commercial speech; *Müller* v. *Switzerland* (1988) 13 EHRR 212, para. 27: artistic speech; as well as matters of general public concern: *Sunday Times* v. *UK* (1979) 2 EHRR 245, *Lingens* v *Austria* (1986) 8 EHRR 407. Within the UK, the PCC is keen to follow the line that the press may behave with complete insensitivity on matters of interest to the public (if not the public interest), and to shock and offend even their readers: see PCC decision on complaint by bereaved partner of Stephen Gately regarding articles in the Daily Mail following Gately's death which received about 25,000 complaints, apparently the most complaints received about an article. PCC decision available at http://www.pcc.org.uk/news/index.html?article=NjIy OA==?oxid=o8q53ebou194fk7483lts42qe5, accessed 27 May 2010. The broadcast media tend to be more aware of such sensitivities, perhaps because they are subject to taste and decency requirements.

speech requires more protection than other, with the role of the media in public discourse being recognised.[16] Nonetheless, the traditional view in the UK is that journalism is accorded no special treatment,[17] though the public interest and objectives supposedly achieved by journalism may weigh heavily in favour of every journalist's free speech rights when weighed against a competing interest, such as defamation or privacy.[18] The decisions of the European Court of Human Rights (ECtHR) show that that court usually treats the position of journalists with some sensitivity and restrictions against them tend to be scrutinised closely.[19] The emphasis lies on the content of the material and whether it is important to form matters of public debate rather than the status of journalists and media *per se*, though their role as 'watchdogs' is highlighted. If the protection given to journalists is essentially functional, is it plausible to suggest that UGC should also benefit from such treatment, in addition to individuals' 'normal' speech rights? There are two problems with this argument: one relating to the nature of the content; and one to the institutional status of journalists.

Looking at the content aspect, there are issues relating to type of expression, its quality[20] and the type of information available. Whilst there are no excluded categories of speech, greater judicial scrutiny of content arises in relation to political speech. Are private individuals more likely to contribute material that relates to the mundane, rather than material relating to democracy and the public sphere, diarists rather than journalists?[21] The mere fact that a mass audience might access a comment in a

---

[16] See e.g. *Observer and Guardian* v. *UK* (1991) 14 EHRR 153, but note comments of Millar, G., "Whither the spirit of *Lingens*?" [2009] *EHRLR* 277 regarding a move in recent jurisprudence away from a presumption of priority for freedom of expression claims to an approach which balances them with other Article 8 interests. This view seems to be reiterated by Barendt, E, "Balancing Freedom of Expression and Privacy: The Jurisprudence of the Strasbourg Court" (2009) 1 *Journal of Media Law* 49, 64–5. See also Amos, chapter 9.

[17] Robertson & Nicol *Media Law* (5th ed) (Penguin Books: London, 2008), xvii. Under the case law of the ECHR, the media relies on the same provision as individuals, Article 10 ECHR: *Goodwin* v. *UK* [1996] 22 EHRR 123. Note that in some political documents, there is a suggestion that the freedom of the media is separate, or perhaps a distinct sub-set of freedom of expression: see Council of Europe, Contribution for the 2009 Internet Governance Forum, *supra* n. 10, 2.

[18] On the significance of reporting see *In Re S* [2004] UKHL 47; In *Re British Broadcasting Corporation* [2009] UKHL 34.

[19] *Jersild* v *Denmark* (1994) 19 EHRR 1 at para. 31.

[20] Quality here is not about production values but rather equates to qualities based in the content itself such as truthfulness, accuracy. These sorts of concerns might be more relevant to factual (news and current affairs) content than to entertainment.

[21] Solove, *The Future of Reputation, gossip, rumor and privacy on the internet* (Yale University Press: New Haven and London, 2007), 24.

blog or a video on YouTube is not going to be enough: popularity does not equate to significance in the public sphere.

In terms of quality, much that is provided by the audience is inaccurate, misinformed, incomplete or nothing more than gossip.[22] From a speaker's perspective, such speech may enjoy protection as a human right, but it is likely to be relatively easily outweighed by other rights and interests. While freedom of expression is not limited to the demonstrably true,[23] the Council of Europe has suggested that trustworthy information is key to the individual's right to information and participation in political, social, cultural and economic life.[24] On this basis, there is a role for professional media in terms of quality assurance and context[25], sometimes seen as curating information or signposting it, and 'Web 3.0' requires a move back away from the "wisdom of crowds".[26] This analysis suggests that the signposting function is specifically relevant in the news and current affairs arena, a view which fits with one which sees the professional media holding those in power to account. So while UGC may offer wider perspectives on matters of importance, 'crowd sourcing' may not be a complete replacement for the role of the professional media, which have some responsibilities towards providing a balanced diet of information. Crowd sourcing may give rise to regulatory issues for the professional media, as we shall see below in regard to impartiality obligations.

This point links to a second problem area, relating to journalism practice and ethics, particularly in terms of the acquisition of information, which are embedded in the institution of journalism. There is an assumption that journalists' "work is carried out in the framework of a professional set of values—the need to be truthful, to be independent and

---

[22] Harrison, J., chapter 8.

[23] By contrast the way the case law was summarised in *Metropolitan International Schools Ltd (t/a Skillstrain and t/a Train2Game) v Designtechnica Corp (t/a Digital Trends), Google UK Ltd, Google Inc* [2009] EWHC 1765 (QB), [2009] E.M.L.R. 27, para. 46 referring to the views of Lord Hobhouse in *Reynolds v. Times Newspapers* [2001] 2 AC 127 at 238, that there is little value in the dissemination of that which is untrue.

[24] Council of Europe, Contribution for the 2009 Internet Governance Forum, *supra* n. 10, 1.

[25] European Federation of Journalist "Trusting Journalism to Make the Best of Democracy" contribution to 1st Council of Europe Conference of Ministers responsible for Media and New Communication Services: A New Notion of Media? (28–29 May 2009, Reykjavik, Iceland), MCM (2009)020, 3; Committee of Ministers Recommendation on measures to promote the public service value of the Internet, Recommendation CM/Rec (2007) 16.

[26] Dokoupil, T., "Revenge of the Experts" Newsweek Web Exclusive, 6th March 2008, available at http://www.newsweek.com/2008/03/05/revenge-of-the-experts.html, accessed 27 May 2010.

to be accountable to the public".[27] In many cases, the ECtHR refers to journalistic ethics or good practice in journalism.[28] The same sorts of ideas are found in the approach of the House of Lords as regards the "defences" to defamation claims in the case of *Reynolds*[29] and *Jameel*.[30] Is it appropriate that such standards, which are ill-defined in case law, be applied to the private individual? The idea that an individual's freedom of expression ought to depend on being employed as a journalist is worrying and may not reflect the reasoning of the courts. Insofar as journalism gets special treatment, it is not generally[31] based on an institutional arguments (that is being regarded as a journalist) but as a result of certain procedures and behaviours on the part of journalists which are more likely to render the story accurate and newsworthy.[32] There is no theoretical reason (though there may be practical resource limitations on UGC) why this sort of endeavour should *only* be carried out by journalists.[33] Nonetheless, freedom of expression must be balanced against the rights of others, such as privacy. The issue of ethics and acquisition of information also looks set to be a problematic area in practice, as well shall see.

---

[27] European Federation of Journalist "Trusting Journalism to Make the Best of Democracy", *supra* n. 25, 2 though there is no explanation of the claimed accountability.

[28] See e.g. *Fressoz and Roire v. France* Application 29183/95, judgment 21 January 1999, though there are now concerns that the requirement for journalistic ethics is limiting freedom of expression in some circumstances: e.g. *Pedersen and Baadsgaard* (2006) 42 EHRR 24; but see Barendt, E., "Balancing Freedom of Expression and Privacy", *supra* n. 16, 66.

[29] *Reynolds* v *Times Newspapers Ltd, supra* n. 23.

[30] *Jameel and others v. Wall Street Journal Europe Sprl* [2006] UKHL 44, though the scope of the *Reynolds* defence has been interpreted narrowly in *Flood* v. *Times Newspapers*, [2009] EWHC 2375 (QB); [2010] EMLR 8, with the Court of Appeal taking a stricter approach than Tuggendhat J at first instance though the Court of Appeal's ruling was overturned by the Supreme Court [2012] UKSC 11.

[31] There are certain limited areas of exception: note the protection for journalists' sources in the Contempt of Court Act and the limited exceptions provided in the Serious Organised Crime and Police Act 2005 and the exception to the data protection regime, see Data Protection Act 1998, s 32. Whilst protection of journalistic sources is perceived as part of freedom of expression, as in *Nordisk Film & TV A/S v. Denmark*, Application no. 40485/02, 8 December 2005, note the problem of giving special treatment to journalists and the possible extension of rights: "... if anyone can be a journalist, then journalistic privilege suddenly becomes a loophole too large to be borne by society" Shirky, quoted by Butterworth, S., and Johannes, J., "Regulating Journalism and Newsgathering" in Goldberg, Sutter and Walden (eds.) *Media Law and Practice* (OUP: Oxford, 2009), 59.

[32] *Steel & Morris v United Kingdom* application no. 68416/01, judgment 15th February 2005 [2005] EMLR 314.

[33] On this point see discussion by Graber, I., "Three Cheers for Subjectivity: or the crumbling of the seven pillars of traditional journalistic wisdom" [2009] *Comms L.* 150. The Privy Council seems to have recognised that the *Reynolds* defence, which is based in journalistic ethics, does not as a matter of principle have to be limited to the professional sphere: *Seaga* v. *Harper* (Jamaica) [2008] UKPC 9 (30 January 2008) Privy Council Appeal No 90 of 2006.

INTERCONNECTION BETWEEN "PROFESSIONAL MEDIA" AND USER GENERATED CONTENT

In principle, freedom of expression arguments may arise just as much in the context of UGC as professional journalism. How then does the law and regulatory regime operate in this sphere, taking into account freedom of expression? While the relationship may be mutually beneficial, it is not unproblematic, as both the general law and the regulatory regime may encourage certain tendencies towards censorship and self-censorship on the part of the professional media as they seek to balance the various rights and obligations, potentially limiting freedom of expression for those contributing UGC. It is this particular aspect of UGC that we will consider. The extent to which contributors of UGC may enforce freedom of expression rights against the media institutions to claim access to airtime (or equivalent) and the conflicting rights within the institutions themselves lies outside this chapter.

There are a number of issues that arise based on obligations under the general law (such as defamation or rules prohibiting hate speech)[34] or arising from the regulatory regimes to which the professional media is subject, whether this be via government imposed regulation[35] or self-regulation.[36] The patchwork of regulatory systems means that the response may vary depending on the regulator involved. Boundaries here are important in terms of determining acceptable behaviour and liability. The heaviest regulatory regime falls on broadcasters, justified on the basis of their impact and on the need to have a range of programmes available, although the negative content obligations to which broadcasters are subject also apply to television-like services, no matter how they are transmitted. Other services provided by electronic communications networks—essentially the Internet and other distance services—fall

---

[34] On the laws against terrorism and their impact on freedom of speech, see Noorlander, chapter 10.

[35] Obligations imposed on broadcasters via the Ofcom Content Code as required by the Communications Act 2003; some of these requirements implement the Audiovisual Media Services Directive, *supra* n. 1.

[36] The Press is subject to a self-regulatory regime run by the PCC; the BBC is partially subject to self-regulation via the BBC Trust, though some aspects of its activities are also subject to regulation by Ofcom. See further, Woods, L., "Regulation and Extra-legal Regulation of the Media Sector" in Goldberg, Sutter and Walden (eds.) *Media Law and Practice* (OUP: Oxford, 2009).

outside the broadcasting regimes,[37] nor are they covered by press self-regulation in this country.[38] Media operators deemed not to be providing an 'audiovisual media service' will fall within the E- commerce directive[39] as implemented in the UK.[40] As already noted, UGC on its own, even if it looks like television, apparently falls outside the broadcasting regulatory regime though it will still be bound by the general law,[41] and individuals blogging where there is no economic element are unlikely to be providing a service for e-commerce purposes.

UGC Incorporated into Professional Content

The first issue concerns UGC which has been incorporated into professional content: the publication in the printed form of a blog, the broadcast of photos or video. While UGC is not directly covered by media regulation, the media organisation itself will be responsible for such content. For example, Ofcom found a violation where a broadcaster was transmitting viewers' text messages as part of a music programme and included one which contained hate speech.[42] This situation places pressure on the

[37] Communications Act 2003 and Wireless Telegraphy Act 2006 both as amended by Audiovisual Media Regulations 2009 (S.I. 2009/2979) and Audiovisual Media Services Regulations 2010 (SI 2010/419) implementing the Audiovisual Media Services Directive (2007/65/EC), *supra* n. 1.

[38] The position of the scope of regulation is far from clear. The PCC's editorial code specifically excluded "user-generated and non-edited material from the Code's remit in online publications" as well as in print. According to the PCC "The test ... is whether the material concerned is subject to editorial control within the terms of the Code of Practice. Comments posted by users in chatrooms or in the form of unedited blogs would generally fall outside the jurisdiction of the PCC". This has been described as "an unrealistic and unworkable fudge—given the increasing use of user-generated material and the blurring of the line between user-generated material and editorial" by the Media Standards Trust: http://www.mediastandardstrust.org/medianews/newsdetails.aspx?sid=4729, accessed 27 May 2010.

[39] Directive 2000/31/EC of the European Parliament and of the Council of 8 June 2000 on certain legal aspects of information society services, in particular electronic commerce, in the Internal Market (Directive on electronic commerce) O.J. [2000] L178/1.

[40] Electronic Commerce (EC Directive) Regulations 2002 regulate "information society service" which is defined as "any service normally provided for remuneration at a distance, by means of electronic equipment for the processing (including digital compression) and storage of data, at the individual request of a recipient of the service."

[41] An area where there may be particular problems is party political broadcasts and the limitations on political advertising, which are subject to a regime additional to the general rules on impartiality. For a brief discussion of the current position see Goldberg, D., "Media, democracy and Reporting Elections" in Goldberg, Sutter and Walden (eds.) *Media Law and Practice* (OUP: Oxford, 2009), especially 184–87.

[42] See also Radio Faza *News Today* (2009) 148 Ofcom Content Bulletin which concerned a community radio station presented by volunteers, one of whom repeatedly read out a 'joke' sent in via text which was anti-Semitic in tone which Ofcom condemned in strong

broadcaster to censor UGC as well as to engage in self-censorship. It should
be noted, however, that although this is an infringement of individuals'
rights (albeit by a non-governmental body),[43] there are public interest
objectives governing mass media content particularly because the reach
and range of broadcasting. When UGC is incorporated into professional
content, it too has that reach. Note that in the example given, the broadcaster was retransmitting in the viewer's words as they were sent in. There
may have been a different outcome had the programme and maker been
engaged in, for example, making a documentary about the problems of
racism and put the material in a critical context,[44] thus contributing to
public debate.[45]

Phone-ins (and 'text-ins') raise other issues, particularly where matters
likely to trigger high public feeling are in issue. As noted above, broadcasters (but not the press) are subject to impartiality requirements; how does
this interact with UGC?[46] Two sets of complaints relating to current affairs
programmes hosted by the controversial MP, George Galloway, illustrate
the regulatory approach and suggest some difficulties in this area. The first
group related to programmes aired on Talksport;[47] the second to programmes aired on Press TV, an Iranian international news network which
broadcasts in English.[48] All programmes concerned the Israeli policy
towards Gaza, with Galloway maintaining a stance critical of the Israeli
actions. In his programmes, he called for audience input, stating on
PressTV, "We want to see your name up here in lights, whether you agree

---

terms even though the station accepted the breach and had notified Ofcom of measures to
prevent further occurrence.

[43] For a discussion of the extent to which other issues arises from the multiple voices
contained within the professional media see e.g. Barendt, E., *Broadcasting Law:
A Comparative Study* (Clarendon Press: Oxford, 1993), 40–41. See also Article XIX,
*Background Paper on Freedom of Expression and Internet Regulation for the International
Seminar on Promoting Freedom of Expression With the Three Specialised International
Mandates*, London, 19–20 November 2001, 9–11, available at http://www.article19.org/pdfs/
publications/freedom-of-expression-and-internet-regulation.pdf, accessed 27 May 2010,
for concerns about the power of third parties to censor speech.

[44] This would seem to affect the speech rights of those contributing UGC, though the
existence and extent of such rights are problematic.

[45] *Jersild, supra* n. 19. Note that in some instances, the mere possession of some forms of
content are offences.

[46] A discussion of the scope of rights of access to the media lie outside this chapter; for
a discussion of impartiality see Feintuck, chapter 4 and Barnett, chapter 3.

[47] George Galloway *Talksport, 22 November 2008; 27, 29 December 2008; 2, 9 January 2009,
22:00* (2009) 136 Ofcom Content Bulletin, 30.

[48] Comment & The Real Deal *Press TV, January 2009, Various dates and times* (2009) 139
Ofcom Content Bulletin, 5.

with us or not", and on Talksport, "you're welcome whatever your point of view but you're especially welcome if you disagree with me...". Ofcom's code requires broadcasters to allow differing views to be heard. The question was whether this requirement was satisfied by invitations to contribute. In the PressTV programmes, most of the UGC reflected Galloway's views; Ofcom noted that 'there were some but extremely limited contributions that could be labelled as being broadly supportive of the actions of the Israeli state in Gaza during January 2009'[49] and that there was not an 'appropriately wide range of *significant* views' [Ofcom's emphasis].[50] Further, when dealing with opposing viewpoints, Galloway used them as an opportunity to explain his points further, thus meaning due weight was not given to those viewpoints.[51] Ofcom concluded that,

> In audience participation programmes, such as *Comment*, where viewers or listeners are encouraged to telephone, email, text or otherwise contribute to the programme, ... it is not the case that broadcasters have to ensure an equal number of points of view are featured. It also has to be recognised that while broadcasters can encourage callers from different perspectives, it cannot 'manufacture' them. ... broadcasters must have systems in place to ensure that due impartiality is maintained.[52]

By contrast, in Talksport a balance had been found, through the inclusion of recognised commentators and also through the inclusion of pro-Israeli callers.[53] This raises questions—particularly for those stations and channels with niche audiences and which themselves might constitute minority access—as to how to ensure that either an appropriate quantity of dissenting views are brought in, or the 'other measures' required by Ofcom to maintain impartiality. It is interesting to contrast the position of such stations (which are sometimes small and with limited resources) with the position of the print media, which are under no such impartiality obligations.[54] Questions about the representativeness of UGC also occur in relation to the second category of media/UGC interface (below).

---

[49] Comment & The Real Deal *Press TV, January 2009, Various dates and times supra* n. 48, 9.

[50] Comment & The Real Deal *Press TV, January 2009, Various dates and times supra* n. 48, 10.

[51] A similar concern was expressed in Talksport, *supra* n. 47.

[52] Comment & The Real Deal *Press TV, January 2009, Various dates and times supra* n. 48, 12.

[53] See also Jeni Barnett *LBC 97.3 FM, 7 January 2009, 14:00* (2009) 136 Ofcom Content Bulletin, 39.

[54] For a summary of the arguments about the distinction between broadcast media and press, see e.g. Hitchens, L., *Broadcasting Pluralism and Diversity*, (Hart Publishing: Oxford, 2006), 47.

An open question is whether broadcasters are seen as broadcasters or as providing information society services when providing discussion forums. Much may depend on context and the degree to which the discussion is linked to broadcast material. If so, do Ofcom's comments about impartiality and UGC apply to that content too? If we see the media's right to freedom of expression as instrumental, then there are obvious links to a requirement for a multiplicity of voices[55] and, as McGonagle discusses, minority access. As Harrison notes, this question has haunted vox pop more generally. The situation is more difficult in cases where we are considering comments posted on websites; here, there is no control—subject to removal of illegal speech (hate speech etc)—and therefore there is a risk of the extreme, the partial, as well as the dull and inaccurate. Harrison's work shows some discomfort within the BBC in this context; the BBC's public service remit (its own and its employees' own freedom of expression) operating under tension with those of its viewers.

Acquisition of Information by Users

A second concern with regard to UGC relates to acquisition of information. A professional using UGC will not be aware of that content's ethical pedigree. As noted, journalistic ethics have been an important factor in the case law on freedom of expression. The broadcasters, and to some degree also the press, have guidelines about how material is acquired and how it is used, with particular regard to issues such as undercover filming[56] and participation by vulnerable people, particularly children. The extension of responsibility for ethics during production of content can be seen in broadcast regulation and in regulation of the press. In a decision involving Sumo TV (which broadcasts clips sent in via its website), the broadcaster was responsible for a clip where due care for the welfare of a child in the filming of the clip had not been taken.[57] Ofcom emphasised that the broadcaster remained under an obligation to ensure that necessary consents have been given, especially where children are concerned. It added a general reprimand:

> Ofcom is concerned that some channels broadcasting considerable amounts of user-generated content may attempt to place too much

---

[55] Hitchens, L., *Broadcasting Pluralism and Diversity, supra* n. 54, 36.
[56] *R v Broadcasting Standards Commission ex parte BBC* (Dixons) [2000] 3 WLR 1327.
[57] Sumo TV—User Generated Content *Andy Milonakis clip, 6 July 2007, 23:46; and Parent/Carer and child clip, 22 July 2007, 00:34* (2008) 101 Ofcom Content Bulletin, 4.

responsibility for ensuring compliance with the Code with the individual user, and not perform sufficient checks themselves. Responsibility for compliance with the Code always remains with the broadcaster.[58]

A similar approach can be seen at the BBC For example, in the context of surreptitious recordings, BBC Editorial Guidelines say *"Secret recordings made by others and offered to the BBC for broadcast should pass the same tests we use for gathering our own material. If it was not gathered according to BBC Editorial Guidelines it should not normally be broadcast".* When a phone call was made by the former Prime Minister, Gordon Brown, to the mother of a dead soldier (Mrs Janes), following allegations that a handwritten letter of condolence that he sent to her contained a number of mistakes, was recorded by Mrs Janes secretly and made available to *The Sun*, BBC News reported the controversy and the contents of the call, but declined to make use of the secretly recorded audio of the Prime Minister.[59]

These examples re-affirm the point that freedom of expression is not unlimited, especially where it comprises the unauthorised use of the speech of others. This is a point of which the professional media should be aware and is certainly covered by the various codes of conduct. Non-professionals might not know this, however, and in the *Sumo case*, Ofcom noted that Sumo's terms and conditions of use were defective as they did not draw to the attention of the audience the limits of acceptable behaviour in terms of content suitable for broadcast. This seems to imply that broadcasters are not just responsible for not broadcasting dubious content, but possibly also under some duty to set standards of behaviour for non-professionals.[60] Highlighting the limits of acceptable behaviour to those contributing makes sense: while some content may on the face of it raises questions about the context in which the content was made or acquired, other content may not. In a case which came before the PCC, a magazine had asked readers to send in photographs, and one reader sent in a photograph of his girlfriend. It transpired that she was actually his ex-girlfriend, under-age (14) and had not consented to his sending the

---

[58] Ofcom, Note to Broadcasters: *User-generated content* (2008) 101 Ofcom Content Bulletin, 11.

[59] BBC *Editorial Policy Newsletter* 24, 12th February 2010.

[60] In a different context, Google executives have been found liable in Italy for breach of data protection rules based on inadequate terms of use, though the reasoning of the Italian court has not yet been published. It seems the obligations on ISPs and other service providers to ensure 'good behaviour' is spreading.

photograph. The PCC rejected the magazine's argument that the teenager looked older, and the fact that the magazine had accepted the assertion by the person submitting the photograph, that the teenager was cohabiting with him. The PCC stated,

> this would have been the case regardless of how old she was, but the Commission was particularly concerned about the impact on the girl in light of her youth. The magazine had clearly not taken any sort of adequate care to establish the provenance of the photograph and whether it was right to publish it.[61]

Obviously, accepting an argument that the newspaper did not know and therefore could not be liable would undercut the effectiveness of the guidelines; the PCC found a violation.

Consent of the subject of the content is a key element, as indeed the PCC recognised here; privacy can outweigh freedom of expression, whether that of the boyfriend or the newspaper.[62] Whilst terms of use may seek to provide protection for the media professional, it is an open question how far a professional content-maker should go to verify whether there has been consent or whether the person is competent to give consent where when material is sent in by a viewer or reader.[63] The issue of privacy will be discussed again below. Of course, where a matter of genuine public interest is raised, privacy may be outweighed by the interest in publication; UGC should not be treated differently in this particular regard.

UGC through Participation in a Website

This situation illustrates a more general concern for a broadcaster, programme-maker, journalist or the press, that of knowing whether the person sending in the content has the right to do so (copyright could also be an issue here) and whether by re-publishing of the material, the media

---

[61] *A Married Couple* v. *FHM* (2007) 75 PCC Adjudication, issued 15/8/07 but cf. *A Woman* v. *Loaded* (2010) PCC Adjudication, 11/05/10.

[62] The courts seemed to take a somewhat censorious view of sexual relationships with sex workers, for example approach of the Court of Appeal in *A* v. *B Plc* [2002] EWCA Civ 337, though whether this approach is still good post *Campbell* v. *MGN Limited* [2004] UKHL 22 and *McKennit* v. *Ash* [2005] EWHC 3003 (QB) has been questioned. Eady J. considered the freedom of expression of parties to intimate (not necessarily sexual) relationships at first instance in *McKennit* v. *Ash*, para. 77 and suggested that freedom of expression should be exercised in such a way as not to infringe privacy of others. His judgment was approved by the Court of Appeal: [2006] EWCA Civ 1714.

[63] See by analogy *T* v. *BBC* [2007] EWHC 1683 (QB).

company infringes copyright or defames someone. Although there is a separate regime for copyright,[64] the e-Commerce Directive,[65] as implemented in the UK,[66] otherwise provides for an exception for criminal or pecuniary liability for all types of illegal content (except data protection breaches) in respect of "information society services", that is

> ... any service normally provided for remuneration, at a distance, by means of electronic equipment for the processing (including digital compression) and storage of data, and the individual request of a recipient of a service.[67]

Internet service providers (ISPs) and others who merely provide access/transmission or services including caching (temporary storage of data)[68] and hosting (storage of information, such as bulletin boards)[69] may be exempt from liability arising from involvement in the publication of material, a provision apparently included in response to fears of the chilling effect of potential liability to freedom of expression. The concern was that the ISPs would be likely to take a cautious view of acceptable content and act as censors accordingly in order to limit exposure to liability arising from UGC.[70]

The position of the professional media under this regime is not clear and different professional media may be categorised differently. Those subject to the broadcasting regime are excluded from the e-Commerce directive and would seem in principle unable to claim the benefit of these exemptions; indeed, given the level of regulatory codes applying to broadcasters directly, exemption regarding liability under the general law seems to have little relevance. It is arguable that some non-linear AVMS can be seen as information society service providers, and therefore able to benefit, subject to the point already made about applicable regulatory

---

[64] Art. 3 e-Commerce Directive, *supra* n. 40. See Directive 2001/29/EC on Copyright in the Information Society which deals *inter alia* with the liability of intermediaries for infringement of copyright and related rights.

[65] Directive 2000/31/EC, *supra* n. 40.

[66] The Electronic Commerce (EC Directive) Regulations 2002 (SI 2013/2002), Regulation 17 *et seq.* Note in relation to terrorism offences and hate speech there are specific provisions clarifying the position: Electronic Commerce Directive (Terrorism Act 2006) Regulations 2007 (312007/1550); The Electronic Commerce Directive (Hatred against Persons on Religious Grounds or the Grounds of Sexual Orientation) Regulations 2010 (SI 2010/894).

[67] Regulation 17, Electronic Commerce (EC Directive) Regulations, *supra* n. 66; this is wider than the definition found in Article 2 of the Directive, *supra* n. 4.

[68] Regulation 18 SI 2013/2002, *supra* n. 66.

[69] Regulation 19 SI 2013/2002, *supra* n. 66.

[70] Valcke, P., and Dommering, E., Comments on Directive 2000/31/EC in Castendyk, Dommering and Scheuer (eds.) *European Media Law* (Kluwer Law International: Alphen a/d Rijn, 2008), para. 49.

codes. Questions remain, however. Are broadcasters excluded from the
e-Commerce directive as regard *all* their activities by virtue of being a
broadcaster, even if some of their activities are not broadcasting and meet
the definition of an information society service? What of the press? Are
their web presences linked to the provision of newspapers and therefore
not provided wholly at a distance?

Assuming the regime is relevant to a service provider, the availability of
the exemption depends on the different levels of knowledge, or lack of it,
of that service provider. In respect of those hosting, the service provider
must not have actual knowledge of unlawful activity or information, and
must not be aware of facts or circumstances from which it would have
been apparent to the service provider that the activity or information was
unlawful. Where a service provider obtains such knowledge or awareness,
it must act expeditiously to remove or disable access to the information.
Service providers are not subject to a general obligation to monitor the
information which they transmit or store, nor to seek facts or circumstances indicating illegal activity.

Many professional media have discussion forums on their Internet sites
and, subject to the comments above, can rely on the hosting exception
found in Regulation 19 of the e-Commerce Regulations.[71] While this will
depend on the facts of each case, where the professional media moderate
the debate, whether moderation arises before the content is seen or after,
it is harder to argue that such body is only an intermediary.[72] It has been
suggested that where there is a link between a discussion forum and the
content provided by the professional media, insofar as that content was
not already caught by a regulatory regime, the intermediary protection
would not be available. This may lead us to making some fine distinctions
between content in which the audience is specifically invited to contribute, and the web site which merely provides a topic based discussion
forum in which members of the audience may discuss subjects but are not
specifically invited to do so.

One of the particular risk areas with regard to UGC is defamation.[73]
Whilst defamatory statements would in most cases not be deliberately
picked up for broadcast,[74] there remains the question of content on

---

[71] *Imran Karim -v- Newsquest Media Group Ltd* [2009] EWHC 3205 (QB)—note that the
offending comments were removed swiftly once brought to the newspaper's attention.

[72] See e.g. *Kaschke* v. *Gray Hilton* [2010] EWHC 690 (QB).

[73] The common law offence of defamatory libel was repealed by s. 73 Coroners and
Justice Act 2009.

[74] The repetition of a defamatory statement itself is caught by the rules on
defamation.

discussion forums of various types.[75] It should be noted that an internet intermediary, if undertaking no more than the role of a passive medium of communication, is not a publisher at common law and would not, therefore, need to turn to any defence.[76] Further, according to s.1 Defamation Act,[77] 'an innocent publisher' has a defence if s/he meets certain criteria listed in the section.[78] S1(3)(e) Defamation Act, which clearly reflects a growing awareness of the impact of the Internet, effectively provides an intermediary style exception. Although these rules have clearly been defined to try to protect those such as ISPs, the relationship between these rules and those deriving from the e-Commerce Directive is not clear.[79] Assuming that the Defamation Act rules are not superseded by the e-Commerce rules, those seeking to rely on the innocent publisher defence are still subject to the requirement that they took reasonable care. This is a difficult balancing act because assuming a level of editorial control will mean the professional media institution falls outside section 1 (3) and will be treated in the same way as a printer publisher.

In *Godfrey* v. *Demon*, the first case to deal with online liability, which concerned a Usenet newsgroup, although the defence was in theory available, in practice it was unavailable: the ISP failed to delete the offending material swiftly once the material had been drawn to its attention.[80] No liability accrued for the period prior to the receipt of the notification, as the ISP hosting the bulletin board (but not editing it) could not reasonably have been expected to be aware of a defamatory statement in a discussion

---

[75] Collins, M., noted that this would cover editors of bulletin boards: *The Law of Defamation and the Internet* (OUP: Oxford, 2005), 62. It is not clear how the courts would assess the scope of publication; all visitors to all parts of the site, or visitors just to that page?.

[76] *Bunt* v. *Tilley* [2006] EWHC 407, paras. 36–37. See also *Kaschke* v. *Gray, supra* n. 72 and *Gatley on Libel and Slander* Milmo et al (eds.) (11th ed) (Sweet and Maxwell, 2008).

[77] The question of whether the common law defence remains is unclear: see discussion in *Metropolitan International Schools Ltd (t/a Skillstrain and t/a Train2Game)* v *Designtechnica Corp (t/aDigital Trends), Google UK Ltd, Google Inc supra* n. 23, para. 65 *et seq.*

[78] They are: the innocent publisher is not the author, editor or publisher of the material (s. 1(1)(a)); it can demonstrate that s/he did not know and had no reason to believe that the statement in question was defamatory (s.1(1)(b)); and it can show it took reasonable care in the publication of the statement (s 1(1)(c)).

[79] The matter was touched on in *Bunt* v. *Tilley, supra* n. 76, but not discussed fully.

[80] Note that archive material may also give rise to liability: *Flood* v *Times Newspapers Ltd, supra* n. 30. Despite the potentially chilling effect for those maintaining on-line archives arising from defamation claims arising from an archive 'publication', the ECtHR has ruled that such a rule is not a violation of Article 10: *Times Newspapers* v. *UK* (Applications3002/03 and 2367/03), judgment 10th March 2009.

of Thai culture. As Eady J commented in *Bunt* v. *Tilley*,[81] 'to impose legal responsibility upon anyone under the common law for the publication of words it is essential to demonstrate a degree of awareness or at least an assumption of general responsibility, such as has long been recognised in the context of editorial responsibility'.[82] While this assists non-notified ISPs[83] and may help blogging sites (though more recent case law[84] has not charted an entirely consistent path) it leaves media hosted sites in a more difficult position as presumably they have that intention. This approach makes context important for the professional media. Where the subject matter of the discussion will usually be innocuous (food, arts),[85] they would not be unreasonable in being unaware of any defamation, until notification thereof. By contrast, where the subject matter of the news-group is likely to be critical of individuals (e.g. celebrity gossip or in response to a news story) the court might adopt the attitude that the body hosting the service could reasonably have been expected to be aware of the statements. More problematically, what is likely to be the view of the court in relation to an "innocuous" newsgroup but which has a long run-ning and highly critical thread?

UGC which is Acquired without Consent

The final concern arises when the professional media uses content that is available on the Internet but which has not been directed specifically to them. Where the provider of the content does not mind the material being re-used, there is still the issue of the content's "ethical pedigree", as noted above. Where the provider of the content does object, or has not consented to the use of the content,[86] the matter is still more problem-atic. Social network sites (SNSs) in particular seem to be giving rise to problems, though the content of blogs have also been picked up by the

---

[81] *Supra* n. 76.

[82] Ibid., para. 22, citing Lord Morris in *McLeod v St Aubyn* [1899] AC 549, 562.

[83] See also *Metropolitan International Schools v Designtechnica, supra* n. 77.

[84] *Davison v. Habeeb, Eyre, Bowden, The Palestine Telegraph Newspapers Ltd, Google Inc., and Google UK Ltd* [2011] EWHC 3031 (QB); Tamiz v. Google Inc [2012] EWHC 449 (QB). *Davison* concerned a blog article; *Tamiz* comments in response to a blog article. In *Davison* there was an arguable claim that Google was a publisher; in *Tamiz* it was found not to be.

[85] See for example discussion on a new presenter for Gardeners' World, though even here there can be personal comments and we never do get to the bottom of pink-dahlia-gate: http://www.bbc.co.uk/dna/mbgardening/F2759004?thread=7244012, accessed 27 May 2010.

[86] That is because someone else has uploaded content about them, or because some-body is pretending to be that person.

professional media.[87] As with the term UGC, there are some variations in defining SNS. In broad terms, they have been described as an online community that allows people to meet and communicate with other community members.[88] Individuals register, create a profile and post comments, upload photographs and videos and communicate with "friends". There are a number of SNS available, with different demographics, as well as different functions (general and social/ business orientated or topic specific). It is remarkable the degree of personal information that some people include on SNS and there has been some suggestion that the approach to sharing information is formed by peer pressure rather than a consideration of privacy concerns.[89] Some information would certainly have the capability of embarrassing that person; perhaps in a different context, perhaps at a later date. It is possible to limit the people who may access the individual's pages, however many people are indiscriminate in accepting 'friends' and the default setting for many social sites is to allow wide access in the interests of ensuring that the SNS provider attracts advertising revenue.[90] Only a minority of users change the default settings,[91] yet there is a feeling of outrage when such material is used by third parties for other purposes: employers checking out the off-duty activities of their employees or would-be employees, for example; and journalists finding stories for republication.[92] This suggests a mismatch between expectation and practice which is the more a concern as it is possible to find individuals' pages by using a search engine. These sites have given rise to a number of privacy issues,[93] which remain even though many of the

---

[87] For examples see e.g. Solove, D., *The Future of Reputation, supra* n. 2.

[88] ENISA, *Online as soon as it happens*, February 2010, 12. ENISA earlier defined the essential characteristics as (1) tools for posting personal content (profile); (2) tools for interactions around the profile; and (3) for defining social relationships which determine who has access to data available on SNSs and who can communicate with whom and how: in October 2007, available at http://www.enisa.europa.eu/act/res/other-areas/social -networks/security-issues-and-recommendations-for-online-social-networks, accessed 27 May 2010.

[89] Acquisti and Gross (2006) cited by The Office of the Privacy Commissioner of Canada Social *Network Site Privacy: A comparative analysis of six sites*, February 2009, 5.

[90] ENISA Position Paper No. 1, 3, *supra* n. 88.

[91] A Article 29 Working Party, Opinion 5/2009, *supra*, 7.

[92] PCC, *Newsletter*, December 2009 referring to research commissioned by the PCC on social networking and privacy: IPSOS MORI, *Public Concern about Social Networking*, March 2008, available at http://www.ipsos-mori.com/researchpublications/ researcharchive/poll.aspx?oItemId=2304, accessed 27 May 2010.

[93] See ENISA Position Paper No 1, *supra* n. 88, 10–15 There are other concerns with the range and detail of information that people are putting on the internet which leads them to be vulnerable to crimes, notably identity theft but see also a site which identifies empty houses, apparently in an attempt to draw attention to how much information people are

SNS providers have signed up to the Safer SNS Principles.[94] For our purposes, the central question is whether professional news organisations can use information they find on such sites as the basis for stories (e.g. humorous stories). The argument from the perspective of the media is that this information is in the public domain;[95] presumably the assumption is that any counter interests limiting the media's freedom of expression are waived or trumped. The problem is that many people either have not considered the consequences of such disclosure, have little sense of the degree of potential exposure, or view SNS as being in some way private; that they are communicating just with their friends.[96] This brings us to our fourth limiting factor noted above and difficult questions about what is in the public domain and what is private.

Privacy is a difficult concept to pin down and can cover a range of concepts.[97] From the Strasbourg case law, and to some extent that of the UK courts,[98] protection is not limited to information that is a complete secret but rather provides an arena within which the individual can develop, in relationship with others.[99] The respect for private life/ privacy interest seems to be a sliding scale, influenced by a number of factors. It allows individuals a certain communicative space, though the extent of this space is somewhat uncertain and may be context and content

---

giving away in the on-line environment: http://news.bbc.co.uk/1/hi/technology/8521598 .stm.

[94] For details see here: http://ec.europa.eu/information_society/activities/social _networking/eu_action/implementation_princip/index_en.htm Note that Facebook has been criticised for changing its default settings: Article 29 Data Protection Working Party, Press Release: European data protection group faults Facebook for privacy setting change, 12 May 2010, available at http://ec.europa.eu/justice_home/fsj/privacy/news/docs/ pr_12_05_10_en.pdf, accessed 27 May 2010.

[95] This argument was accepted by the PCC in *A Woman v. Loaded, supra* n. 61.

[96] International Working Group on Data Protection in Telecommunications, *Report and Guidance on Privacy in Social Network Services*, 4th March 2008 (675.36.5) (Rome Memorandum) warn against a false sense of 'community' inculcated by the way SNS are set up and the terminology used, 2. 30th International Conference of Data Protection and Privacy Commissioners, *Resolution on Privacy Protection in Social Network Services*, 17 October 2008, 1.

[97] Wacks, R., "Introduction" in Wacks (ed.) *Privacy*, Vol 1 (1993), xi. We will not cover data protection issues here, given the existence of an exception to the data processing rules at both EU and UK level. Note, however, that although the ECJ has ruled that an individual may claim the benefit of this exemption, there are conditions attached to its use, including the fact that publication be in the public interest. Given that this is to be determined, according to The Data Protection (Designated Codes of Practice) (No.2) Order 2000, S.I. No. 1864, the media codes of conduct, the limitation may not provide significant constraints on the operation of the exemption.

[98] *R v. BSC* ex parte *BBC* [2001] QB 885, 900.

[99] *Botta* v. *Italy* (1998) 26 EHRR 241, at para. 32.

dependent.[100] Of course, the desire to protect privacy does not mean that individuals cannot chose to make personal information public. There is a distinction between the potential existence of a private zone and the infringement or loss of privacy: information and context may be of the type which engages privacy but that right can be waived, or outweighed. Here we should note the difference between particular pieces of information, for example a picture of a bride signing the marriage register, and a general topic, with a willingness to talk about the fact of the upcoming ceremony. Caution, especially post-*Campbell*,[101] should be exercised if trying to infer a generalised consent to intrusion where individuals have 'opened up' issues to debate.[102] Likewise, we should remember that not all material on the internet is there with consent, as the Max Mosley case illustrates (discussed by Amos), even if it appears to be in the individual's name. The position of information that is potentially available may lead to questions beyond that of consent or implied consent (and consent to what: uploading in the first place or further dissemination of the material?). Here we need to consider whether the information is protected by privacy even if public and whether the potentially public nature of it constitutes a waiver of the right to privacy.

Whilst the natural inclination is to talk of privacy, privacy is protected in England and Wales by the doctrine of confidentiality,[103] now sometimes referred to as the tort of misuse of private information,[104] rather than a free standing right to privacy.[105] Whilst information in the public domain

---

[100] This suggestion is based on the case law of the English courts and the ECtHR, but it seems also to fit with suggestions made in the American literature (but not the case law there): Nissenbaum, H., "Privacy as Contextual Integrity" (2004) 79 *Washington Law Review* 119, 136–7.

[101] *Campbell, supra* n. 62, clarified the line of reasoning that seemed to be developing even prior to the Human Rights Act, that even public figures have the right to some private life.

[102] Phillipson, G., and Fenwick, H., "Breach of Confidence as a Privacy Remedy in the Human Rights Act Era" (2000) 63 *MLR* 660, 680 discussing cases such as *Woodward* v. *Hutchins* [1977] 1 WLR 760 (CA) and *Lennon* v. *News Group* [1978] FSR 575. See comments of Eady J in *McKennit* v. *Ash, supra* n. 62 at first instance and the ECtHR in *Von Hannover* v. *Germany* (No. 2), judgement 7 February 2012, para. 111.

[103] A discussion of the relationship between confidentiality and the tort of the misuse of private information lies outside this chapter though some confusion seems to exist: see *Campbell, supra* n. 62, *McKennit* v. *Ash, supra* n. 62, and more recently *Terry* (*previously known as LNS*) v. *Persons Unknown* [2010] EWHC 119 (QB).

[104] *Campbell supra* n. 62, *McKennit* v. *Ash, supra* n. 62, *John Terry* (*previously referred to as LNS*) *v Persons Unknown,* Ibid., though it is not consistently referred to as such in cases: see e.g. *Mosley* (*II*) [2008] EWHC 1777 (QB).

[105] *Wainwright* v *Home Office* [2003] UKHL 53; [2003] 3 WLR 1137 despite suggestion to the contrary by Sedley J., in *Douglas* v *Hello* [2001] QB 967, 997.

is not protected by confidentiality,[106] not everything that is known by others is in the public domain;[107] the court has suggested that a substantial number of people need to be aware for a matter to lose its confidentiality.[108] Indeed, the issue may not even be resolved by a pure numerical calculation, but also the question of whether the information has leaked out of a particular circle or group of people;[109] it has also been suggested that confidentiality (or privacy) is about the control of the dissemination of private information.[110] Further, there has been a shift in the understanding of confidentiality, reflecting to some degree the approach taken by the ECtHR. Originally, the focus was on the relationship in which the information was imparted, as well as on the fact that the information was not publicly known. Whilst circumstances which fit the 'old' version of confidentiality will clearly still be protected, the law has broadened to include the misuse of private information whether or not there was a relationship between the subject and the person who discloses the information. Instead, the focus is on whether there was a reasonable expectation of privacy, an assessment which takes into account the nature of the information disclosed, as well as context. Whilst location (public or non-public place) or the fact that the information is not known by others may be factors, they are not necessarily determinative. Confidentiality can arise where the recipient should have realised from the nature of the material that it was confidential. Such a suggestion pre-dates the Human Rights Act, with Goff L.J.'s suggestion in the *Guardian* case that a diary in the street would, by its nature, be recognised as obviously confidential,[111] though the case law now seems to be influenced by the approach to private life under Article 8 ECHR.

---

[106] *AG v Guardian Newspapers* (no 2) (1990) 1 AC 109; and the fact that information has been disseminated in breach of confidence may affect the remedies available: see *Mosley* (I) [2008] EWHC 687 (QB) in which an interim injunction was refused; this aspect of the case was the subject of an unsuccessful action against the UK before the European Court of Human Rights.

[107] Franchi v. Franchi [1967] RPC 147, p. 152; more recently see Associated Newspapers v. Prince of Wales [2006] EWCA Civ 1776, [2007] 2 All ER 139, [2007] 3 WLR 222.

[108] Stephens v. Avery [1988] Ch 449, 454; Barrymore -v- News Group Newspapers Ltd [1997] FSR 600.

[109] The case of *Douglas v Hello supra* n. 105 could be an example of this, even where there was an intention to disseminate the photographs subsequently anyway. We can also argue that there are issues about control over information which links to concerns in other cases about the harm with covert surveillance being that as we do not know it is there we do not have the opportunity to object and have lost control over the information consequently acquired.

[110] *Douglas v. Hello!* (no 1), *supra* n. 105; Campbell v MGN, *supra* n. 62.

[111] *A.G. v. Guardian Newspapers* (No 2) [1990] 1 AC 109, 281.

Information and activities may be private, even if they occur in a public place, a point that is repeated in the Strasbourg jurisprudence. In *Peck*, a case which originated in the UK, the ECtHR held that a Article 8 protected 'a zone of interaction with others, even in a public context'. While this appeared to be justified by the exceptional circumstances—Peck had been caught on CCTV footage trying to commit suicide in a public street—in *von Hannover*[112] the ECtHR held that photographs depicting the princess in a range of mundane activities which did not involve her personal sphere were likewise protected by Article 8. Even celebrities and public figures *par excellence*, who traditionally have a lower expectation of privacy especially in public, have a right to some private life. What was notable in *von Hannover* was that the photos did not relate to circumstances in which she was seeking seclusion even within a public space—as would have been the case had the photos related, for example, to a candlelit dinner with her boyfriend at an obscure table. Rather, the photographs related to everyday life, such as the princess shopping. In *Von Hannover II*,[113] the Princess again argued that the German courts were not sufficiently protecting her privacy in relation to the publication of photographs of the Princess and her husband on holiday skiing. This time, Germany (and the press) won. *Von Hannover II* is not an overturning of the original *Von Hannover* judgment, as the question was really about the margin of appreciation of national authorities and whether the courts had taken the relevant factors into consideration. What *Von Hannover II* does do is give more guidance on the factors to be taken into account in balancing Article 8 and Article 10. Nonetheless, it is far from clear whether the UK courts would go this far.[114] It has been suggested that the decision in *von Hannover* may have been a reaction to the constant media attention which the princess endured[115] though subsequent case law suggests that a broader range of protection for public activities might be now accepted in English law than might have seemed to be the case immediately after *Campbell*.[116] What is clear is the mere fact that an activity is open to view does not necessarily defeat a claim for confidentiality, while attempts to seek seclusion would buttress (though not necessarily guarantee) a confidentiality claim.

---

[112] *Von Hannover v. Germany* (application no. 59320/00), (2005) 40 EHRR [63].

[113] *Von Hannover v. Germany* (No 2), *supra* n. 102.

[114] See Baroness Hale in *Campbell*, *supra* n. 62, *Murray* v. *Big Pictures* [2008] EWCA Civ 446, [2008] 3 WLR 1360 and *Elton John* v. *Associated Newspapers* [2006] EWHC 1611 (QB) (Eady, J.,).

[115] Fenwick, H., and Phillipson, G., *Media Freedoms under the Human Rights Act*, (Oxford: OUP, 2006), 681 referring to the text of judgment, *supra* n. 112, at paras. 44, 68 and 59.

[116] *Murray* v. *Big Pictures, supra* n. 114.

So how does this analysis suggest the law should regard material on the internet, particularly that on SNS? One argument is to suggest that even if the material was made public by a third party, if sufficiently available it will lose its confidentiality or protection through privacy.[117] The question is whether inclusion on a website automatically has that consequence. Case law suggests that it does not[118] though the position is ambiguous. In *Barclays Bank* v *Guardian*, a case concerning a traditional confidentiality claim, Blake J. distinguished between that which was readily available and that which was more difficult to find, such as specialist websites.[119] It seems that the likely audience may also have an impact; for dissemination to the public a broader scope of dissemination will be needed for the information to lose its confidentiality. In *Mosley I*, Eady, J. emphasised the number of hits on the relevant website before determining that—although a privacy claim could still go forward—injunctive relief would not be available.[120] The type of information as well as the type of person—public or private—posting will have an impact on the outcome, as will the type of website. It is clear that a binary approach which sees the Internet as public, rather than allowing any private speech is not consistent with the case law. How then might we characterise 'public' sites as opposed to private? *Barclays Bank* may suggest some answers, but it is important to note that the case dealt with a website that was designed to publish material, albeit in an online form. UGC may well be different, as it is often intended for a limited audience.

There has been a tendency to view the Internet as a place or a separate space.[121] If we accept the metaphor, we must consider whether we regard it as a single, probably public, space, or instead allow for a variety of spaces. Technology allows differentiation through firewalls, encryption systems and geolocation programs,[122] and differentiation seems at least a possibility in the English case law to date. SNS, although used in many ways, are more likely to be regarded as a living room (or a teenage bedroom) where

---

[117] It certainly affects the remedies available; injunctive relief was not available to Mosley as the material was already too well known. On this issue see further, Phillipson, G., "Max Mosley goes to Strasbourg: Article 8, Claimant Notification and Interim Injunctions" [2009] 1 *Journal of Media Law* 73.

[118] *Mosley II, supra* n. 104.

[119] *Barclays Bank PLC* v *Guardian News & Media Ltd* [2009] EWHC 591 (QB), see also the approach to assessing publication in respect of defamation cases.

[120] *Mosley I, supra* n. 106.

[121] See approach of US Supreme Court in *Reno v. American Civil Liberties Union*, 521 *U.S.* 844 (1997), in the early days of the Internet.

[122] Goldsmith and Wu, *supra* n. 3.

existing friends 'meet'.[123] The fact that individuals use SNS to maintain existing relationships on-line has led some commentators to emphasise that SNS are social network sites rather than social network*ing* sites,[124] a distinction which suggests that such networks come replete with exceptions about the relationship between members, and the use of information disclosed in group. That is, there is an expectation of privacy, an assumption potentially reinforced by the fact such sites can be accessed whilst individuals are in the home.

It may be that the space metaphor is not helpful,[125] and that we may wish to consider internet use as primarily about communication. Nonetheless, we would have to return to the same analysis, that of looking at context and, crucially, content. Matters of personal interest alone should be treated as falling within private life, which would seem to protect significant private events, such as attempted suicide, but also—possibly— the trivial and mundane.[126] Even where there might be a public interest in the story (for example the information on Facebook posted by the wife of the head of MI5), there is a difference between reporting the story, and repeating the content, especially where photographs are used.[127] This position can be contrasted with using SNS to try to launch a musical career or with blogging on a matter of public interest, which has been held to be a public activity.[128]

At this point it is worth highlighting and then dismissing two, linked misunderstandings about 'reasonable expectation of privacy'. The first misunderstanding is factual and found in the suggestion that those who

---

[123] Marwick et al, *Youth, Privacy and Reputation* Research Publication, 2010 5 Berkman Center for Internet and Society. The binary approach of Facebook, where a person is either a 'friend' or not, and no shades of acquaintanceship are allowed has been criticised in terms of understanding privacy.

[124] Canadian Commissioner for Privacy, *supra* n. 89.

[125] A key difference between seeing internet communication as real space activity is that unlike a chat in a coffee shop, Internet communication leaves a record: boyd "Social Network Sites: Public, Private or What?" (Knowledge Tree, 2007) available at www.danah .org/papers/knowledgere.pdf. In this context the proposed changes to the single publication rule may have harsh consequences.

[126] *McKennitt* v. *Ash, supra* n. 62 per Eady J at 138.

[127] The distinction between the spoken word and images has been noted—see e.g *Campbell, supra* n. 62.

[128] See comments of Eady J. in *The Author of a Blog* v. *Times Newspapers* [2009] EWHC 1358 (QB)—but note does this apply to all blogs; the majority are diaries not journalism. See Solove D., *The Future of Reputation, supra* n. 2. Eady also misses the freedom of expression point about whether anonymity is necessary for freedom of expression; the same sort of argument one sees with regard to the protection of journalists' sources, and which has been recognised where the BBC world service broadcasts comments from its audience anonymously.

put information on-line in the context of SNS (usually characterised as
'youth' and therefore digital natives) are not concerned with privacy and
therefore do not have a reasonable expectation of privacy. Quite apart
from a lack of evidence to support it (and some complaints brought before
the PCC suggest the opposite) this suggestion makes far too many assumptions about the intentions of people using SNS with regard to the dissemination of information and ignores the context: the fact that often the
information is being shared to friends, what may be perceived as a small or
closed group.[129] Disclosure within closed groups is, as we have noted, covered by confidentiality, and control of dissemination of information is an
aspect of this.[130] Secondly, there are problems with the legal analysis; that
is, the assumption that public disclosure means we all lose any expectation of privacy. The jurisprudence from both the ECtHR and the English
courts makes it clear that the public nature of an activity does not necessarily remove all expectation of privacy. Further, while the behaviour of
individuals may play a role in the determination of whether there is a reasonable expectation of privacy, the question is not totally subjective. In
most cases, the test considers the response of the reasonable person and
includes external factors such as the type of information disseminated, as
well as the behaviour of those acquiring the information. As we have seen
above, surreptitious acquisition should generally be justified. This
approach is currently reflected by the PCC. In a ruling concerning the sur-
vivors of the Dunblane massacre, *Mullen, Weir and Campbell*,[131] the PCC
ruled that there had been a violation of privacy. As the PPC itself summarised, this case, 'demonstrates clearly that newspapers cannot automatically justify the use of material simply on the basis that it has appeared
previously on the internet and is, therefore, 'publicly available'.[132] Even if
an individual has not taken steps to protect their personal information (by
hiding it behind strict privacy settings), newspapers will have to consider
whether republication of the material shows respect for the individual's
privacy. Rather worryingly, the PCC in the *Loaded* case,[133] the PCC
appeared to backtrack. The complaint concerned a number of photographs of the complainant, described as having the "best breasts on the

---

[129] See literature cited by Marwick et al, *Youth, Privacy and Reputation, supra* n. 123,
especially 12–14 and 60–61.
[130] *Douglas* v. *Hello, supra* n. 105; *Prince of Wales v Associated Newspapers*[2006] EWCA
Civ 1776—leave to appeal to the House of Lords was refused.
[131] *Mullen, Weir and Campbell* v. *Scottish Sunday Express* (2009) PCC Report 79.
[132] "Privacy in the Age of Social Networking" (2009) *PCC Newsletter* December 2009.
[133] *A Woman* v. *Loaded, supra* n. 95.

block", and which offered readers a reward of £500 for assistance in encouraging her to do a photo shoot with it. According to the complainant, the magazine had published her name and the photographs, which had been uploaded to her Bebo site in December 2006 when she was 15 years old, had been taken from there and published without permission. The PCC found there was no violation on the basis that the pictures were not taken from Bebo, but from other sites which were already discussing the material in this salacious way and that the material was already widely available. This stable door reasoning seems to blur aspects of confidentiality with aspects of privacy, and leave a handy get out clause for newspapers wishing to use such material. It is also a warning about the dangers of putting material on the Internet.

If we assume that such material is confidential to what extent has the media's right to freedom of expression been damaged? Barendt has suggested that it is a misunderstanding of the argument from truth to suggest that everyone has the right to know everything about everybody and so this justification of freedom of expression does not support media claims, save perhaps where a public figure is in issue. Here the argument is blending in to that which sees the media's freedom of expression as being related to the functioning of democracy. Again, on that reasoning the limitations on the dissemination of private information about private individuals would not interfere much with media freedom of expression. This seemed to be the point the ECtHR was making in *von Hannover* when it drew a distinction between

> reporting facts ... capable of contributing to a debate in a democratic society relating to politicians and the exercise of their functions, for example, and the reporting of details of the private life of an individual who ... does not exercise official functions.

In the latter situation, freedom of expression should be given a "narrow interpretation".[134] So while neither freedom of expression nor privacy take priority,[135] there seems to be a clear message coming from the courts that freedom of expression claims are tied to matters of public interest and not 'the most vapid tittle-tattle about the activities of footballers' wives and girlfriends',[136] irrespective of whether the statements are true or not. Even

---

[134] *von Hannover, supra* n. 112,—one judge observing that the ECHR had (under American influence) to some extent "made a fetish of freedom of the press". This approach matches that taken in a number of Council of Europe documents.

[135] *Re S, supra* n. 18.

[136] Baroness Hale in *Jameel, supra* n. 30, para. 147.

where the information is provided by a third person who has an individual
right to autobiographical speech, where this involves intimate part of life,
a cautious balancing act seems to be required.[137]

CONCLUSIONS

UGC has the possibility to widen the range of stories portrayed in the
media and the views of those stories, ameliorating potentially the traditional control of the professional media on the public agenda. In terms of
freedom of expression, this allows individuals to speak to an audience
wider than might otherwise have been the case. While we may seek to
overlay the structure of freedom of expression analysis in this framework,
it is clear that the interrelationship of audience, creator of UGC and professional media means that the issue is more complex than simply that of
more speech equals more freedom. Qualitative issues can filter into a freedom of expression analysis. In this context, it seems that media institutions will face a difficult balancing act: whilst they seek to respect the
freedom of expression of contributors, we must be aware of other freedom
of expression claims as well as competing societal interests. For both the
creator of UGC and the media institutions there lies the risk of penalties if
this balance is misjudged. In this, there might be nothing new qualitatively; however, the modern technological environment increases the risk
quantitatively. For those who contribute UGC, it is important to remember that freedom of expression is an individual right as well as an institutional one; and that however ill-informed and trivial their expressions,
individuals should not be expected to meet journalistic standards to communicate electronically, though these considerations may affect the question of whether that speech can be outweighed by other interests, or
whether amateur expressions can be further disseminated by the professional media. For media institutions, while UGC may offer opportunities,
it also contains risks. The media position to some extent is privileged, but
this privilege is not an absolute. Media professionals when dealing with
the amateur should not forget that while content may be provided volun-
tarily, appearances can be deceptive and that familiarity should not be
allowed to breed contempt for the dignity of the audience.

---

[137] Although not involving UGC, consider *Barrymore -v- News Group Newspapers Ltd*
[1997] FSR 600, 602–3; *McKennitt -v- Ash, supra* n. 62 contrast *LDS, supra* n. 104.

FREEDOM OF EXPRESSION: THE BBC AND USER GENERATED CONTENT[1]

Jackie Harrison

...if any freedom of discussion is permitted to exist, it is only because it cannot be repressed; the reason why it cannot be repressed, being, the dread of public opinion.[2]

According to Thomas Hobbes (1588–1679), freedom of expression was a threat to effective statehood because it was a threat to government and to civil order. It was, in his mind, associated with religious and political dissent, which he always feared would lead to a repetition of the chaos he had seen at first hand during the English civil war (1642–1651). Freedom of expression he believed was contrary to the interests of rational people who desired a legitimate order, which not only accommodated their collective and agreed self interests, but required a political authority to protect them in the pursuit of these interests. In short, what was required was an authority which had a legitimate duty to underwrite a harmonious and collectively well understood political and civil order. Such an authority was charged with this duty because it was bound by virtue of a contract that existed between the state and its citizens; the former to guard against disorder and, the latter free to pursue their own shared self interests within the setting of the contracted to and subsequently established order. With the former came further responsibility to guard against dissent and, with that, to guard against unregulated freedom of expression. With the latter came a certain form of political security and civil society, inevitably accompanied by the acceptance of a certain form of expressive (both intellectual and artistic) rectitude.

For John Milton (1608–1674) such a contract as Hobbes described laid the way open to handing over a stifling form of dogmatic censorship to the

---

[1] A shortened (and less contextualized in terms of freedom of expression) version of this chapter was presented at the 'Freedom of Expression and the Media', conference sponsored by the Clemens Nathan Research Centre and subsequently published in the conference proceedings as J. Harrison, "UGC: Free Expression and Gatekeeping at the BBC" in Gray, T. (ed.) *Media and Human Rights* (London: Clemens Nathan Research Centre Publications, 2009).

[2] John Stuart Mill, "Law of Libel and Liberty of the Press", *Westminster Review*, 111, 1825.

state which was contrary to the interest of a desirable or peaceful civil
order. Milton argued this was so for two reasons: prosaically the state censorship that Hobbes wanted was dangerously inefficient, merely sending
dissenters underground. More idealistically Milton believed that it was
freedom of expression that generated commonly recognisable truths that
bound people together in a way that political suzerainty and ecclesiastical
dogma could not. As Christopher Hill puts it, Milton 'abandons the attempt
at (or pretence of) a one-minded community,'[3] believing instead that freedom of expression and tolerance went someway together to establish
political and civil harmony, though not in any modern liberal way, since he
also believed that the discovery of these common truths belonged primarily to bible reading Protestants who were tolerant of each others' different
views, although he also extended his views on tolerance to include Jews.
Ultimately, Milton's sense of tolerance and freedom of expression was
dependent upon his belief in the 'liberty of printing,'[4] the responsibility of
an essentially Protestant form of republican citizenship, the role of the
poet, his disapproval of the demagogue and with this his constant insistence that only those who themselves advocated censorship and violence,
and were themselves deeply intolerant, should be censored. The 'proponents of unfreedom—Rome, Charles 1st, [and] Presbyterians,'[5] were
according to Milton, the most deserving of censorship.

   Archaic as Hobbes and Milton's language may sound, their respective
views over the value of freedom of expression have been used in discussions ever since in terms constantly reminiscent of their disagreement. In
other words since at least the 1640s we have debated freedom of expression according to a variety of formulae which have simply defined how
much or how little freedom of expression was acceptable and permissible
in order to maintain political order, promote individual freedom and to
be of benefit to civil society. A case in point is the current debate over
the extent to which anti-terrorism laws do or do not require limitations to
be imposed upon the press.[6] In this country, since Hobbes and Milton,
freedom of expression has been understood in the context of a balancing
act between what is regarded as necessary press legislation required for
reasons of state (for example, to ensure national security) and responsible
press self-governance, where the press regulate themselves over matters of

---

3 Hill, C, *Milton and the English Revolution* (London: Faber and Faber, 1997), 153.
4 Ibid., 157.
5 Ibid., 157.
6 See the chapter by Peter Noorlander in this volume.

expression (for example over matters of political openness and public interest). To put the matter another way, both Hobbes and Milton would recognise that freedom of expression now belongs to an evolved conception of the limits of the state and the extent of civil rights.

Today however, we have an interesting and possibly incorrigible twist to this way of thinking about freedom of expression and the balancing act between the needs of the state and the needs of an institutional and civil press,[7] and correspondingly about the way we must now think about press freedom. Following Onora O'Neill's lead,—in order to think about current conceptions of freedom of expression and the way the press upholds this freedom, we must also understand the material circumstances under which today's press operate. These circumstances O'Neill believes show the press to be too powerful and ultimately unaccountable.[8]

Traditionally the press response to the challenge that they have too much power operates from a combination of the following five defensive arguments: a) they are the fourth estate; b) attempts to 'gag' or censor the press are unnecessarily secretive and usually wrong; c) they are a civil conduit for freedom of expression; d) they enhance democratic well being through the representation of the public interest and public opinion and that e) self regulation works. Indeed, there is some truth and authority to be found in these five well understood defences, but addressing the truth or untruth of these five defences is not what I take O'Neill's point to be about, nor do they serve as an adequate response to her argument. Rather than curtail responsible criticism of government, return to excessive 'gagging' and censorship, reduce democracy and jeopardise the expression of public opinion, O' Neill asks should we not consider new forms of press accountability. These new forms would require that the press remain within the purview of a more modern balancing act between necessary but essentially liberally inspired legislation and responsible self governance. The balancing act remains true to the historic purposes of the press, which she regards as being: truthful; supporting freedom of expression and supporting deliberative debate essential to any democracy.[9] These are all purposes that she argues were established at a time when the

---

[7] See J. Alexander, *The Civil Sphere* (New York, Oxford: Oxford University Press, 2006).

[8] O. O'Neill (2004) "Rethinking Freedom of the Press Royal Irish Academy" available at http://www.ria.ie/reports/pdf/pressfreedom.pdf; and "Conceptions of Press Freedom in a Globalising World" (2008) available at http://www.admin.cam.ac.uk/offices /communications/community/ideasfestival/reports/conceptions-of-press-freedom -transcript.pdf.

[9] O. O'Neill, "Rethinking Press Freedom", Ramsey Murray Lecture, Selwyn College, Cambridge, April 2003.

press was weak and which are now distorted by a contemporary press which has become too powerful and whose members are 'the least accountable players in public affairs.'[10] With that latter point it appears that the debate about the press and freedom of expression changes and turns to hinge upon the meaning and the extent of press accountability and with that responsibility. One version of the ways the press regards itself as accountable and responsible, and which it has recently used to justify its own conduct and by extension the power it has (and should be allowed to keep), is via what I shall call the participation defence.

The participation defence goes as follows: audiences can now participate in the mainstream press and television news.[11] Or so we are told. And what makes this so? A culture of increasing participation in domains once regarded as the sole preserve of experts and professionals which has been reinforced by the potential and capacity of information communication technology (ICT). This is technology whose virtues are listed as: so personally adaptive that they enable diverse, heterodoxical and previously inaccessible data sources to be mined; alternative opinions to be heard and different views to be engaged with; facilitate the questioning of official or received versions of contemporary events; is good for democracy and social well being; allows geographically remote networks of individuals moved by the same issues to work together and simultaneously liberates the hitherto repressed desire for responsible free expression, beyond the confines of the old didactic press; and, more widely (and more profoundly) that ICT 'opens a range of possibilities for pursuing the core political values of liberal societies—individual freedom, a more genuinely participatory political system, a critical culture, and social justice.'[12]

Today we are supposed to have a new multi-platform media environment and inclusive press culture aligned in a contemporary 'technics' which supports active citizens working outside (but alongside and with) professional news gathering organisations who are concerned about public affairs; civic issues; ensuring that the public sphere is lively;

---

[10]   Ibid.

[11]   I abide throughout to the clear distinction made to me by people at the BBC that UGC is defined as 'where the audience does it for the BBC' and citizen journalism is defined as 'where the audience does it for themselves'. This is by no means accepted by all and other distinctions and definitions are made. For example Wardle, Claire and Williams, Andy (2008) *ugc@thebbc Understanding its impact upon contributors, non-contributors and the BBC News* (Cardiff School of Journalism, Media and Cultural Studies: Cardiff University, 2008), argue that UGC represents five different types of audience material.

[12]   Y. Benkler, *The Wealth of Networks* (New Haven: Yale University Press, 2006) 7–8.

government and official criminality are uncovered; and in equal measure censorship and spin are exposed. Such participation in the news by news audiences is presented by the press and their spokespersons as representing a new model of journalism, 'converged journalism': where the story marks the beginning of a conversation between the journalist and the citizen; which demonstrates an increase in daily democracy which adds qualitatively to its deliberative character; which is more adapted to the reporting of public opinion; which guarantees the survival of public affairs journalism at the local and community level; which enables the 'cry in the dark' to be heard and which is a hallmark of a genuinely civil press that can challenge the political sphere.[13] In short, 'converged journalism' is supposed to represents the contemporary opportunities of developments in ICT in establishing integrated and ubiquitous multi-platformed news outlets and at the same time the civil and political benefits of news audiences participating in the news. It is the latter I wish to focus on and ask—has participation in news in the form of user generated content (UGC) actually changed anything very much where news journalism and the power and accountability of the press are concerned? In short is the participation defence valid—are the users and active contributors really breaking down the bipolar categories or producers and consumers, professionals and amateurs?

Current research about UGC reveals that using terms which blur and conflate such bipolar categories might be premature.[14] Indeed, the often used term of 'produser'[15] seems to belie the reality of participatory engagement which in fact may be better represented by degrees of inactivity and passivity which more accurately reflects the way most of us respond to mediated content.[16] This is not to deny user agency but to suggest that it needs also to be considered in the context of traditional journalistic practices and their corresponding unwillingness to relinquish editorial control

---

[13] Views like this resonate throughout with discussions on new models of journalism. For example, see *New Models for News The 2008 Breaux Symposium Report* (Louisiana State University: LSU Manship School of Mass Communication: 2008) available at http://www.lsu.edu/reillycenter/breauxsym.htm, or *World Editors Forum Trends in Newsrooms 2008; Innovative Ideas for Newspapers in the Digital Age* (World Association of Newspapers 2008).

[14] J. Van Dijck (2009) "Users like you? Theorizing agency in user-generated content", *Media Culture and Society* (2009) 31(41), 41–58.

[15] A. Bruns (2007) "Produsage: Towards a Broader Framework for User-led Content Creation", http://snurb.info/files/.

[16] Organisation for Economic Co-operation and Development (OECD) *Participative Web: User-generated Content, OECD Committee for Information, Computer and Communications Policy Report*, cited in Van Dijck (2009), Ibid.

over content. Journalists remain the practical gatekeepers of content even in a highly participatory format.[17] Thurman (2008) found that due to their strong reliance on news agencies and other institutions as sources, time constraints, their belief in the ability to distinguish newsworthy from non-newsworthy items, journalists viewed their news selection practices and routines as an important way of distinguishing their professional status from that of non-professionals.[18] The reluctance of many journalists to share the newsmaking process with users was observed by Paulussen and Ugille who noted that the 'mainstream media are reacting to the trend of UGC in a rather ambivalent way'.[19] A point developed by Domingo et al multi-national study of UGC on media websites which found that professional newsrooms were reluctant to open up most of the news production process to users and that news organizations tend to view participation as an opportunity for readers to debate current events rather than introduce new ones.[20] What these studies point to is the way in which the core journalistic cultural assumption of it being a case of 'only fellow journalists are able to make news selection and editing decisions at each stage of the news production process,' remained unchanged even in supposed participatory environments.[21] Indeed one study found that even high quality audiences' pictures were only accorded high UGC status and not high quality journalistic status.[22] Such levels of retained control over selection and editing by journalists is not surprising given that there is also growing evidence that the ideal of participation does not sit too well with the journalists' own view that they should keep their professional distance from the sources of content whether from users or through more

---

[17] J. Singer, "The political j-blogger: 'Normalizing' a new media form to fit old norms and practices", *Journalism: Theory, Practice and Criticism*, (2005) 6(2), 173–98; J. Harrison "User generated content and gatekeeping at the BBC Hub", *Journalism Studies*, (2011) in press.

[18] N. Thurman, "Forums for citizen journalists? Adoption of user generated content initiatives by online news media", *New Media and Society* (2008) 10(1), 139–57.

[19] Paulussen, Steve and Ugille, Pieter, "User Generated Content in the Newsroom: Professional and Organisational Constraints on Participatory Journalism", *Westminster Papers in Communication and Culture* (2008) 5(2), 24–41, 25.

[20] Domingo, David, Quant, Thorsten, Heinonen, Ari, Paulussen, Steve, Singer, Jane and Vujnovic, Marina, "Participatory Journalism Practices in the Media and Beyond: An international comparative study of initiatives in online newspapers", *Journalism Practice* (2008) 2(3), 326–42.

[21] See also Hermida, Alfred and Thurman, Neil, "A Clash of Cultures: The integration of user-generated content within professional journalistic frameworks at British newspaper Web sites", *Journalism Practice* (2008) 2(3), 343–56.

[22] H. Ornebring, "The consumer as producer—of what? User-generated tabloid content in The Sun (UK) and Aftonbladet (Sweden)", Paper presented at the 'Future of Newspapers' Conference, Cardiff, UK, September 2007, 19.

traditional sources.[23] Further reinforcing the idea of retained control is the fact that in practice many journalists remain concerned about the quality of UGC.[24] Indeed, Thurman's study of online UGC in ten British online news organizations documents this concern and breaks it down accordingly: concerns about newsworthiness, quality, balance, and decency. These concerns frequently resulted in 'conflicts between editor's professional gatekeeper roles and their perceptions of user participation'.[25] For some journalists the 'management and moderation of UGC seem to be counter-intuitive to the work place discussion, daily routines and professional values of the newsrooms'[26] and because of this many journalists 'still perceive audience participation as a problem to manage rather than a benefit for the news product'.[27]

Never the less despite these finding there are signs of some kind of participatory compact between the press and its audiences. With the emergence of UGC, audiences' participation in news has in principle extended the ability of audiences to create content and not to wait for the professional to approach them. In considering the development and significance of audience participation the House of Lords Select Committee on Communications described UGC accordingly:

> This is content provided by the public, often recorded on the cameras or video functions of mobile telephones. The term also encompasses users providing comment and "analysis of stories on web based news' sites."[28]

To which they subsequently noted that there are two contrasting views about UGC. First, Stewart Purvis gave evidence which referred to the idea that, 'unmediated content is back to the printing press in the first place. It is about people putting forward their views; it is about citizens having a voice suddenly. If we do not like what they say, that is a small price to pay for the freedom those people are being given to air their views.'[29] Second and contrastingly the Pew Research Centre suggested, 'The prospects for user-created content, once thought possibly central to the next era of journalism, for now appear more limited, even among "citizen" sites and blogs.

---

[23] M. Deuze, A. Bruns and C. Neuberger "Preparing for an age of participatory news", *Journalism Practice*, (2007) 1(3), 322–338.

[24] Singer 2005, Harrison 2010.

[25] Thurman (2008), 27.

[26] Thurman (2008), 38.

[27] Domingo (2009), 698.

[28] House of Lords, *The Ownership of the News* (Select Committee on Communications, 2008), 29–30, S106.

[29] Ibid., 29–30.

News people report the most promising parts of citizen input currently
are new ideas, sources, comments and to some extent pictures and video.
But citizens posting news content has proven less valuable, with too little
that is new or verifiable'.[30] These two views broadly reflect the two different interpretations of participation. The former represents the optimism
of a 'bottom-up process of individual and collective self-expression'[31]
which allows the citizen to speak and be heard, the latter a more hard
headed or a 'top-down (industry-driven) customer-provider relationship'[32] which uses the news audience as a source of information while
maintaining a stringent gatekeeping role. To find out which view of participation was more accurate and to see if the 'participation defence' discussed above has any real merit in terms of audience involvement in news
I undertook a study of the management and impact of user generated content at the BBC's UGC Hub.[33]

My initial research assumption was that in order to understand these
two views of participation we must find the answer to two questions. First,
is user generated content (UGC) routinely fed straight into the mix of BBC
established news priorities without altering news selection criteria or editorial values? Second, does UGC represent the extension of BBC news
from a civil and participatory point of view? From my admittedly limited
study I found that the answers to my two research questions were as
follows.[34]

---

[30] Ibid., 30. On this last point the House of Lords report is citing *The State of the News
Media 2008: An annual report on American Journalism*, The Pew Research Centre's Project
for Excellence in Journalism, 2008.

[31] Deuze et al. (2007), 322.

[32] Deuze et al. 2007, 322.

[33] I was generously given access to the UGC Hub at the BBC between 4 and 10 November
2007. I was granted observer status and allowed to watch whatever I wished too. I was not
allowed to formally interview using recording equipment staff (this was seen as being
potentially disruptive), though I was provided with an exceptionally helpful minder who
introduced me to people and acted as catalyst for my being able to talk informally with all
members of staff. The latter proving far more valuable than formal interviews given the
limited amount of time I had available. I took field notes in shorthand, which I found
encouraged greater freedom of expression than I had noticed when on previous ethno-
graphic work I had taped conversations and conducted formal interviews in J. Harrison
Terrestrial TV News in Britain: The Culture of Production (Manchester: Manchester
University Press, 2000). The study was funded by the British Academy to whom I express
my gratitude, my gratitude also goes to the BBC particularly to Vicky Taylor and to all those
who were then working on the UGC Hub.

[34] A more empirically and ethnographically detailed set of findings of this study are to
be found in Harrison (2010) though I draw upon them in what follows.

Q1) UGC is something that is just routinely fed straight into the mix of BBC established news priorities without altering news selection criteria or editorial values.
There is little doubt that what now counts as newsworthy has been extended to include UGC as a form of source material. As one BBC news journalist remarked 'things are a lot more open,' and UGC is acquiring a status as a standard source of pictures or information. One of the reasons for the recent growth in use of UGC is because of its perceived convenience and availability, and importantly its increasing ease of use and the recognition that it can play a role alongside pre-existing news styles or ways of selecting news. UGC has been absorbed into newsroom practices and is now routinely considered as providing an aspect or value-added dimension to many stories. In this sense UGC has the capacity to enhance stories and more rarely may elicit new ones, potentially affecting some of the stories that are selected and their prominence in the news agenda. Overall it is the addition of new UGC material such as pictures, testimony and video clips to a story that can make a new story more newsworthy. Though it is important not to overstate this. Television news journalism has, since the advent of ITN (and in the USA before that) recognised that ordinary people's testimony from witnessing an event or their opinion can move a story on.[35] Even so, UGC is very carefully moderated at the BBC and it is here we see the extent to which audience free expression is controlled through moderation as a form of gatekeeping.

The BBC is quite clear on its attitude towards moderation. The guidelines unequivocally say that: *'Every online space where user generated content is published must have someone editorially responsible for that content and should have a host to provide a visible and active presence and a moderator who can remove illegal or inappropriate content'.*[36] To achieve this end the BBC require that *UGC is moderated in one of two ways. First pre-moderation, this* is undertaken to ensure that on-line material cannot be accessed by visitors to the website until a moderator has seen the material and decided it is suitable for posting. Sites designed to appeal to children are pre-moderated, as are online debates about contentious issues such as immigration. *Secondly post-moderation, this* occurs where a moderator sees the material after it has been posted and decides whether it is suitable

---

[35] See J. Harrison, "A History of ITN" in (eds.) C. Johnson and R. Turnock, *ITV Cultures: Independent Television Over Fifty Years* (London: Open University Press, 2005), 120–137.
[36] See the BBC's Editorial Guidelines at http://www.bbc.co.uk/guidelines /editorialguidelines/edguide/interacting/gamesusergenera.shtml#3.

enough to remain on the site. As such this type of post-moderation is often reactive, being activated because visitors to the website have pressed the 'alert the moderator' key in order to flag up what they regard to be an inappropriate or offensive message. This type of post/reactive moderation is more common amongst mature online communities, or discussions groups that are likely to elicit extreme views or overly aggressive responses. Added to these two forms of moderation is the presence of an internal investigations team which has been set up to deal with pornography, racist abusive and very offensive posts.[37] And added to this, though on the technical rather than more interpretative human side of moderation, a profanity filter has been installed and is designed to pick up words that the BBC would deem inappropriate for its web sites, although users can easily confound the filter by adding asterisks or spaces to words. Given this, it is unsurprising that the filter is growing in sophistication, size and intervention.

From the extent of moderation alone it can be seen that UGC is not a cheap option for the BBC and never will be. The BBC's impartiality rules do not allow for a partisan viewpoint to dominate and as such UGC is seen as requiring careful scrutiny (sometimes legal and always editorially and journalistically) an exercise which is both labour intensive and expensive. Adding to this expense is the fact that UGC is further supported by: the 'Have Your Say' website,[38] creative commons licensing; the BBC open 'creative archives;' payments for received content; conferences and training; access to mainstream news site; support and solicitation for audience engagement. In short, moderation as a form of gatekeeping UGC has proven to be one of the most time consuming and resource hungry elements of the user generated phenomenon.

The extent of moderation and the trappings that go to support UGC at the BBC should not be viewed as suggesting that there is unanimity of opinion when it comes to judging the worth of UGC for the News. For example opinion in the BBC is divided about how many and what types of online conversations should be hosted and whether licence fee money should be used to encourage heated debate, or to provide a platform for the opinions of only the more 'responsible' members of the public. Interestingly the UGC phenomenon has provided rich pickings for comedians and satirists. The BBC 4's programme *Newswipe* recently referred to

---

[37] The BBC also has a list of people who are problems. Some of the people posting obscenities are well known and their posts are taken off.
[38] 'Have Your Say' had over 200,000 registered users in November 2007.

the BBC's adoption of UGC as being akin to 'switching on the idiot magnet'. The programme criticised the BBC's use of audience opinion as being irrelevant non-news, dressed up as news. In their send up of UGC in 2007, the British comedians, David Mitchell and Robert Webb asked:

> Are you personally affected by this issue? Then email us. Or if you're not affected by this issue, can you imagine what it would be like if you were? Or if you are affected by it, but don't want to talk about it, can you imagine what it would be like not being affected by it? Why not email us? You may not know anything about the issue, but I bet you reckon something. So why not tell us what you reckon. Let us enjoy the full majesty of your uninformed, ad hoc reckon, by going to bbc.co.uk, clicking on 'what I reckon' and then simply beating on the keyboard with your fists or head.[39]

In contrast to these humorous, but nonetheless very negative views expressed both within and outside the BBC[40] about the use of UGC material in news, some journalists are less mocking and scornful. In particular those working in the BBC's UGC Hub feel that while it is time consuming to trawl through the thousands of emails, pictures, video clips as well as online posts, case studies and debates hosted by the 'Have Your Say' website, the effort is worth it to find those 'nuggets of pure gold' and valuable contacts that might arise from public participation. This is particularly the case where a debate question has been posed by the BBC online and the public's input provides useful material for other outlets which may also be covering the same issues/stories. Frequently the BBC will also congratulate itself on the sheer volume of material it solicits from the public. On its breakfast programme (during a week of heavy snow in the UK in February 2009) it celebrated the fact that it had had the highest number of stories from viewers that it had ever received. The BBC presenters of the morning news show congratulated the programme for receiving 35,000 pictures and emails from viewers. This public display of pride shows the extent to which parts of the organisation have embraced the ability to solicit content from the ordinary public and its sense of achievement in having as many people as possible who want to communicate with it.

In managing the sheer volume of UGC the lack of unanimity of opinion at the BBC over its true worth for News further reveals itself. Decisions on removing an online comment or ignoring an email are time consuming and vary from person to person (although a moderator will check with other colleagues if he or she is unsure). Some journalists moderated online

---

[39] Quoted by Eddie Mair in the BBC's in house magazine, *Ariel* (30 October 2007), 4.
[40] See for example Edward Docx, "If I ruled the world", *Prospect*, September 2009, 7.

posts of content quite quickly others more slowly though what was more interesting was the different levels of tolerance for diverse content shown with the net result that material which did not clearly break BBC guidelines, but which is difficult to assess, was moderated in slightly different ways by different members of the UGC hub. Also as a result of the volume of UGC, moderators were having to deal with complaints made by the public about other people's comments which further adds to the time pressures of moderation especially in this case since it requires that judgements have to be made quickly. Compounding this problem is the fact that if a complaint is upheld and material removed the person who posted the material may also complain and so once again there needs to be a formal response. To be clear: I saw no evidence of UGC Hub journalists removing posts from the website because they did not agree with the sentiment expressed, though there was evidence of discussion amongst journalists over views they disagreed with or found difficult to understand. One UGC Hub journalist said to me that she found herself asking the following question: 'when a dictator or fascist dies and someone writes a positive tribute—should it be removed?, although when pressed by colleagues she said it should not, while another asked if it is a public service broadcaster's job to provide a platform for unrepresentative public opinion and comment.

The discussions on the BBC's 'Have Your Say' website between the members of the public generally do not meet the same standards of taste and decency as the BBC in its broadcast programmes, particularly in its factual programmes, but those moderating are heard to remind themselves that this is a different forum. Problematically, some pre-moderated debates such as immigration policy tend to attract people with strong views and often those views become more strident as others challenge them or reinforce them. This leads to the problem of amplification where the debate creates a kind of 'echo chamber' or 'information cocoon,'[41] where people's opinions are reinforced rather than challenged. Amplification of views can occur where the debate become more strident or extreme because other like-minded individuals push the ideas so hard that there is little to challenge them. This reflects a type of 'discussion' that is far from the ideal of a 'public sphere' and some news journalists at the BBC recognise that there is a wide gulf between the more utopian aims for public discussion and comment and its quotidian online reality. Indeed some BBC journalists spoke of the danger of allowing a few extreme views

---

[41] C.R. Sunstein, *Republic.com 2.0* (New Jersey, Princeton: Princeton University Press, 2007), 212–213.

to be seen as reflecting widely held public views and the challenge they faced in being inclusive of diverse views. The uncomfortable world of online public comment and the BBC's attempts to be inclusive is in contrast to the way UGC is managed on television and radio (and the BBC's own news website). Here its use can be managed in much more circumspect way and made more easily to fit into the BBC's news selection criteria and news styles. Ultimately, in spite of the BBC's careful approach to moderation however, there is a guardedness and genuine worry among its journalists about the threat that non-moderated UGC poses to editorial values and to news standards.[42]

What now counts as newsworthiness has for the BBC been extended to include UGC as a routine form of source material and story enhancement. And it needs to be noted that far less contentious and requiring far less moderation than online public discussion, and of more practical use to the BBC, is UGC that comes in the form of numerous emails, texts and pictures sent in by the public. Only rarely does UGC inaugurate a new news story or alter a news story that is already being run.[43]

Overall though moderation ensures that there is little sign of UGC changing or challenging the BBC's editorial values and UGC is now systematically used to enhance or provide value-added to news stories by conforming to pre-determined BBC news selection processes and styles. This observation leads us to the answer to the second question.

Q2) UGC does not represent the extension of BBC news from a civil and participatory point of view
It is easy to be overly optimistic about UGC and regard it as signalling new age which is variously referred to as citizen journalism, participatory journalism, public insight journalism, public journalism, occasionally and more recently open source journalism or crowd-sourcing journalism. These are, it is usually argued, the domain of active citizens who usually do not work for a professional media organisation, are untrained as journalists and who pass on their own news stories, sources or views of news stories to professional journalists and then collaborate with them, a public news site or a professional news organisation. They are sometimes paid but their motivation is usually described in civil terms. But this belies the

---

[42] See also Singer (2005) who found that most journalists held concerns about the quality of UGC.

[43] For a similar point see Domingo et al (2008). See also Ornebring (2007) who noted that users' pictures tend to be seen as more useful for story enhancement than text even in an online environment which is both text and picture driven.

reality of UGC at the BBC. To begin with UGC was routinely understood at
the BBC, as we have seen above in the following way: 'where the audience
does it for the BBC' and citizen journalism was defined as 'where the audience does it for themselves'. So from the start it was obvious that talk of
citizen journalism in any meaningful sense was irrelevant as the heuristic
distinction used at the BBC makes abundantly clear.

Heterodoxical opinions are not in themselves seen as a problem or
automatically 'moderated out', but the public service duty at the BBC is
one that pushes it towards adopting a position of negative tolerance, that
is of not tolerating speech that it appears to them to breach fundamental
civil (or human) rights, or contravenes human dignity. This means that
moderation errs on the side of what I shall call a 'BBC news consensus'
which operates through the careful moderation of content and with constant reference to the BBC's own core editorial values. To some extent,
these core editorial values serve as a vehicle for restraining and limiting
the broadcasting or hosting of UGC by the BBC. How drastic and censorious this is, is an open question, if only because 'the BBC's news consensus'
may be judged by others to be for example 'too establishment', 'centre left',
'too liberal', 'too restrictive', 'out of touch', or 'middle class' etc. Naturally
enough, the BBC journalists I spoke to thought differently and regarded
BBC news values as both inclusive of diversity and tolerant. Whatever the
case, it is these core editorial values which mark the boundaries for acceptance or non-acceptance of UGC.

One of the unpalatable sides of UGC, and which is noted by Helen
Boaden,[44] is the fact that 'the simplicity of digital technology means it's
never been easier for audiences to make judgements about our judgements'.[45] She also observed that 'When we said we were going to show
Jerry Springer The Opera on BBC 2, we received more than 60,000 complaints—most by e-mail. When we said we would show a glimpse of the
Danish cartoons on the News, Radio 5Live was subject to an organised text
campaign by angry Muslims. In all those cases, we stuck to our guns and
made our judgements based on our values of being independent and
impartial.'[46] The problem is clear, technological change has made orga-
nized, co-coordinated and large scale protest very much easier and the
spectre of on-line bullying that much more real. Again as Boaden notes

---

[44] At the time of writing Helen Boaden is Head of BBC News.
[45] H. Boaden, "The role of citizen journalism in modern democracy", available at http://
www.bbc.co.uk/blogs/theeditors/2008/11/the_role_of_citizen_journalism.html 2008.
[46] Ibid.

'the sheer volume of e-mail and text traffic possible because of digital technology could have the effect of bullying a less confident organisation'. And certainly bullying by blog is a phenomenon that many newspapers are struggling with in relation to their columnists, and is 'one of the darker sides of the great push to more connection and transparency.'[47]

Nevertheless the BBC recognises, again hard headedly and understandably, that UGC can be used to engage audiences and therefore does represent an extension of the BBC's own way of going about newsgathering. In this way, the BBC regards UGC as an extension of its public service obligations to engage and involve its audiences and in an era where the BBC has to make claims to be both distinctive and able to engage with its audiences, UGC is seen by the senior news management to be worth supporting. The decision to move the UGC hub from the online newsroom into the heart of the newsroom at the BBC's News Centre indicates that UGC is now a central part of the BBC's conventional news journalism mix but, as outlined above, the reality is that it is only playing an ancillary and supportive role to pre-existing ways of selecting news. Because of this, the civil and participatory aspect of UGC is very limited. It is worth considering the following observations from the Guardian writing about a report by Neil Thurman:[48]

> Looking at a debate on the BBC's news site, Thurman found that one of the most popular discussions on the Have Your Say section typically attracted contributions from only 0.05% of the site's users in one day. That's half the 'social media rule of thumb' which says around 1% of a site's user base will actively contribute, but I don't think that is a sign that UGC is failing—the web is a medium for niche services, after all, and nothing on a site at the scale of the BBC is that niche; last month the site had 2.1 million users in one day.[49]

Certainly UGC is not failing as far as the BBC is concerned it is extensively solicited and used by the organisation. It is also in terms of volume, and as the Guardian make clear, widely created. It is not however, the domain of the active citizen or of citizen journalism which is radicalising the BBC and forcing a change to core editorial values. Thus far the civil significance of UGC seems minimal. But then UGC needs to be assessed not so much in terms of citizen journalism or citizen's activism, but in terms of the

---

[47] Ibid.
[48] N. Thurman, "Forums for citizen journalists Adoption of user generated content initiatives by online news media", *New Media & Society* (2008) 10 (1), 139–157.
[49] http://www.guardian.co.uk/media/pda/2008/feb/25/isugcviablefornewssites/print.

issues it raises for gatekeeping and moderation and for news gathering
and selection and it is these issues which help us understand modern day
news journalism. And I believe that it comes down to this: what is the
relationship (at the BBC) between core editorial values and the diversity
and plurality engendered by UGC? It is this question which points to the
problem posed by using UGC. This is a problem which consists of two
related parts, the first part, and by far the easier to deal with is with regard
to civil or some other form of change (social political scientific etc); and
the second part, which is much more worrying, is with regard to public
knowledge.

First there is the problem of change. At BBC news there is an active
attempt to balance views impartially and so it judges UGC both for its utility and for its partiality. This judgment occurs against a background BBC
news consensus that stands for a specific set of core editorial values which
have been built up over time and are officially endorsed. As we also know
any consensus, particularly one where understanding civil relationships is
concerned, must be constantly challenged less it ossify and fail to capture
wider progressive changes in society, or worse, become repressive. As
Jeffrey Alexander puts it, the factual audiovisual media are anchored in
the life world of public opinion and they help to articulate,

> ... the inclusive and exclusive relationships established by civil society ...
> [the] structures of feeling, the diffusely sensed obligations and rights
> that represent, and are at the same time evoked by, contrasting solidary
> ties... The structures of feeling that such institutions produce must be con-
> ceptualized as influence rather than authoritative control, or power in a
> more structural sense. They institutionalize civil society by creating mes-
> sages that translate general codes into situationally specific evaluations and
> description.[50]

And those specific evaluations and descriptions of who or what should
count as part of a civil society are constantly changing. One possibility is
worth considering. Within the volume of UGC, it is perfectly possible that
voices or as yet uncoordinated but widely held views for civil or other
kinds of change could be being expressed. This possibility only raises the
question of how these voices might be regarded from the vantage point of
a BBC News consensus particularly if such views questioned what is currently regarded as 'common sense' or what are 'common and convention-
ally held truths'. Recently Peter Horrocks[51] argued that the BBC News

---

[50] J. Alexander (2006), 70.
[51] Peter Horrocks, "Finding TV News' lost audience" (Oxford: Reuters Institute, November 2006). Also see Barnett's chapter in this volume, "Freedom of speech, broadcasting

needed to provide the opportunity for people to encounter alternative points of views, risk broadcasting views that some might consider abhorrent, and to set next to each other views that are diametrically opposed to each other. In summarising this approach he called it the application of 'radical impartiality' and, to be fair, the application of 'radical impartiality' certainly would permit a diverse form of UGC to be aired. Nevertheless, questioning fundamentally held values can still appear 'cranky' and be dismissed as absurd (think of the early ecology movement in this regard). In other words, is it the case that the current procedures and newsroom routines within which UGC is contained, sifted and selected are sufficiently sensitive to recognise the heterodoxical as worthy of consideration or is it just moderated out? And while I saw no evidence of such insensitivity news agendas do evolve, the BBC has constantly changed its news formats and extended its news reach all with the net result that for the future much depends on the critical ability of an increasing number of moderators to recognise the heterodoxical as legitimate (and of course still weed out the 'cranky') and to apply 'radical impartiality,' which is in the last analysis is to ask an awful lot of moderators and the process of moderation.

The second part is with regard to public knowledge. Ultimately, at the moment UGC is managed and edited at the BBC as a supply of news content designed to enhance the BBC's own news provision without undermining the BBC's core values: a case of 'professionals moderating amateurs'. But while this appears reassuring, it may also hide the fact that UGC rather than being the herald of an emerging civil debate actually reinforces a tendency toward soft journalism and human interest, as exemplified by the rise of stories centred on crime, calamities and accidents all supported by role of the UGC. If content of this nature leads to a decline of political and economic coverage and hard edged journalistic interpretation then there is likely to be an attendant decline in public knowledge, the consequences of which could well be to diminish the quality of civil debate and limit civil engagement. At the BBC UGC material is now placed at the heart of the newsroom. The temptation to use material that may move a story on is growing, but if it begins to move stories out of a hard news agenda and into a soft one then it undermines the architecture of public service news. Ultimately the paradox of UGC might be that, by extending reach and audience involvement, in the long run it diminishes the public service

---

and impartiality: Imposition or empowerment?" for a fuller discussion of this point and of the BBCs inclusive conception of impartiality.

standards of BBC news through the spread of soft journalism. In short, UGC may prove to be corrosive where public service journalism is concerned.

Given the above with regard to how UGC is dealt with at the BBC it is now time to return to the question of how the 'participation defence' holds up against O'Neil's view that the press is too powerful and ultimately unaccountable. From the way UGC was regarded at the BBC, audience participation is managed in terms of the flexibility by which core editorial values were applied to the setting of a particular platform and the context in which it was used. Mainstream news programmes are more rigid in their applications of core editorial values and therefore tougher on the use of UGC than online chat rooms which are more flexible and provide the public with some degree of latitude. In both cases UGC is marginal, by which I mean in the former case it usually supports extant news agendas and in the latter cases is without much influence. I do not mean that it is unimportant just that it has a supportive function at the margins of what has been determined to be newsworthy. Where it might have influence is, as I noted above, over the longer term as news journalists become more and more dependent of the constant flow of soft stories provided by audiences to fill in more and more news slots—the corrosive drift toward soft journalism. For a news organisation such as the BBC, the growth of UGC invites the rhetoric of meaningful collaboration with the audience, but in reality this would require a different set of relationships with audiences than those currently in place. It is clear that talk of citizen participation actually means individuals working 'for' the BBC. This is not to contradict the fact that greater audience participation and the many various means of engaging its audience(s) are all initiatives linked to the BBC's claims to be taking a more contemporary approach to public service broadcasting (PSB) goals such as universality of access, and quality and diversity of output.[52] With UGC the BBC is doing no more than maintaining (or returning to) the old mass PSB philosophy of catering for all. The use of UGC is seen as attracting a diverse range of people, ethnic minorities, young and old as well as serving as a call to those disenchanted with conventional news suppliers to supply content relevant to their interests.[53] In this light it is of

[52] See the DCMS Green Paper 2005 on the Future of the BBC, March 2005; BBC Response to Green Paper, "Review of the BBC's Royal Charter: The BBC's Response to 'A strong BBC independent of government'", May 2005 and Ofom, "Second Public Service Broadcasting Review: Phase One: the Digital Opportunity", April 2008; "Phase Two: Preparing for the Digital Future", September 2008, and the final Second Public Service Broadcasting Review, "Putting Viewers First", January 2009.
[53] See Ofcom reports, "New News, Old News" and "New News, Future News".

real value and goes some little way to support to the 'participation defence'. But in the final analysis, O'Neil's charge is not rebutted by appeals to serious and meaningful audience involvement in News, or at least not from what I observed at the BBC. For the press to claim serious and meaningful audience involvement more is required from both audiences and the media.

WHAT HAS HUMAN RIGHTS LAW DONE FOR THE MEDIA?

Merris Amos

INTRODUCTION

When the Human Rights Act 1998 (HRA) came fully into force on 2 October 2000, there was cause for the media to celebrate. Article 10 of the European Convention on Human Rights (ECHR), which protects the right to freedom of expression, had at last been given legal effect in United Kingdom law, empowering the media, amongst others, to assert this right before domestic courts without the "inordinate delay and cost" of taking a claim to the European Court of Human Rights (ECtHR) in Strasbourg.[1] However, more than ten years later, it is apparent that the media is no longer celebrating. Prominent editors of national newspapers are concerned at the restriction imposed upon them by Article 8 of the ECHR, the right to respect for private life, which has been given direct legal effect against the private sector, in particular media companies, by the courts.[2] And there is general dismay about the very limited advancements which have been achieved by the media utilising their new Art.10 right. Some commentators have even suggested that the way in which Art.10 is drafted, setting out possible lawful "proportionate" interferences with expression, has actually encouraged Parliament and the courts to permit more limitations on freedom of expression than would have occurred without it.[3] Echoing this, prior to the 2010 General Election, the Conservative Party bolstered its call for a new bill of rights with the observation that the HRA had failed to protect against the erosion of historic liberties and may have even provided a "veneer of respectability".[4] Recently the media's opinion of the HRA has plummeted even further. One journalist commented that 2009 "saw the most sustained assault on free expression in the UK for two

---

[1] *Rights Brought Home: The Human Rights Bill* (Cm 3782) (London, TSO, 1997) at [1.14].

[2] See, for example, the speech of Paul Dacre, Editor of the Daily Mail, to the Society of Editors in December 2008. Available at www.societyofeditors.org.

[3] See, for example, Henry Porter, "Small sops to freedom can't hide what Labour has stolen" *The Observer*, 28 October 2007, 27.

[4] A. Travis, "Cameron pledges bill to restore British freedoms" *The Guardian*, 28 February 2009, 11.

decades."[5] Editorial comments in *The Daily Mail* frequently call for the repeal of the HRA[6] and editorials in *The Sun*, the national daily newspaper with the highest circulation[7], are similar.

The purpose of this chapter is to consider the framework of domestic human rights law which now supports, as well as interferes with, media activities. The advantages of human rights law for the media, in particular the right to freedom of expression, will be considered as well as the disadvantages. Observations will be made about the media's perceptions of the HRA and the right to freedom of expression, and conclusions offered concerning possible future directions for the law of human rights as it relates to the media.

THE HUMAN RIGHTS LAW FRAMEWORK

The HRA gives further effect to most of the "Convention rights" contained in the European Convention on Human Rights (ECHR).[8] Of particular relevance to the media are Art.10, the right to freedom of expression, Art.8, the right to respect for private life, Art.6, the right to a fair trial and Art.14, the prohibition of discrimination in the enjoyment of the Convention rights. Of these rights, only Art.6 is, in part, an absolute right. Article 10(1), for example, provides that everyone has the right to freedom of expression. This right includes freedom to hold opinions and to receive and impart information and ideas without interference by public authority and regardless of frontiers. However, Art.10 specifically does not prevent states from requiring the licensing of broadcasting, television or cinema enterprises.[9] Furthermore, under Art.10(2), permitted interferences with the right to freedom of expression are set out. These must be "prescribed by law" and "necessary in a democratic society" but permit restrictions "in the interests of national security, territorial integrity or public safety, for

---

[5] J. Kampfner, "Libel reform: A year of gagging, and fightbacks" *The Guardian*, 14 December 2009, 4.

[6] See for example "Another human rights victory for terrorism" *The Daily Mail*, 3 November 2008, 12 and "The terrorists' friend" *The Daily Mail*, 1 Nov 2007, 14. See further J. Petley, "Podsnappery; or Why British Newspapers Support Fagging" *International Journal of Communications Ethics* 3 (2006), 42.

[7] Circulation for May 2009, as reported by the Audit Bureau of Circulation, was 2,984,103.

[8] These are defined in section 1 as Articles 2–12 and 14 of the ECHR, Articles 1–3 of Protocol No.1 to the ECHR, and Articles 1–2 of Protocol No.6 to the ECHR. All must be read with Articles 16–18 of the ECHR and have effect subject to any designated derogation or reservation.

[9] Art.10(1).

the prevention of disorder or crime, for the protection of health or morals, for the protection of the reputation or rights of others, for preventing the disclosure of information received in confidence, or for maintaining the authority and impartiality of the judiciary." Arts.8 and 14 are also subject to exceptions.

The key part of the majority of human rights litigation is the notion of proportionality, a part of the larger principle of necessity. For example, where there is a potential interference with freedom of expression as a result of finding a media company liable in defamation, much of the court's judgment will concern a discussion of whether or not this restriction is proportionate to the objective of protecting reputation.[10] When carrying out this balancing process, courts are obliged, by s.12 of the HRA, to have particular regard to the importance of the Convention right to freedom of expression. However, it is important to note that this section was inserted into the Human Rights Bill during the parliamentary debates in response to press fears that the HRA would lead to untrammelled restrictions on freedom of the press[11], and it has actually proved to be of very little influence.[12]

The HRA is designed to mirror the international system for the enforcement of the ECHR. The objective is to ensure that it is possible to bring any claim that could be brought before the European Court of Human Rights (ECtHR) in Strasbourg under the HRA before the domestic courts. Victims of a violation of Convention rights, including media companies and individual journalists, may bring proceedings under the HRA, or rely on Convention rights in any legal proceedings, but they must be directly affected by the alleged violation.[13] In accordance with Strasbourg authority, domestically "[t]here is no scope for proceedings to be brought by a person who has not himself been affected by the alleged violation"[14] so test case challenges by NGOs and other public interest groups are not possible.

---

[10] See for example *Reynolds v Times Newspapers Ltd* [1999] 4 All ER 609.

[11] HC Deb, Vol 315, col 543 (2 July 1998), Secretary of State for the Home Department, Mr Jack Straw.

[12] *Ashdown v Telegraph Group Ltd* [2001] EWCA Civ 1142, [2001] 3 WLR 1368 at [27].

[13] S.7 HRA.

[14] *Eastaway v Secretary of State for Trade and Industry* [2007] EWCA Civ 425 at [49] per Arden LJ in reliance upon *Klass v Germany* (1978) 2 EHRR 214. See also *R. (Johnson) v Secretary of State for Health* [2006] EWHC 288 (Admin).

Under the HRA, the burden of compliance with the Convention rights is imposed upon public authorities, including the BBC and OFCOM.[15] As the courts are also considered to be public authorities, they are bound by the HRA to take the Convention rights into account when developing the common law. As a direct result of this obligation, Art.8, the right to respect for private life, now applies to private media companies via the existing pre-HRA tort of breach of confidence. When such claims are considered by the courts, media respondents can raise their Art.10, freedom of expression right in their defence and courts are equally bound to take this right into account.[16] It is via this type of development of the common law in purely private sector litigation that human rights law has had its greatest impact on the media.

The HRA also affects the relationship between Convention rights and primary legislation, or Acts of Parliament. As the HRA has been carefully drafted to preserve the sovereignty of Parliament, if a public authority can demonstrate that it was acting in accordance with primary legislation when breaching Convention rights, this provides a complete defence.[17] However, sections 3 and 4 of the HRA provide some respite. If a court decides that the primary legislation is indeed incompatible with a Convention right, it may utilise s.3 and interpret the legislation compatibly with the Convention rights "so far as it is possible to do so" provided a meaning inconsistent with a fundamental feature of the legislation is not adopted. If it is not possible to use s.3, a court may issue a declaration of incompatibility under s.4. A government minister, if he or she considers that there are compelling reasons, may by order make such amendments to the legislation as considered necessary to remove the incompatibility.[18]

Finally, it is important to note that when interpreting and applying the Convention rights under the HRA in the domestic context, British courts adhere closely to the jurisprudence of the European Court of Human Rights. Although s.2 of the HRA provides that this case law need only be taken into account where relevant, it has been held by the House of Lords that although these judgments of the ECtHR are not binding, absent a

---

[15] See for example, *R. (on the application of Prolife Alliance) v British Broadcasting Corporation* [2003] UKHL 23, [2004] 1 AC 185 and *Gaunt v OFCOM* [2010] EWHC 1756 (Admin). On the meaning of public authority, see generally M. Amos *Human Rights Law* (Oxford: Hart, 2006), chapter 2.

[16] See for example *Campbell v MGN Ltd* [2004] UKHL 22, [2004] 2 AC 457.

[17] S.6(2) HRA.

[18] S.10(2) HRA. See further, M. Amos *Human Rights Law* (Oxford: Hart, 2006), chapter 5.

"strong reason" domestic courts should regard themselves as bound.[19] Whilst this prevents domestic courts from adopting an interpretation of a Convention right more narrow than that of the ECtHR, it also means that a more generous interpretation of Convention rights is not usually possible.[20]

THE ADVANTAGES OF THE CURRENT LEGAL FRAMEWORK FOR THE MEDIA

A New Legal Right to Freedom of Expression

Being able to argue for a concrete legal right to freedom of expression before the British courts, without the "inordinate delay and cost"[21] of lodging an application in Strasbourg with the ECtHR, obviously carries with it some advantages for the British media. Whilst a right to freedom of expression was recognised in the common law prior to the coming into force of the HRA[22], it was not always predictable what the outcome would be where this was argued a part of a defence to a claim such as defamation or contempt of court, or as a ground for judicial review of the decision of a public authority. Furthermore, the common law right was particularly powerless in the face of encroachments on freedom of expression as the result of an Act of Parliament. The limits of the common law right were clearly demonstrated in the case of *Brind*[23] an application, brought by journalists, for judicial review of the Home Secretary's directive that the BBC and Independent Broadcasting Authority refrain from broadcasting the direct statements by a person who represented an organisation involved in terrorism. The House of Lords concluded unanimously that whilst freedom of expression was compromised, the Home Secretary's actions were lawful and it was not possible to employ an Art.10 proportionality analysis in relation to the restriction. As Lord Ackner observed:

---

[19] *R. v Special Adjudicator, ex p Ullah* [2004] UKHL 26, [2004] 2 AC 323 at [20] per Lord Bingham.

[20] See for example *N v Secretary of State for the Home Department* [2005] UKHL 31, [2005] 2 AC 296. See further M. Amos, "The principle of comity and the relationship between British courts and the European Court of Human Rights" in P. Eeckhout and T. Tridimas (eds.) *Yearbook of European Law 2009* (Oxford: Clarendon Press, 2009).

[21] *Rights Brought Home*, Op. cit., at [1.14].

[22] See for example *Cassell & Co v Broome* [1972] 2 WLR 645 per Lord Kilbrandon at 726; *Harman v Secretary of State for the Home Department* [1982] 2 WLR 338 per Lord Scarman at 351; and *Secretary of State for Defence v Guardian Newspapers Ltd* [1984] 3 WLR 986 per Lord Fraser at 1001.

[23] *Brind v Secretary of State for the Home Department* [1991] 1 All ER 720.

Unless and until Parliament incorporates the convention into domestic law, a course which it is well known has a strong body of support, there appears to me to be at present no basis upon which the proportionality doctrine applied by the European Court can be followed by the courts of this country.[24]

Using the HRA as a Sword

Under the HRA, it is now possible for individual journalists, media companies, and other individuals connected with the media, to bring legal proceedings to challenge the compatibility of a particular Act of Parliament, court order or act of a public authority, with Art.10. For example, *Rusbridger*[25] concerned proceedings brought by Alan Rusbridger, editor of *The Guardian*, and Polly Toynbee, a journalist, for a declaration that s.3 of the Treason Act 1848, when read in the light of Art.10, did not apply to persons who evinced in print or in writing an intent to depose the monarch or deprive her of her imperial status or to establish a republican form of government unless their intent was to achieve this by acts of force, constraint or other unlawful means. Whilst there were some question marks over the status of the claimants as victims given no prosecution had actually been brought, Lord Steyn did state that "[t]he idea that s.3 could survive scrutiny under the Human Rights Act is unreal. The fears of the editor of The Guardian were more than a trifle alarmist."[26]

With respect to the actions of public authorities, in particular the courts, increasingly the media are using the HRA to challenge what are perceived to be disproportionate restrictions on reporting. For example, in *Re Attorney General's Reference (No.3 of 1999)*,[27] utilising Art.10, the BBC successfully applied to the court to have an anonymity order protecting an acquitted defendant set aside so that it could reveal his identity in connection with a proposed programme inspired by the removal of the double jeopardy rule. And in *Webster*[28] the parents of a child, the BBC, Associated Newspapers Ltd and others succeeded in overturning reporting restrictions made on care proceedings taking place in relation to the couple's fourth child.

---

[24] at 735.
[25] *R. (on the application of Rusbridger) v Attorney General* [2003] UKHL 38, [2004] 1 AC 357.
[26] at [28].
[27] [2009] UKHL 34, [2009] 3 WLR 142.
[28] *Re Webster (A Child) v Webster* [2006] EWHC 2733 (Fam).

Using the HRA as a Shield

Whilst such claims on the part of media companies and individuals as potential victims remain possible, what is far more common is for a challenge to primary legislation, or existing common law encroachments on freedom of expression, to be raised as a defence in legal proceedings. Sections 3 and 4 HRA arguments can be raised wherever a restriction is imposed as a result of primary legislation. And courts, as public authorities, are bound by s.6 of the HRA to take into account Convention rights, including the right to freedom of expression, when applying and developing the common law. In these types of cases, judicial pronouncements are often made concerning the importance of freedom of expression. It has been frequently held that there is a public interest *per se* in freedom of expression and freedom of the press. For example, in *R. v Shayler* Lord Bingham observed:

> Modern democratic government means government of the people by the people for the people. But there can be no government by the people if they are ignorant of the issues to be resolved, the arguments for and against different solutions and the facts underlying those arguments.[29]

It is generally recognised in the courts that the media have a positive duty to act as a watchdog or as the eyes and ears of the general public and to inform their readers about matters of public interest.[30] It has been held that the existence of a free press is in itself desirable and in the public interest[31] irrespective of whether a particular publication is in the public interest.[32] It has also been held that the press are entitled to a reasonable margin of appreciation in taking decisions as to what details need to be included in an article to give it credibility as this is an essential part of the journalistic exercise.[33] Particular advantage might be gained where it can be established that the subject matter of the publication is a matter of public interest. Whilst there remains considerable confusion over the definition of "public interest publication",[34] it is usually accepted that

---

[29] [2002] UKHL 11, [2002] 2 WLR 754 at [21].

[30] *R. v Sherwood, ex p The Telegraph Group plc* [2001] EWCA Crim 1075, [2001] 1 WLR 1983 at [17]–[18].

[31] *Ashdown v Telegraph Group Ltd* [2001] EWCA Civ 1142, [2001] 3 WLR 1368 at [66].

[32] *B & C v A* [2002] EWCA Civ 337, [2002] 3 WLR 542 at [11(iv)].

[33] *Campbell v Mirror Group Newspapers Ltd* [2004] UKHL 22, [2004] 2 AC 457 at [112] per Lord Hope and [143] per Baroness Hale.

[34] See further M. Amos "Can we speak freely now? Freedom of expression under the Human Rights Act" *European Human Rights Law Review* 6 (2002), 750.

the definition in the Press Complaints Commission Code is a good starting point. Here public interest expression is defined to include detecting
or exposing crime or a serious misdemeanour; protecting public health
and safety; and preventing the public from being misled by some statement or action or an individual or organisation. The highest level of protection is afforded to "political information" Lord Nicholls observing in the
Prolife Alliance[35] case that freedom of political speech "is a freedom of the
very highest importance in any country which lays claim to being a democracy. Restrictions on this freedom need to be examined rigorously by all
concerned, not least the courts."[36] It has also been recognised that news is
a perishable commodity and that encompassed with Art.10 protection is
not just content, but also the timing of a communication.[37]

Examples of individual journalists and media organisations employing
Art.10 in argument before the courts are numerous. Art.10 has continued
to shape the law of defamation ensuring that the interference posed is
proportionate to the aim of protecting reputation. The defence of qualified privilege has now developed under Art.10. Where publication is to the
world at large, the publication will be privileged if the public is entitled to
know the particular information. A number of factors must be taken into
account in determining whether the test is satisfied, the touchstone being
"responsible journalism".[38] As was explained by the Court of Appeal in
Loutchansky:

> The interest is that of the public in a modern democracy in free expression
> and, more particularly, in the promotion of a free and vigorous press to keep
> the public informed.. The corresponding duty on the journalist (and equally
> his editor) is to play his proper role in discharging that function. His task is
> to behave as a responsible journalist. He can have no duty to publish unless
> he is acting responsibly any more than the public has an interest in reading
> whatever may be published irresponsibly ... Unless the publisher is acting
> responsibly privilege cannot arise.[39]

Art.10 has been employed in argument against the granting of injunctions
contra mudum (against the world at large) to protect an individual's

---

[35] *R. (on the application of Prolife Alliance) v British Broadcasting Corporation* [2003]
UKHL 23, [2004] 1 AC 185.
[36] at [6].
[37] *R. v Sherwood, ex p The Telegraph Group plc* [2001] EWCA Crim 1075, [2001] 1 WLR 1983
at [16] and *Attorney General v Punch Ltd* [2002] UKHL 50, [2003] 1 AC 1046 at [31].
[38] *Reynolds v Times Newspapers Ltd* [1999] 4 All ER 609.
[39] *Loutchansky v Times Newspapers Ltd (No.2)* [2001] EWCA Civ 1805, [2002] 2 WLR 640.

identity or whereabouts.[40] For example, in *Re S*[41] the House of Lords concluded that the right of the press to freedom of expression outweighed the request for an injunction protecting the identity of a boy whose mother was to be tried for the murder of his older brother. It has also had some beneficial influence on the law of copyright,[42] the tort of breach of confidence,[43] *Norwich Pharmacal* orders, which give a court the power to order a journalist to disclose his or her source,[44] and the law of contempt of court.[45]

Art.10 has also played a large part in shaping the development of the tort of modified breach of confidence, which now protects Art.8 privacy rights from disproportionate interference by private sector media companies. As noted by Lord Hope in *Campbell*:

> [T]he right to privacy which lies at the heart of an action for breach of confidence has to be balanced against the right of the media to impart information to the public. And the right of the media to impart information to the public has to be balanced in its turn against the respect that must be given to private life.[46]

If the invasion of private life is held to be a matter of legitimate public interest because, for example, a public figure has previously lied about the matter, the claim to freedom of expression will be particularly strong and will often defeat the strongest privacy claim. For example, in *Campbell*[47] the House of Lords concluded unanimously that Naomi Campbell had no claim in relation to the fact of her drug addiction or to the fact that she was receiving treatment at as she had lied about these facts and also sought to benefit from this by comparing herself with others in the fashion business who were addicted.

---

[40] See for example *Venables v News Group Newspapers Ltd* [2001] WLR 1038 and *X (a woman formerly known as Mary Bell) v O'Brien* [2003] EWHC (QB) 1101, [2003] 2 FCR 686.

[41] *Re S (A Child) (Identification: Restriction on Publication)* [2004] UKHL 47, [2005] 1 AC 593.

[42] *Ashdown v Telegraph Group Ltd* [2001] EWCA Civ 1142, [2001] 3 WLR 1368.

[43] *London Regional Transport v The Mayor of London*, Divisional Court, 31 July 2001 and *H (A Healthcare Worker) v Associated Newspapers Ltd* [2002] EWCA Civ 195, [2002] EMLR 23.

[44] *Ashworth Hospital Authority v MGN Ltd* [2002] UKHL 29, [2002] 1 WLR 2033.

[45] *R. v Sherwood, ex p The Telegraph Group* [2001] EWCA Civ 1075, [2001] 1 WLR 1983.

[46] *Campbell v MGN Ltd* [2004] UKHL 22, [2004] 2 AC 457 at [105].

[47] Ibid.

Protection for the Providers of Information

Finally, it is important to note that Art.10 might also offer protection to those who wish to communicate information to the media. In *Hirst*[48] the Home Secretary had denied a serving prisoner's request that he be entitled, in certain circumstances, to speak to the media by telephone on matters of legitimate public interest relating to prisons and prisoners. In the Home Secretary's view, he could exercise his right to freedom of expression by expressing his views in writing. The Administrative Court disagreed and found the blanket ban to be a disproportionate interference with freedom of expression.[49] Art.10 was also employed by David Shayler, a former member of the security services who was indicted on three counts of breach of the Official Secrets Act 1989 following his disclosure of documents to journalists from the *Mail on Sunday*.[50]

The Disadvantages of the Current Legal Framework for the Media

A Framework for Interference

Whilst the HRA has given the media the benefit of Art 10, as discussed in the preceding section, it has also imposed a new layer of regulation upon it. As it is drafted, and interpreted, Art.10 does not offer legal protection for an *absolute* right to freedom of expression. Within the parameters of "prescribed by law" and "necessary" it actually permits a wide range of interferences and the media relies upon Parliament, public authorities and the courts, to ensure that the balance struck between the interference and the objective is a proportionate one. Put simply, Art.10(2) does actually provide a framework, within which to work, if the objective is to impose new restrictions upon freedom of expression. Utilising this framework, a number of new laws, restrictive of freedom of expression and the media, have been passed by Parliament in recent years including the controversial Racial and Religious Hatred Act 2006 which created the new offence of stirring up hatred against persons on religious grounds, and the Terrorism

---

[48] *Hirst v Secretary of State for the Home Department* [2002] EWHC (Admin) 602, [2002] 1 WLR 2929.
[49] See also *R (on the application of A) v Secretary of State for the Home Department* [2003] EWHC (Admin) 2846.
[50] *R. v Shayler* [2002] UKHL 11, [2002] 2 WLR 754. His Art.10 arguments were not successful.

Act 2006 which includes offences relating to the encouragement of acts of terrorism and the dissemination of terrorist publications.[51] An example of the impact such laws can have is the case of *Malik*[52] where a respected freelance journalist complained that it was incompatible with Art.10 for the court to grant a production order under Sch.5 of the Terrorism Act 2000 seeking all material in his possession concerning the terrorist activities of a particular individual about whom he was writing a book. The Administrative Court concluded that the order should be made in principle but that the terms of the order were too wide observing as follows:

> Where, as in the present case, such material is in the possession of a journalist, there is a potential clash between the interests of the state in ensuring that the police are able to conduct terrorist investigations as effectively as possible and the rights of a journalist to protect his or her confidential sources. Important though these rights of a journalist unquestionably are, they are not absolute. Parliament has decided that the public interest in the security of the state must be taken into account. A balance has to be struck between the protection of the confidential material of journalists and the interest of us all in facilitating effective terrorist investigations. It is for the court to strike that balance applying the carefully calibrated mechanism enacted by Parliament in schedule5 of the 2000 Act.[53]

New Convention Rights, New Obligations

In addition to the framework for interference provided by Art.10, other Convention rights have had a restrictive impact on the activities of the media. Art.2, the right to life, Art.6, the right to a fair trial, Art.8, the right to respect for private life, and Art.14, the right to no discrimination in the enjoyment of Convention rights, have all impacted directly, or indirectly, on the activities of the media. Media public authorities, such as the BBC, the Press Complaints Commission[54] and OFCOM, are directly subject to the obligation imposed by s.6 of the HRA to act compatibly with these Convention rights. For example, in 2003 the Prolife Alliance, a political party opposed to abortion, euthanasia, destructive embryo research and human cloning, participated in the general election in 2001 and thereby qualified for a party election broadcast in accordance with the rules of allocation agreed by all broadcasters. The BBC chose not to transmit its

---

[51] See further D. Murray, "Freedom of expression, counter-terrorism and the internet in the light of the UK Terrorist Act 2006 and the jurisprudence of the European Court of Human Rights" *Netherlands Quarterly of Human Rights* 27 (2009), 331.

[52] *Malik v Manchester Crown Court* [2008] EWHC 1362 (Admin)

[53] at [110].

[54] *R. v Press Complaints Commission, ex p Ford* [2001] EWHC Admin 683.

proposed broadcast under s.6(1)(a) of the Broadcasting Act 1990 on the grounds that it offended good taste, decency and public feeling and utilising the HRA, the Prolife Alliance sought a legal remedy. In a widely criticised decision, the House of Lords found that Art.10 did not entitle the Prolife Alliance to make a free television broadcast. However, it determined that access should not be refused on discriminatory, arbitrary or unreasonable grounds. Nor should access be granted subject to discriminatory, arbitrary or unreasonable conditions. Here it concluded that the BBC had applied the statutory criteria correctly.[55]

In addition to the obligation imposed upon these media public authorities, the courts are also obliged, as public authorities themselves to act compatibly with the Convention rights when interpreting, applying and developing the law. Due to this obligation, important Convention rights have had a serious impact on the activities of the media with Art.8, the right to respect for private life, having the most significant impact. Prior to the HRA, the right to respect for private life was relatively underdeveloped in English law and no statutory or common law tort of invasion of privacy had developed. Post HRA it has been held that there is no logical ground for saying that a person should have less protection against a private individual than he would have against the state for the publication of personal information for which there is no justification.[56] As already discussed, courts, as public authorities, are bound by s.6 of the HRA to act compatibly with Convention rights and if "there is a relevant cause of action applicable" it "must act compatibly with both parties' Convention rights."[57] The tort of breach of confidence has now been modified and the "values embodied in Arts 8 and 10 are as much applicable in disputes between individuals or between an individual and a non-governmental body such as a newspaper as they are in disputes between individuals and a public authority.[58]

> Instead of the cause of action being based upon the duty of good faith applicable to confidential personal information and trade secrets alike, it focuses upon the protection of human autonomy and dignity—the right to control the dissemination of information about one's private life and the right to the esteem and respect of other people.[59]

---

[55] *R. (on the application of Prolife Alliance) v British Broadcasting Corporation* [2003] UKHL 23, [2004] 1 AC 185.

[56] *Campbell v MGN Ltd* [2004] UKHL 22, [2004] 2 AC 457 at [50] per Lord Hoffmann.

[57] *Campbell v MGN Ltd* [2004] UKHL 22, [2004] 2 AC 457 at [32] per Baroness Hale.

[58] *Campbell*, Ibid., at [17] per Lord Nicholls.

[59] *Campbell*, Ibid., at [51] per Lord Hoffmann.

A duty of confidence arises whenever the party subject to the duty is in a situation where he knows, or ought to know, that the other person can reasonably expect his privacy to be protected.[60] It has been established that, depending on the circumstances, there might even be a reasonable expectation of privacy in a public place, such as a public street.[61] An intrusion in such a situation will be capable of giving rise to liability in an action for breach of confidence unless the intrusion can be justified.[62] This is a balancing act for the court:

> The right to privacy which lies at the heart of an action for breach of confidence has to be balanced against the right of the media to impart information to the public. And the right of the media to impart information to the public has to be balanced in its turn against the respect that must be given to private life.[63]

This new avenue for redress against the media is increasingly being utilised by celebrities and other public figures anxious to protect their private lives from unwarranted intrusion or to punish an intrusion when it has already occurred. In *Douglas*[64], Michael Douglas and Catherine Zeta-Jones established that although their wedding was not private, as they had sold their privacy to OK! magazine, they still retained an aspect of Art.8 protection with respect to their autonomy, in particular, their right of veto over publication of the photographs in order to maintain the kind of image professionally and personally important to them. Footballer Gary Flitcroft established in *B&C v A*[65] that there was a difference between the confidentiality which attaches to permanent relationships and that which attaches to affairs but nevertheless, there was still a modest degree of privacy concerning those relationships to which he was entitled. However, this was outweighed by Art.10 on the facts of the case.

Model Naomi Campbell did not manage to obtain a remedy from Mirror Group Newspapers Ltd for publishing the facts that she had been misleading the public about her drug addiction and that she was receiving therapy for her drug addiction. However, other confidential details she had chosen not to put in the public domain were off limits including the fact that she was receiving treatment at Narcotics Anonymous, the details of the

---

[60] *Campbell*, Ibid., at [85] per Lord Hope.
[61] *Murray v Big Pictures (UK) Ltd* [2008] EWCA Civ 446.
[62] *B & C v A* [2002] EWCA Civ 337, [2002] 3 WLR 542 at [11(ix)]-[11(x)].
[63] *Campbell*, Ibid., at [105] per Lord Hope.
[64] *Douglas v Hello! Ltd* [2001] QB 967.
[65] [2002] EWCA Civ 337.

treatment and the visual portrayal of her leaving a specific meeting with other addicts.[66] And Formula One boss Max Mosley was awarded damages of £60,000 against News Group Newspapers Limited for publication of an article in the *News of the World* concerning a party he attended where it was alleged, by the *News of the World*, that he had engaged in a "Nazi orgy".[67] Art.8 has also been utilised by private individuals who have found themselves the subject of media attention. For example, a mother, T, successfully obtained an injunction to prevent the BBC from identifying her in a television programme broadcast in 2007 concerning adoption.[68]

The Impact of Other Convention Rights

In addition to Art.8, other Convention rights have had an impact on the media, forming a new, and in most cases, very unwelcome, layer of regulation. For example, in *Venables*[69] the claimants sought injunctions to restrain the publication of information relating to their identities and whereabouts. They had both been convicted of the murder of two year old James Bulger in 1993 when they were ten years old. The injunction was sought *contra mundum*—against the world at large. The Family Division found that it had the jurisdiction, in exceptional cases, to extend the protection of confidentiality of information where not to do so would be likely to lead to serious physical injury, or to the death, of the person seeking that confidentiality.[70] Here it was satisfied that if the claimant's identities were discovered, neither of them would have the chance of a normal life and there was a real and strong possibility that their lives would be at risk.[71] It therefore concluded that the extension of the tort here was proportionate to the legitimate aim of protecting the claimants from serious and possibly irreparable harm.[72]

Art.6, the right to a fair trial, has also had some impact on the media both directly and via the medium of the law of contempt of court for which provision is made in Art.10(2) for "maintaining the authority and impartiality of the judiciary". It is possible for orders to be made under

---

[66] *Campbell*, Op. cit.

[67] *Mosley v News Group Newspapers Limited* [2008] EWHC 1777 (QB), (2008) EMLR 20.

[68] *T (by her litigation friend the Official Solicitor) v British Broadcasting Corporation* [2007] EWHC 1683 (QB). See also Secretary of State for the Home Department v AP [2010] UKSC 26.

[69] *Venables v News Group Newspapers Limited* [2001] WLR 1038.

[70] at [81].

[71] at [94].

[72] at [86]. See also *Times Newspapers Ltd v R.* [2008] EWCA Crim 2559, [2009] 1 WLR 1015.

s.4(2) of the Contempt of Court Act 1981 postponing the reporting of court cases. In its judgment in *ex p The Telegraph Group plc*[73] the Court of Appeal held that it was important to consider whether there was a way to overcome the risk of prejudice to the administration of justice by less restrictive means although in the present case, it was not possible and the order was made. However, in its judgment in the case of *B*[74] the Divisional Court lifted an order postponing reporting until the trial of co-defendants stating as follows:

> An equally precious principle, hallowed by custom and the tradition of the common law, is the freedom of the media to act as the eyes and ears of the public at large and, among their other responsibilities, to observe and contemporaneously to report the criminal proceedings involving the same defendant whose birthright to a fair trial must be protected. The administration of criminal justice must be open and transparent. The freedom of the press to report the proceedings provides one of the essential safeguards against closed justice.[75]

THE BALANCING PROCESS—ARE THE COURTS BIASED AGAINST THE MEDIA?

In addition to the new layer of regulation which the HRA represents for the media, there is another possible disadvantage which it is important to consider and assess. Increasingly the media is almost universally complaining that in addition to the Convention rights they must now strive to act in accordance with, they are more often than not on the losing side when the proportionality balance is struck between rights under Art.10 and other rights or interests. There is a feeling amongst some that particular judges are actually biased against the media. Most concern is usually directed at judgments concerning the impact of Art.8, the right to respect for private life, but there are also others in different areas. In order to assess whether the media has a valid point, these key judgments are briefly discussed in the following paragraphs.

The Right to Respect for Private Life

In *Campbell*[76] although it was unanimously concluded that Naomi Campbell had no claim in relation to the fact of her drug addiction or to

---

[73] *R v Sherwood, ex p The Telegraph Group* [2001] EWCA Civ 1075, [2001] 1 WLR 1983.
[74] *In the matter of B* [2006] EWCA Crim 2692.
[75] at [19].
[76] Op. cit.

the fact that she was receiving treatment as she had lied about these facts
and also sought to benefit from this, a majority of the House of Lords did
conclude that the balance fell in her favour in relation to the fact that she
was receiving treatment at Narcotics Anonymous, the details of the treatment and the visual portrayal (photograph) of her leaving a specific meeting. She was awarded damages of £3,500 and in further litigation
established before the House of Lords that it was not incompatible with
Art.10 for the publishers of the Daily Mirror to be ordered to pay her costs
in the Court of Appeal and House of Lords amounting to the sum of
£1,086,295.47, including a success fee agreed by Campbell under a conditional fee agreement.[77]

In *Mosley*[78], Eady J in the High Court concluded that Max Mosley,
President of the FIA,[79] had a reasonable expectation of privacy in relation
to sexual activities carried on between consenting adults on private property. He further concluded that there was no element of public interest in
the story as he found no evidence that the gathering was intended to be an
enactment of Nazi behaviour or an adoption of any of its attitudes and
that there was "no genuine basis at all for the suggestion that the participants mocked the victims of the Holocaust."[80] Applying established principles to the facts, Eady J concluded:

> [T]here was no public interest or other justification for the clandestine
> recording, for the publication of the resulting information and still photo-
> graphs, or for the placing of the video extracts on the News of the World
> website—all of this on a massive scale. Of course, I accept, that such behav-
> iour is viewed by some people with distaste and moral disapproval, but in
> the light of modern rights-based jurisprudence that does not provide any
> justification for the intrusion on the personal privacy of the Claimant.[81]

In determining the amount of damages to be awarded, Eady J observed
that no amount could fully compensate the Claimant for the damage

[77] *Campbell v MGN Ltd* [2005] UKHL 61, [2005] 1 WLR 3394. See also *Associated Newspapers Limited v HRH the Prince of Wales* [2006] EWCA Civ 1776, [2008] Ch 57 where it was held that publication of extracts from the Prince of Wales' journals was in breach of confidence and an infringement of copyright; *X and Y v Persons Unknown* [2006] EWHC 2783 (QB) where X and Y successfully maintained an injunction against persons unknown to prevent the further dissemination of allegations about the state of their marriage; and *CC v AB* [2006] EWHC 3083 (QB) where an interim injunction was granted to prevent the respondent from publicising the fact that C had had an affair with his wife.
[78] *Mosley v News Group Newspapers Ltd* [2008] EWHC 1777.
[79] Fédération Internationale de l'Automobile.
[80] at [232].
[81] at [233]

done. £60,000 was awarded the judge observing that his life was ruined and what could be achieved by a monetary award in the circumstances was limited.[82] This judgment, and others, prompted Paul Dacre, Editor of the *Daily Mail*, in his 2008 Annual Lecture to the Society of Editors to observe:

> ...inexorably, and insidiously, the British Press is having a privacy law imposed on it, which—apart from allowing the corrupt and the crooked to sleep easily in their beds—is, I would argue, undermining the ability of mass-circulation newspapers to sell newspapers in an ever more difficult market . . This law is not coming from Parliament—no, that would smack of democracy—but from the arrogant and amoral judgments ... of one man ... I am referring, of course, to Justice David Eady who has, again and again, under the privacy clause of the Human Rights Act, found against newspapers and their age-old freedom to expose the moral shortcomings of those in high places.[83]

National Security

Whilst privacy claims, because these are relatively new, have formed an intense focus for the media, there is also much disappointment on other fronts. For example, David Shayler did not succeed in his argument that the absence of a public interest defence from the Official Secrets Act 1989 was incompatible with Art.10.[84] The House of Lords concluded that the ban on disclosure was not an absolute ban but a ban on disclosure without lawful authority. It was open to Shayler to have tried to make his disclosures via the routes provided for in the Act—as he did not do so, it was concluded that his prosecution was compatible with Art.10. National security was also employed to justify the conclusion in A[85] that it was proportionate for the Home Secretary to permit Category A prisoners detained under s.21 of the Anti-Terrorism Crime and Security Act 2001 only to be interviewed by journalists if the interviews were conducted within the earshot of officials and tape recorded.

Defamation Law

A cause for particular concern has been the absence of improvements in defamation (libel) law as a result of Art.10. In their 2009 report, *Free Speech*

---

[82] at [236]
[83] www.societyofeditors.org.
[84] *R. v Shayler* [2002] UKHL 11, [2002] 2 WLR 754.
[85] *R. (on the application of A) v Secretary of State for the Home Department* [2003] EWHC (Admin) 2846.

is not for Sale[86] the NGOs Index on Censorship and English PEN concluded as follows:

> English libel law has a negative impact on freedom of expression, both in the UK and around the world. Freedom of expression is a fundamental human right, and should only be limited in special circumstances. Yet English libel law imposes unnecessary and disproportionate restrictions on free speech, sending a chilling effect through the publishing and journalism sectors in the UK. This effect now reaches around the world, because of so-called 'libel tourism', where foreign cases are heard in London, widely known as a 'town named sue'. The law was designed to serve the rich and powerful, and does not reflect the interests of a modern democratic society.[87]

Whilst there have been improvements in the defamation defence of qualified privilege, the courts have not gone as far as the media would like. In *Reynolds*[88], the Sunday Times argued that there should be a new category of occasion when privilege derives from the subject matter of alone if it was a "political communication". This was rejected by the House of Lords. Although it appreciated the important role played by the media, it was also concerned that the reputation of public figures "should not be debased falsely".[89] It concluded that where publication was to the world at large, the publication would be privileged if the public was entitled to know the particular information. However, all the circumstances, particularly whether responsible journalism had been exercised, had to be taken into account in determining whether the test was satisfied. Lord Nicholls listed the following ten matters which may be taken into account, depending on the circumstances:

> (1) The seriousness of the allegation. The more serious the charge, the more the public is misinformed and the individual harmed, if the allegation is not true. (2) The nature of the information, and the extent to which the subject matter is a matter of public concern. (3) The source of the information. Some informants have no direct knowledge of the events. Some have their own axes to grind, or are being paid for their stories. (4) The steps taken to verify the information. (5) The status of the information. The allegation may have already been the subject of an investigation which commands respect. (6) The urgency of the matter. News is often a perishable commodity. (7) Whether comment was sought from the plaintiff. He may have information others do not possess or have not disclosed. An approach to the plaintiff will

---

[86] London: Index on Censorship and English PEN, 2009 available at www.libelreform.org.
[87] p. 3.
[88] *Reynolds v Times Newspapers Ltd* [1999] 4 All ER 609.
[89] per Lord Nicholls.

not always be necessary. (8) Whether the article contained the gist of the plaintiff's side of the story. (9) The tone of the article. A newspaper can raise queries or call for an investigation. It need not adopt allegations as statements of fact. (10) The circumstances of the publication, including the timing.[90]

Other aspects of the law of the defamation have not changed dramatically as a result of the HRA. It has been confirmed that the rule that each individual publication of libel gives rise to a separate cause of action is compatible with Art.10.[91] A defendant who relies on the defence of justification must still justify the essence or sting of an assault on reputation rather than a diminished version of it.[92] In *Campbell*[93] the House of Lords concluded that it was not incompatible with Art.10 to allow success fees to be charged under conditional fee agreements in cases brought against the media involving defamation or breach of confidence although it was conceded that such fees constituted a "chill factor".[94] The pre-existing rule, that a company with a trading reputation in England and Wales was entitled to recover damages for defamation without proving that the publication had caused it special damage, was not altered as a result of Art.10 by the House of Lords in *Jameel*.[95]

Disclosure of a Journalist's Source

There was considerable hope in the media that Art.10 would bring with it some change to "*Norwich Pharmacal* orders"[96] whereby a court may order a journalist's source be disclosed. Many hoped that such orders would be found incompatible with Art.10 given the obvious "chilling effect" on the freedom of the press. However, this was not to be the case and orders were made in two very high profile cases. The first, *Ashworth Hospital Authority v MGN Ltd*[97] concerned an article published in the Daily Mirror

---

[90] at 626. The House of Lords concluded in *Jameel v Wall Street Journal Europe* [2006] UKHL 44, [2007] 1 AC 359 that the defence was established on the facts. However, the Court of Appeal concluded in *Galloway v Telegraph Group Ltd* [2006] EWCA Civ 17, [2006] HRLR 13 and the Divisional Court concluded in *Flood v Times Newspapers Ltd* [2009] EWHC 2375 (QB) that the defence was not established on the facts.

[91] *Loutchansky v Times Newspapers Ltd (No.2)* [2001] EWCA Civ 1805, [2002] 2 WLR 640.

[92] *Berezovsky v Forbes* [2001] EWCA Civ 1251, [2001] EMLR 45.

[93] *Campbell v MGN Ltd* [2005] UKHL 61, [2005] 1 WLR 3394.

[94] at [55] per Lord Carswell.

[95] Jameel v Wall Street Journal Europe [2006] UKHL 44, [2007] 1 AC 359.

[96] *Norwich Pharmacal Co v Customs and Excise Commissioners* [1973] 2 All ER 943.

[97] *Ashworth Hospital Authority v MGN Ltd* [2002] UKHL 29, [2002] 1 WLR 2033.

concerning Ian Brady. The article included a series of verbatim extracts
from information held on a database maintained by staff of Ashworth
Hospital Authority. The journalist had received these extracts from one of
his regular sources (the intermediary) who had in turn received the information from a member of staff at Ashworth (the source). Ashworth wished
the identity of the intermediary to be disclosed as a means of identifying
the source. The House of Lords concluded that given the probability that
the source was a member of staff, they were undoubtedly wrongdoers as
they were acting in breach of their contract of employment or in breach of
confidence.[98] Furthermore, it did not matter if the wrongdoing was in
breach of confidence or in breach of contract: all that mattered was that
there was involvement or participation on the part of the journalist and/
or newspaper. This requirement was undoubtedly satisfied in the view of
the House of Lords as the information wrongfully obtained was published.[99] Furthermore, the jurisdiction applied whether or not the victim
intended to pursue action in the courts against the wrongdoer.[100] Taking
into consideration the importance of maintaining confidentiality in medi-
cal records, particularly in the case of the class of patients that the authority was responsible for caring for at Ashworth, the House of Lords
concluded that the situation was exceptional and orders to disclose were
necessary and justified.[101]

Compliance with the order revealed the name of an intermediary,
Mr Ackroyd, not the actual source. When he declined to reveal his source,
the hospital sought an order for disclosure against him. However, applying
the principles established by the House of Lords, on appeal the Court of
Appeal concluded that in all the circumstances the trial judge was entitled
to hold that it was not convincingly established that there was in 2006 "a
pressing social need that the source or sources should be identified."[102] It
also stated that he was entitled to hold "that an order for disclosure would
not be proportionate to the pursuit of the hospital's legitimate aim to seek
redress against the source, given the vital public interest in the protection
of a journalist's source."[103]

---

[98] at [31]–[32].
[99] at [34].
[100] at [49].
[101] at [63] and [66].
[102] at [80].
[103] Ibid.

Contempt of Court

The media also had high hopes that Art.10 would have some impact on contempt of court laws, in particular, third-party contempt which was notoriously applied in the "Spycatcher" case.[104] However, this was not to be the case. In July 2000 *Punch* notified the Treasury Solicitor that it intended to publish an article by former member of the security services, David Shayler against whom an order had been made in 1997[105] restraining the disclosure of information. The article was published, amended from the draft version, but did not reflect the amendments notified. The Attorney General brought proceedings for contempt. It is a contempt of court for a third party, with the intention of impeding or prejudicing the administration of justice by the court in an action between two other parties, to do the acts which the injunction restrains the defendant in that action from committing if the acts done have some significant and adverse effect on the administration of justice in that action.[106] Obviously *Punch* was hoping that Art.10 would have some dramatic impact on the existing law. It did not. It was admitted that Punch did the relevant act[107] and the House of Lords concluded that there was no doubt with respect to intent concluding that the Editor "must, inevitably, have appreciated that by publishing the article he was doing precisely what the order was intended to prevent, namely, pre-empting the court's decision on these confidentiality issues. That is knowing interference with the administration of justice."[108]

Confidentiality

Finally, it was hoped that the law of confidentiality would be modified to make greater allowances for freedom of expression. Art.10(2) specifically provides that freedom of expression may be subject to proportionate restriction "for preventing the disclosure of information received in confidence." In a high profile battle with The Guardian newspaper, Barclays Bank succeeded in maintaining an injunction on seven documents leaked by a Barclays employee to a Member of Parliament.[109] The documents related to financial transactions that Barclays was proposing to set up between 2005 and 2007 using a series of interrelated transactions in

---

104   *A-G v Times Newspapers Ltd* [1992] 1 AC 191.
105   the order was also made against Associated Newspapers.
106   *A-G v Times Newspapers Ltd* [1992] 1 AC 191 at [4].
107   at [20].
108   at [52].
109   *Barclays Bank plc v Guardian News and Media Ltd* [2009] EWHC 591 (QB).

the hope that these arrangements would lead to a saving of tax otherwise payable in the United Kingdom. For a brief period the documents were available to the public at large on The Guardian's web site. The Divisional Court concluded that whilst the Guardian could continue to make use of the contents of the documents "to inform their opinions and to express them and to stimulate public debate"[110] this did not mean that they had complete freedom to publish in full confidential documents leaked in breach of a fiduciary duty. Blake J. observed as follows:

> Responsible journalists must themselves consider whether publication of personal details that they may be in possession of, even about the affairs of corporations not alleged to have done any wrongdoing in the sense of violation of the laws, is appropriate. The more that is sought to be published, the more sensitive or confidential the data is, the self-direction of a responsible journalist is to consider whether the justification of full verbatim quotation as part of the exercise of freedom of expression is made out with particularity to the form of publication that is intended.[111]

Disputes concerning confidentiality and freedom of expression reached a peak in 2009 with the battle between the commodity trading company Trafigura and *The Guardian* concerning the discharge from the Probo Koala, a Trafigura chartered vessel, in August 2006 of gasoline slops in Abidjan in the Ivory Coast in West Africa. A draft report on the incident, commissioned by Trafigura, was the subject of an injunction granted in September 2009 following its leaking to the media. Trafigura maintained that "the injunction was designed to prevent misuse in the media of a legally privileged, outdated and incomplete document, which had been obtained unlawfully and leaked to the media. There has never been any intention of preventing any discussion of these matters by MPs or any reports of Parliamentary proceedings."[112] The Guardian maintained that under the terms of the "super injunction" it was prevented from publishing the report and that it was also banned from revealing that Trafigura had been to court to obtain an injunction. It stated that when it became aware that the existence of the injunction had also been mentioned in a parliamentary question, it sought to publish but was advised that this would be in contempt of court.[113] Trafigura eventually abandoned attempts to keep the report secret following, as Alan Rusbridger editor of the

---

[110] at [29].
[111] at [30].
[112] "Eight key facts about the draft Minton report" 16 October 2009, available at www .trafigura.com.
[113] Editorial, *The Guardian*, 14 October 2009, page 32.

Guardian described it a "combination of old media—the Guardian—and new—Twitter—turned attempted obscurity into mass notoriety."[114]

Are the Complaints by the Media about the Balancing Process Justified?

Whilst the media feels that the balancing process is biased against it, representing a further intrusion into freedom of expression and media freedom generally, it is important not to simply accept this criticism of the HRA without further examination. Art.10(1) of the ECHR has never protected an absolute right to freedom of expression. Art.10(2) is now also given further effect in UK law by the HRA and courts are obliged to balance freedom of expression against other important interests such as national security, maintenance of confidence, protection of reputation and the rights of others. Whilst the media may believe these rights and interests should be subordinate to freedom of expression, those on the opposing side of the balance would not agree. For example, in those cases where Art.10 has been balanced against the right to respect for private life, often it is not a trifling matter which the claimant is seeking to protect from public disclosure. For example Max Mosley in his evidence to the House of Commons' Culture Media and Sport Committee's inquiry into press standards, privacy and libel stated as follows:

> One does not realise when you read these things, where certain people say they should be allowed to publish because it sells newspapers, the appalling impact on the family. It is the most terrible thing you can imagine ... It is like imposing on someone the most enormous penalty. It is like taking all your goods, taking all your money; in fact it is worse because it someone took all your good and your money you have some chance of replacing it ... but if someone takes away your dignity . . you can never replace it. No matter how long I live, no matter what part of the world I go to, people will know about it.[115]

In respecting these rights and interests, British courts are not only following what is required of them by Art.10, but the interpretation and application of Art.10 established by the European Court of Human Rights. In a recent judgment concerning the decision of an Austrian court against a

---

[114] Alan Rusbridger, "The lessons of Trafigura" *The Guardian*, 15 October 2009, 32.
[115] House of Commons Culture, Media and Sport Committee *Press standards, privacy and libel* Second Report of Session 2009–2010 Volume II Oral and written evidence HC 362-II (London: TSO, 2010) at Ev 56.

daily newspaper, the Court, concluding that the judgment was not a disproportionate interference with freedom of expression, observed as follows:

> . . the reasons given by the Austrian courts were relevant and sufficient to justify the interference. It observes that the courts fully recognised that the present case involved a conflict between the right to impart ideas and the right of others to protection of their private life. It cannot find that they failed properly to balance the various interests concerned. In particular the courts duly considered the claimants' status as public figures but found that the article at issue failed to contribute to any debate of general interest ... idle gossip about the state of his or her marriage or alleged extra-marital relationships ... does not contribute to any public debate in respect of which the press as to fulfil its role of public watchdog, but merely serves to satisfy the curiosity of a certain readership[116]

Media self regulation would not produce a similar outcome for those seeking some remedy, as Louis Blom-Cooper has observed, the role of the courts is crucial:

> ... the scope and flow of information is ours to be controlled in so far as it is necessary to protect other cultural values. Self-regulation of the press ... cannot begin to act as a protector or enhancer of these other cultural values. Something much more is needed to instil an attitude of responsibility on the part of newspaper owners, editors, journalists and all disseminators of information whatever the medium.[117]

The media is in actually in a position of advantage when it comes to the balancing process. As already noted, judicial pronouncements are often made concerning the importance of freedom of expression. And it has been frequently held that there is a public interest per se in freedom of expression and freedom of the press. The courts are willing to accept that the media has a positive duty to act as a watchdog or as the eyes and ears of the general public and to inform their readers about matters of public interest. Often the balancing process can result in a victory for the media, a fact which is usually not reported with as much fanfare as a loss in the courts but there are a number of examples, particularly in the area of court imposed reporting restrictions. In 2009 the House of Lords ruled that the BBC could broadcast a programme concerning the circumstances of an

---

[116] *Standard Verlags GMBH v Austria (No.2)*, European Court of Human Rights, Application no.21277/05, 4 September 2009 at [52]. See also *Times Newspapers Ltd (Nos. 1 and 2) v United Kingdom*, Applications 3002/03 and 23676/03, 10 March 2009.

[117] L. Blom-Cooper, "Press freedom: constitutional right or cultural assumption?" *Public Law* (2008) 260.

individual's acquittal on a charge of rape, lifting an anonymity order and concluding that the individual's right to reputation did not outweigh the right of the BBC to imperil that reputation by their proposed broadcast which was of undoubted public interest.[118] Early in 2010, on the application of *The Guardian*, the Supreme Court set aside anonymity orders made in relation to five individuals who had been granted anonymity in proceedings to challenge their designation by the Treasury as persons reasonably suspected of facilitating acts of terrorism.[119] The Supreme Court stated that a requirement to report in some austere, abstract form, devoid of much of his human interest, could mean that the report would not be read and the information would not be passed on. It found that ultimately such an approach could threaten the viability of newspapers and magazines which could only inform the public if they attracted enough readers and made enough money to survive. It also found that the possibility of some sectors of the press abusing their freedom to report could not, of itself, be a sufficient reason for curtailing that freedom for all members of the press.

The touchstone is now "responsible journalism", responsible journalism as defined by Lord Nicholls in his speech in *Reynolds*. Where responsible journalism has been exercised, and the subject matter is a matter of public interest, the media has an excellent chance of the balancing process resulting in a decision in its favour.

CONCLUSION

Article 10, as given further effect by the HRA, has not granted the media an absolute right to freedom of expression. Whilst it has resulted in some advantages, making it possible for the media to bring legal proceedings seeking to vindicate their right to freedom of expression, or to use it as a shield when interferences with freedom of expression arise, there are also clear disadvantages. However, it is not possible for the media to put forward a convincing case that in the interpretation and application of the HRA, the British judiciary has been biased against it. The case law has developed in this way as a direct result of the nature of Art.10 which is, and has always been a Convention right qualified by other rights and interests. It does not enshrine an absolute right to freedom of expression and has not been interpreted or applied by UK courts or the European Court of

---

[118] *Re Attorney General's Reference No.3 of 1999* [2009] UKHL 34, [2009] 3 WLR 142.
[119] *Application by Guardian News and Media Ltd in Her Majesty's Treasury v Ahmed* [2010] UKSC 1.

Human Rights to produce this result. Nevertheless, there are clear advantages if the subject matter is a matter of public interest and responsible journalism has been exercised. In such instances, the case law demonstrates that the courts are almost always willing to find in favour of the media. As the European Court of Human Rights has held:

> Article 10 does not guarantee a wholly unrestricted freedom of expression to the press, even with respect to press coverage of matters of serious public concern. When exercising its right to freedom of expression, the press must act in a manner consistent with its duties and responsibilities, as required by Article 10(2). These duties and responsibilities assume particular significance when, as in the present case, information imparted by the press is likely to have a serious impact on the reputation and rights of private individuals. Furthermore, the protection afforded by Article 10 to journalists is subject to the proviso that they act in good faith in order to provide accurate and reliable information in accordance with responsible journalism.[120]

To achieve a different outcome, it would be necessary to get rid of Art.10 from UK law and seek to establish, in a British Bill of Rights or the common law, a right to freedom of expression not quite so qualified. However, assuming the UK maintains a Contracting State to the ECHR and member of the European Union, such a development is unlikely. As a Contracting State it is not possible for the UK to cherry pick the Convention rights it would like to have—here one of the media's most desired outcomes would obviously be to have the right to freedom of expression without the right to respect for private life. A more realistic solution is incremental change addressing what are perceived to be some of the worst inroads into freedom of expression. There are signs that this process is already underway. The House of Commons Culture, Media and Sport Committee made a number of recommendations in its report *Press Standards, Privacy and Libel*[121] and in July 2010 the Ministry of Justice announced plans to review the law on defamation to protect free speech and freedom of expression and promised to publish a draft defamation bill for consultation and pre-legislative scrutiny in 2011.[122] Provided such changes also remain respectful of the rights and interests which must be placed in the balance against the media's freedom of expression, everyone might be a little happier and the media just might stop complaining so much about the HRA.

---

[120] *Times Newspapers Ltd (Nos 1 and 2) v United Kingdom*, Applications 3002/03 and 23676/03, 10 March 2009 at [42].

[121] Second Report of Session 2009–2010, Volume I, HC 362-I (London: TSO, 2010).

[122] Ministry of Justice, "Plans to reform defamation law announced", at www.justice.gov. uk. Lord Lester of Herne Hill Q.C. introduced the Defamation Bill, a private member's bill, to the House of Lords on 26 May 2010.

FIGHTING WORDS—THE WAR ON TERROR AND MEDIA FREEDOM

Peter Noorlander

The war on terror has led governments in many countries to introduce legislation that has had a serious impact on the enjoyment of human rights. Most governments have claimed that this crackdown has been necessary to preserve safety and security, that if its citizens wish to continue to live a comfortable life then they will need to accept some restrictions on their freedoms. Two rights in particular have been affected: the right to liberty, and the right to freedom of expression. For example, legislation has been brought in to outlaw various forms of conspiracy to commit terrorist acts, as well as many forms of expression that can be construed to constitute support for terrorism. This legislation has been extended to indirect incitement to terrorism and expressions of support for terrorist acts as well as to direct incitement to violence. In addition, restrictions have been placed on photography of 'restricted' sites such as bridges and railway stations, and journalists' confidential sources are increasingly under pressure. In this chapter, the various restrictions that have been placed on journalism in recent years and the impact of these measures on media freedom will be examined. The extent to which the traditional safeguards against abuse of state power, as provided under constitutional and international human rights law, have been sufficient to protect media freedom will also be considered. Given its self-proclaimed place in the vanguard of the war on terror, much of the focus of this chapter will be on legislative developments and practices in the UK. However, it should not be assumed that the problem referred to in the title of this chapter is limited to the UK. There are also many examples from France, Russia and Turkey which illustrate the pan-European (some would argue, global) nature of the impact of the war on terror on media freedom.

ANTI-TERROR LAWS AND THE MEDIA

Legislation and practices adopted as part of the fight against terror have impacted on the media in three distinct areas. First, journalists have been hindered in their ability to gather and access information. For example, freedom of information laws have been interpreted more restrictively as regards the extent to which the public are able to access information which is alleged to pertain to issues of national security. There are also greater restrictions on the possession of material that may 'aid' terrorism, which impacts in particular the ability of investigative journalists to gather materials to research terrorism-related issues. Second, newly introduced legislation has limited what can be published in the media. This is particularly true of the ever greater restrictions on material that might incite— whether directly or indirectly—terrorism. Finally, the ability of journalists to protect confidential sources has been affected.

Restrictions on Access to Information

Journalists cannot report on the news unless they have access to information, including access to locations as well as to official documents. All of these have been affected by recently introduced anti-terror laws.

Across Europe in the last few years, state secrets laws or UK-type Official Secrets Acts in particular have been frequently relied upon to restrict information available to the public in general and to sanction the media for releasing information supposedly sensitive to national security. For example, the Irish Freedom of Information Act 1998 has been amended to lower the threshold for access to documents relating to national security or defence interests to be refused;[1] and in the Netherlands, the editor-in-chief and two journalists working for the country's biggest newspaper, *De Telegraaf*, had their phones tapped over a long period of time following the publication by the newspaper of leaked government documents relating to the Iraq war.[2] A 2008 report commissioned by the Council of Europe, '*Speaking of Terror*', revealed a catalogue of misuse of state secrets laws, including the prosecution of journalists in Denmark for publishing leaked material from the Ministry of Defence revealing that there were doubts about the existence of weapons of mass destruction in Iraq; the detention of Croatian journalists who reported on war crimes; and the shutting down of a Bulgarian website for posting allegedly classified documents revealing corruption.[3]

---

[1] Freedom of Information (Amendment) Act 2003, number 9 of 2003.

[2] The phone taps were declared legal by the Dutch Review Committee on the Intelligence and Security Services: *inzake de klacht van De Telegraaf c.s. betreffende gedragingen van de AIVD*, decision of 10 November 2009.

[3] D. Banisar, *Speaking of terror: A survey of the effects of counter-terrorism legislation on freedom of the media in Europe*, Media and Information Society Division, Directorate General of Human Rights and Legal Affairs, Council of Europe, November 2008.

There has been occasional condemnation of the overuse or excessive reliance on secrecy laws to shield documents. The UN Human Rights Committee, the independent body set up to supervise the implementation of the International Covenant on Civil and Political Rights, stated in its latest official report on the UK:

> The Committee remains concerned that powers under the Official Secrets Act 1989 have been exercised to frustrate former employees of the Crown from bringing into the public domain issues of genuine public interest, and can be exercised to prevent the media from publishing such matters. It notes that disclosures of information are penalized even where they are not harmful to national security.[4]

The Committee recommended that the UK should "ensure that its powers to protect information genuinely related to matters of national security are narrowly utilized and limited to instances where the release of such information would be harmful to national security."[5]

Other restrictions on access to information are found—perhaps counter intuitively—in freedom of information laws. These have been enacted across Eastern Europe at a very rapid pace throughout the 1990s (they existed in western Europe—except for the UK and Spain—for much longer). These laws typically grant a fairly general right of access with the one hand, but take much of it back with the other—they often contain a good dozen or so clauses detailing the circumstances in which access to government information may be refused. Typically, this includes a fairly broadly worded exemption allowing governments to refuse to disclose material harmful to national security. These exceptions are frequently relied upon. But in some cases, restrictions go further. For example, the UK Freedom of Information Act allows for access to be refused to protect what is known as "the confidentiality of decision-making" in government generally and allows government ministers to override formal enforcement notices against them. Infamously, the former UK Justice Minister, Jack Straw, relied on the concept of "cabinet confidentiality" to veto the release of the minutes of Cabinet meetings held in the run-up to the Iraq war.[6] In a statement to the House of Commons, he explained:

> The Freedom of Information Act has profoundly changed the relationship between citizens, and their elected representatives and the media on the

---

[4] Concluding Observations of the Human Rights Committee, United Kingdom of Great Britain and Northern Ireland, 21 July 2008, CCPR/C/GBR/CO/6, para. 24.

[5] Ibid.

[6] He acted under Section 53 of the Freedom of Information Act 2000.

one hand, and the Government and public authorities on the other. It has, as intended, made the Executive far more open and accountable. The Act provides a regime for freedom of information which is one of the most open and rigorous in the world ... There was, however, a key balancing measure written into the Act, and accepted by Parliament. This was to provide ... that in specific circumstances Ministers and certain others could override a decision of the commissioner or tribunal requiring the release of information ... In December 2006, the Cabinet Office received a freedom of information request for Cabinet minutes and records relating to the meetings that it held between 7 and 17 March 2003, where the Attorney-General's legal advice concerning military action against Iraq was considered and discussed. There were two such meetings, on 13 and 17 March. The Cabinet Office refused the request, citing the Act's exemptions for information relating to policy development and ministerial communications ... The [Information Tribunal] decided that the public interest balance fell in favour of release of the minutes... To permit the commissioner's and the tribunal's view of the public interest to prevail would, in my judgment, risk serious damage to Cabinet government—an essential principle of British parliamentary democracy. That eventuality is not in the public interest. Cabinet is the pinnacle of the decision-making machinery of government. It is the forum in which debates on the issues of greatest significance and complexity are conducted. Whether the nation was to take military action was indisputably of the utmost seriousness. However, I disagree with the reasoning of the majority of the tribunal ... [7]

The Binyam Mohamed litigation in the UK courts provides another interesting example of the depth of the desire of security services not to reveal information they believe to be damaging to national security interests. Binyam Mohamed was an Ethiopian national who was detained in Guantanamo Bay prison between 2004 and 2009, when he was eventually released and allowed to return to the UK, the country where he had been granted asylum several years earlier. He was captured and transported under the US extraordinary rendition program, and since his release has claimed that evidence used against him by the US was obtained through torture. Litigation is currently ongoing (at the time of writing) concerning this claim as well as the extent of UK knowledge of the torture he suffered. In the course of the litigation the High Court took the unusual step of

---

[7] Hansards, House of Commons, 24 February 2009, col. 153 et seq. This was the first time the veto had ever been used. The second time was on 10 December 2009, when Jack Straw issued a notice overruling a decision by the Information Commissioner while an appeal to the Information Tribunal was still pending: Certificate of the Secretary Of State for Justice, made in accordance with Section 53(2) of the Freedom Of Information Act 2000, 10 December 2009, published at http://www.justice.gov.uk/news/docs/section53-certificate .pdf.

inviting the press to make an application for the publication of details of Binyam Mohamed's 'treatment' at the hand of US agents which had been excised from an earlier judgment at the request of the UK Government.[8] The press duly applied, and the UK Foreign Secretary responded that if publication was allowed then the US would cut its intelligence sharing ties with the UK. This, he argued, would be harmful to the public interest. After several more rounds of litigation and a change in US Administration which had seen the new US President announce an 'era of openness' which had already resulted in the release of some CIA memos that detailed torture, the High Court ruled on 16 October 2009 that there was a "compelling public interest" in disclosing the paragraphs from the judgment that had initially been removed.[9] The paragraphs summarised CIA documents that had been passed on to MI5 which related to the treatment suffered by Binyam Mohamed. The judges stated that "we cannot accept the assertion that there is anything of an intelligence nature in the redacted paragraphs ... it cannot be suggested that information as to how officials of the US Government admitted treating Binyam Mohammed during his interrogation is information that can in any democratic society governed by the rule of law be characterised as 'secret' or as 'intelligence'."[10] In a further judgment, in November 2009, the judges agreed that the paragraphs should remain excised pending the government's appeal but expressed surprise that the Foreign Secretary wished to withhold material that had already been released into the public domain by the new US administration.[11] The appeal failed[12] and the government eventually published the excised paragraphs—prompted in large part by a US judgment from December 2009 that acknowledged the torture suffered by Mohamed.[13] The case amply demonstrates the traditional anxieties of many governments when it comes to releasing information that pertains to national security or defence interests.

---

[8] *Mohamed, R (on the application of) v Secretary of State for Foreign & Commonwealth Affairs (3)* [2008] EWHC 2519 (Admin) (22 October 2008).

[9] *Mohamed, R (on the application of) v Secretary of State for Foreign & Commonwealth Affairs (Rev 1)* [2009] EWHC 2549 (Admin) (16 October 2009).

[10] Ibid., paras. 103, 93.

[11] *Mohamed, R (on the application of) v Secretary of State for Foreign & Commonwealth Affairs* [2009] EWHC 2973 (Admin) (19 November 2009).

[12] Mohamed, R (on the application of) v Secretary of State for Foreign & Commonwealth Affairs [2010] EWCA Civ 65 (10 February 2010).

[13] Farhi Saeed Bin MOHAMMED, et al., Petitioners, v. Barack H. OBAMA, et al., Respondents., United States District Court, District of Columbia, 689 F.Supp.2d 38 (2009). See Hansard, HC, 10 Feb 2010 col.913 for the Foreign Secretary's statement on the matter.

Anti-terror laws have also placed important restrictions on other journalistic activities. Many countries already have legislation in place prohibiting photography in 'restricted places'; and recent years have seen an increased use of these laws. One infamous incident occurred in Greece in late 2001, when a group of Dutch and English 'plane spotters' were arrested and served prison sentences for taking photograph of military planes at an air show. They were finally acquitted after a year-long legal battle.[14] Similarly, the editor of Swiss weekly *Sonntags Blick* had to battle in court for nearly two years to get his conviction overturned following the publication of photos of an underground bunker.[15]

Across Europe, it is increasingly common practice for police—often acting without any clear legal basis—to harass photographers who take pictures of sensitive situations (large public demonstrations, for example, or at airports) and demand they delete their photographs. The Council of Europe's 'Speaking of Terror' report catalogues instances of such cases in Russia, Montenegro and Spain, amongst others.[16] In September 2009, the Finnish Supreme Court rejected a claim from a photojournalist who had been convicted for ignoring a police order to stop reporting on a demonstration at the Asia-Europe meeting in Helsinki in 2006.[17] There has been particular controversy in the UK, where legislation has been introduced specifically targeted at photographers. Under Section 76 of the UK Counter-Terrorism Act 2008, it is a criminal offence to take any photographs that are "likely to be useful to a person committing or preparing an act of terrorism."[18] UK photographers are extremely wary of this new provision which became law in February of 2009. Experience has taught them that police have interpreted their anti-terror powers very broadly—many photojournalists have been harassed by police and even arrested under the stop and search powers of Section 44 of the Terrorism Act 2000[19]—and following concern that this new power was being used to stop photographers taking pictures of demonstrations or of police officers, the Home

---

[14] *Greek Appeals Court Overturns Conviction of 14 Plane Spotters*, New York Times, 7 November 2002.
[15] As detailed in *Speaking of Terror*, note 4, 17.
[16] *Speaking of Terror*, note 4, 17.
[17] *Finland's Supreme Court Denies Reporter's Appeal over Conviction for Ignoring Police Order to Stop Filming Demonstration*, International Press Institute, 7 September 2009.
[18] Counter-Terrorism Act 2008, Ch. 28.
[19] Terrorism Act 2000 (c. 11).

Office and Metropolitan Police were forced to issue new guidance on the implementation of the powers in August 2009.[20]

Restrictions on what can be Published

As well as restricting access to information and limiting the ability of journalists to gather information, laws and practices introduced in the war against terror have placed increasingly vague and wide-ranging restrictions on what can be published. This has been particularly true of legislation put in place to criminalise not only direct incitement to terrorism, but also "indirect" incitement, "apology" of terrorism and in the UK, the "encouragement" of terrorism.

All European countries prohibit incitement to murder and terrorism, and from a free speech perspective this is uncontroversial. International human rights law has long recognised that direct incitement to hatred and violence is not a protected form of expression.[21] However, until the mid-2000s, only France and Spain had specific legislation prohibiting 'apology' of terrorism—the expression of support for terrorism, but falling short of direct incitement.[22] The list of States with these laws grew rapidly with the adoption of the Council of Europe's Convention on the Prevention of Terrorism in May 2005[23] which called on States to prohibit "public provocation to commit a terrorist offence ... where such conduct, whether or not directly advocating terrorist offences, causes a danger that one or more such offences may be committed."[24] In 2008, the EU Framework Decision on Combating Terrorism was amended to include similar language.[25] As a result, a growing number of States now ban indirect forms of incitement to terrorism, and the Council of Europe has itself expressed

---

[20] Home Office circular 012/2009, *Photography and Counter-Terrorism legislation*, 18 August 2009. See also the Met's *Photography Advice*, http://www.met.police.uk/about/photography.htm.

[21] See, for example, Article 20(2) of the Covenant on Civil and Political Rights, adopted by General Assembly resolution 2200A (XXI) of 16 December 1966, entry into force 23 March 1976, which states: "Any advocacy of national, racial or religious hatred that constitutes incitement to discrimination, hostility or violence shall be prohibited by law."

[22] See the Council of Europe's report *'Apologie du terrorisme and 'incitement to terrorism'*, Committee of Experts on Terrorism (CODEXTER), July 2004.

[23] Council of Europe Convention on the Prevention of Terrorism, Warsaw, 16 May 2005, CETS No. 196, entry into force 1 June 2007.

[24] Ibid., Article 5.

[25] Council Framework Decision 2008/919/JHA of 28 November 2008 amending Framework Decision 2002/475/JHA on combating terrorism, Official Journal L 330, 09/12/2008, 21.

concern and called on its Member States to review the impact these laws have had on human rights and media freedom.[26]

The laws that have been adopted on 'indirect incitement' have had a particular impact on small and minority publications. Police and prosecution authorities often judge that mainstream media are a low-risk venture when it comes to inciting terrorism but place minority publications under enhanced scrutiny. In France and Spain, for example, this has resulted in prosecutions of Basque outlets for publications that might have been published elsewhere without any problems. In the immediate aftermath of 9/11, a Basque cartoonist was convicted for publication of a cartoon of the twin towers falling down, with the caption "we've all dreamt of it—Hamas did it".[27] The French courts judged that there was a real risk that the cartoon would incite others to similar violence.[28]

Of all European states, the UK undoubtedly has the most vaguely worded and potentially far-reaching restrictions on inciting and 'encouraging' terrorism. Under the Terrorism Act 2006, a criminal offence is committed if a person:

> ... publishes a statement to which this section applies or causes another to publish such a statement; and
> at the time he publishes it or causes it to be published, he—
> (i) intends members of the public to be directly or indirectly encouraged or otherwise induced by the statement to commit, prepare or instigate acts of terrorism or Convention offences; or
> (ii) is reckless as to whether members of the public will be directly or indirectly encouraged or otherwise induced by the statement to commit, prepare or instigate such acts or offences.[29]

The next paragraph clarifies what it means to "indirectly encourage or otherwise induce" someone to commit terror:

> the statements that are likely to be understood by members of the public as indirectly encouraging the commission or preparation of acts of terrorism or Convention offences include every statement which—
> (a) glorifies the commission or preparation (whether in the past, in the future or generally) of such acts or offences; and
> (b) is a statement from which those members of the public could reasonably be expected to infer that what is being glorified is being glorified as conduct that should be emulated by them in existing circumstances.[30]

---

[26] Committee of Ministers Resolution, MCM(2009)011, 29 May 2009.
[27] As published in the magazine *Ekaitza*, 13 September 2001, 3.
[28] Court of Appeal, Pau, 24 September 2002; Court of Cassation, 25 March 2003, as summarised in *Leroy v. France*, 2 October 2008, no. 36109/03.
[29] Terrorism Act 2006 (c. 11), Section 2.
[30] Ibid., Section 3.

The final paragraphs state:

> For the purposes of this section the questions how a statement is likely to be understood and what members of the public could reasonably be expected to infer from it must be determined having regard both—
> (a) to the contents of the statement as a whole; and
> (b) to the circumstances and manner of its publication.
> ...
>
> It is irrelevant for the purposes of subsections (1) to (3)—
> (a) whether anything mentioned in those subsections relates to the commission, preparation or instigation of one or more particular acts of terrorism or Convention offences, of acts of terrorism or Convention offences of a particular description or of acts of terrorism or Convention offences generally; and,
> (b) whether any person is in fact encouraged or induced by the statement to commit, prepare or instigate any such act or offence.[31]

This is probably the most poorly drafted criminal offence in English parliamentary history. What makes it particularly offensive to media freedom is its vast potential scope of application, and the reference to context and circumstances and manner of the publication. In essence, this sends a signal that the section is most likely to be used against minority publications—it is telling Muslim publications in particular that they'd better watch what they publish.[32]

Parliament's Joint Committee on Human Rights assessed the legislation in its First Report of 2007, and concluded that "the encouragement of terrorism offence in section 1 of the Terrorism Act 2006 [is] incompatible with the requirement ... that the establishment of any new offence of public provocation to commit a terrorist offence be compatible with the right to freedom of expression, and proportionate to the legitimate aim pursued".[33] It advised, ironically, that because of this shortcoming, the UK could not ratify the Council of Europe Convention on the Prevention of Terrorism which requires any newly introduced offences to be compatible with human rights.

There do not appear to have been many prosecutions under the encouragement provisions of the 2006 Act;[34] earlier law criminalising incitement

---

[31] Ibid.

[32] In parliamentary debates, the Home Secretary refused to narrow down the range of publications that would be caught under the provision, stating that he wished to send a "strong message to all those who are involved in recruiting terrorists": Hansard, HC, 15 February 2006, col. 1434.

[33] Joint Committee On Human Rights—Thirteenth Report, Session 2007–08.

[34] One of the rare prosecutions, against Muslim preacher Abu Izzadeen, ended with the jury unable to reach a verdict—although it did convict Izzadeen on charges of inciting

to murder and directly inciting terrorism is more commonly used against suspects such as hate preachers.[35] But the chilling effect of the law has been serious. Because of its very broad wording and the indication that it is likely to be used against minority Muslim publications, the prohibition of encouragement of terrorism has resulted in significant self-censorship—publishers will not want to fall foul of a terrorist offence. Thus, it has dampened public debate precisely at a time when a free, open and frank debate about terrorism and its causes is most needed.

The UN Human Rights Committee has called on the UK to revise Section 1. It has stated:

> The Committee notes with concern that the offence of "encouragement of terrorism" has been defined in section 1 of the Terrorism Act 2006 in broad and vague terms. In particular, a person can commit the offence even when he or she did not intend members of the public to be directly or indirectly encouraged by his or her statement to commit acts of terrorism, but where his or her statement was understood by some members of the public as encouragement to commit such acts.

> The State party should consider amending section 1 of the Terrorism Act 2006 dealing with "encouragement of terrorism" so that its application does not lead to a disproportionate interference with freedom of expression.[36]

While the encouragement provision in the UK's Terrorism Act 2006 is particularly poorly drafted, other European countries do have similar broad-ranging provisions—and, unlike the UK, they have used them. In Spain, for example, an often-quoted example of the use of the criminal law prohibition on 'apology' of terrorism was the trial of a Basque punk band[37]— who were eventually acquitted. There have been numerous other prosecutions in Spain over the last few years, and the Supreme Court has devoted considerable time to narrowing down the scope of the offence.[38] The most recent reported prosecution for 'glorification' of terrorism (*enaltecimiento del terrorismo* being the Spanish term used) is of a young man who posted comments that were disrespectful of two policemen

---

terrorism overseas and fundraising for terrorism. BBC news, 17 April 2008: http://news.bbc.co.uk/1/hi/uk/7352969.stm.

[35] See, for example, the conviction of Abu Hamza in February 2006 for inciting murder.

[36] Concluding Observations of the Human Rights Committee, United Kingdom of Great Britain and Northern Ireland, 21 July 2008, CCPR/C/GBR/CO/6, para. 26.

[37] Supreme Court judgment 656/2007, 17 July 2007 (Criminal).

[38] Most recently in its judgment of 5 June 2009, Resolution 676/2009 (Criminal).

killed in a terrorist attack in Spain in July 2009[39]. In Turkey, wide-ranging prohibitions on terrorist propaganda are often used against members and supporters of the Kurdistan Workers Party (the PKK). The illegitimacy of the PKK prosecutions in particular is highlighted by the very high percentage of violations of the right to freedom of expression found by the European Court of Human Rights when these cases eventually reach it.

In Russia, laws prohibiting "extremism" (used as the equivalent of terrorism elsewhere) have even been used to keep the US cartoon *South Park* off the air as well as to target dissident political voices. As it did with the UK, the UN Human Rights Committee issued very critical comments on the Russian legislation, citing concerns "that the extremism laws are being used to target organizations and individuals critical of the Government" and regretting "that the definition of "extremist activity" in the Federal Law on Combating Extremist Activity remains vague, allowing for arbitrariness in its application."[40] It recommended that the Russian government "should revise the Federal Law on Combating Extremist Activity with a view to making the definition of "extremist activity" more precise so as to exclude any possibility of arbitrary application".[41]

Protection of Sources and Associated Issues

From time to time, journalists rely on confidential sources for information. This is particularly true for investigative journalists and journalists reporting on sensitive matters. Government employees and others witnessing wrong-doing are often hesitant to 'go public' with their concerns and will approach journalists with information only on the condition that their names are kept confidential. Hundreds of stories are reported in this way every year and many in-house codes of ethics remind journalists that sources are not to be revealed. For example, the English *Times* Code of Conduct states: "Journalists have a moral obligation to protect confidential sources of information." And the ethical code adopted by the Dutch *Society of Editors-in-Chief* ("Nederlands Genootschap van

---

[39] *Detenido un hombre por enaltecimiento del terrorismo a través de Internet*, EUROPA PRESS 1 December 2009.

[40] Concluding observations of the Human Rights Committee, CCPR/C/RUS/CO/6, 29 October 2009, para. 24.

[41] Ibid.

Hoofdredacteuren") states that journalists "must protect sources who have been promised confidentiality".[42]

It is well-established that journalists are entitled as a matter of principle to keep sources confidential. In a landmark judgment, the European Court of Human Rights held in 1996 that:

> Protection of journalistic sources is one of the basic conditions for press freedom as is reflected in the laws and professional codes of conduct in a number of Contracting States and is affirmed in several international instruments on journalistic freedoms. Without such protection, sources may be deterred from assisting the press in informing the public on matters of public interest. As a result, the vital public-watchdog role of the press may be undermined and the ability of the press to provide accurate and reliable information may be adversely affected.[43]

However, while most countries will agree that journalistic sources should be protected as a matter of principle,[44] it is not an absolute privilege—meaning that in certain circumstances, journalists can be compelled to disclose who their sources are. The important question that arises is: under what circumstances can a journalist be compelled to disclose their sources? This is a highly contentious issue. It is tempting for police and prosecution authorities, when they see a publication that has been written by someone who has obviously had good access to, say, a terrorist group, to demand that the journalist concerned hand over all their documents—it is probable that there is something there that will aid their investigations. But to allow this would be to misunderstand both the function of journalism in society—to report on matters of public interest (and there can be fewer matters of as high importance as terrorism)—and the fact that, as soon as it becomes known that police have access to journalists' sources, these sources will soon run dry.

Precisely the above scenario occurred in the UK in the case of Shiv Malik, last year. Shiv Malik had written a book on terrorism which included a number of interviews with a terrorist suspect. Police thought he must have information and material of interest and obtained an order requiring Mr Malik to hand over "all material" connected with the book. Mr Malik appealed and the High Court, on review, agreed that police had gone on a

---

[42] Code for Journalism, published at http://www.genootschapvanhoofdredacteuren.nl/het_genootschap/code-voor-de-journalistiek.html.

[43] *Goodwin v. the United Kingdom*, no. 17488/90, 27 March 1996, para. 39.

[44] With the notable exception of the United States, where there is no federal legislation to protect sources although the vast majority of the US States do have so-called 'shield laws'.

fishing expedition: they had obtained an extremely wide order in the hope that among the materials Mr Malik would hand over, there might be something of interest. This, the Court ruled, was disproportionate and breached the right of Mr Malik to protect his sources of information. Mr Malik's victory turned out to be a pyrrhic one, however, since the judge ruled that a narrower production order could be made[45] and he was ordered, a week later, to hand over a cache of journalistic materials.[46]

There have been similar cases across Europe, and journalists have even served time in prison for refusing to hand over material that could identify their sources of information—a strong illustration of how important their sources are to them. For example, in France in 2007, a journalist was detained for two days for refusing to disclose the source of leaked documents concerning the 9/11 attack;[47] and in the Netherlands, two journalists served two days in prison in 2006 for refusing to disclose the source of intelligence dossiers they had published concerning the case of a notorious criminal.[48]

The case of the Dutch journalists, which at the time of writing is pending before the European Court of Human Rights,[49] had another worrying aspect: not only were they subject to a demand for disclosure of their sources, they were also placed under surveillance and their phones were tapped. The case has dragged on for several years and the Dutch Review Committee on the Intelligence and Security Services recently ruled that the phone taps had been legal "but premature".[50] The UN Human Rights Committee has expressed its concern about the Dutch practice in this regard.[51]

---

[45] *Malik v Manchester Crown Court & Ors* [2008] EWHC 1362 (Admin) (19 June 2008).

[46] *Shiv Malik given seven days by court to hand over terror notes*, Press Gazette, 26 June 2008.

[47] *Gardé à vue, reportage à froid*, Guillaume Dasquié, Le Monde, 26 December 2007.

[48] See Villamedia news archive: http://www.villamedia.nl/n/nieuwsarchief/2006nov .htm.

[49] A partial admissibility decision has been adopted striking out the journalists associations who had joined in the application since they could not be regarded as 'victims' under article 34 ECHR, and adjourning the remainder for further consideration: *Uitgeversmaatschappij De Telegraaf B.V. and others v. the Netherlands*, Application no. 39315/06, partial admissibility decision of 18 May 2010.

[50] Review Committee on the Intelligence and Security Services: *inzake de klacht van De Telegraaf c.s. betreffende gedragingen van de AIVD*, Note 3. See http://www.rnw.nl/english/ article/phone-taps-dutch-journalists-were-legal for a report on the case.

[51] The UN Human Rights Committee recently criticised Dutch intercept laws stating its concern that "that any use of wire and telephone taps should be minimized so that only pertinent evidence is gathered and that a judge should supervise its use." Concluding observations of the Human Rights Committee, CCPR/C/NLD/CO/4, 25 August 2009, para. 14.

The use of surveillance to undermine source protection laws is a particularly concerning development that seems to have spread to other countries. According to the Council of Europe's *Speaking of Terror* report, police in Germany have gone so far as to pay journalists to spy on their colleagues;[52] while in the United States, ABC news reporters had their phones tapped and New York Times and Washington Post journalists were placed under surveillance in the name of the 'war on terror'.[53] In reality, they had done nothing more heinous than to report on CIA practices in Eastern Europe. Practices such as these severely undermine not just the confidentiality of journalists' sources but strike at the heart of media freedom.

ANTI-TERROR LAWS AND THE EUROPEAN COURT OF HUMAN RIGHTS

Most States have not denied that many of their anti-terror laws and practices have impacted on media freedom and freedom of expression. However, they have argued that the impact has been a proportionate restriction necessary to protect public order and national security. In this section, I will review how the European Court of Human Rights, the ultimate arbiter on human rights questions for Council of Europe Member States, has dealt with that claim.

The European Convention on Human Rights (and international human rights law generally) allows restrictions on the right to freedom of expression if three conditions have been satisfied.[54] First, the interference must be provided for by law. The European Court of Human Rights has stated that this requirement will be fulfilled only where the law is accessible and "formulated with sufficient precision to enable the citizen to regulate his

---

[52] *Speaking of Terror*, note 4, 29.

[53] *Federal Source to ABC News: We Know Who You're Calling*, 15 May 2006: http://blogs .abcnews.com/theblotter/2006/05/federal_source_.html.

[54] This 'three-part test' follows from the text of Article 10(2) of the European Convention of Human Rights, which states: "The exercise of these freedoms, since it carries with it duties and responsibilities, may be subject to such formalities, conditions, restrictions or penalties as are prescribed by law and are necessary in a democratic society, in the interests of national security, territorial integrity or public safety, for the prevention of disorder or crime, for the protection of health or morals, for the protection of the reputation or rights of others, for preventing the disclosure of information received in confidence, or for maintaining the authority and impartiality of the judiciary." Convention for the Protection of Human Rights and Fundamental Freedoms, Adopted 4 November 1950, E.T.S. No. 5, entered into force 3 September 1953. Paragraph (3) of the Covenant on Civil and Political Rights, the main global human rights treaty, contains a similar 'clawback' formula: Covenant on Civil and Political Rights, adopted by UN General Assembly Resolution 2200A (XXI), 16 December 1966, entered into force 3 January 1976.

conduct."[55] Second, the interference must pursue one of the legitimate aims listed in the treaty in question. These aims include public order and national security, which are commonly invoked to justify the war on terror. Third, the restriction must be necessary and proportionate to secure the legitimate aim. Addressing terrorism is clearly a legitimate aim, but where measures have an excessive impact on freedom of expression, or could be drafted more narrowly and still achieve the aim, they cannot be justified.

In practice, it is the third part of this test that is most contentious. It is usually not contested that a measure complained of pursued the aim of protecting national security[56] or maintaining public order. However, what is a 'necessary' restriction is the subject of much debate.

As a preliminary matter, it should also be noted that the definition of 'national security' is not internationally agreed on. International courts have generally accepted at face value governments' claims that restrictions on freedom of expression were aimed at protecting national security. For example, in the *Observer and Guardian v. United Kingdom*, the European Court of Human Rights did not question whether a British ban on the memoirs of a former secret agent served a national security goal, even though the book had already been published and circulated widely in Australia and the USA. Instead, the Court found that the ban failed the necessity test since any possible harm to national security had already become irreversible due to prior publication.[57]

The Human Rights Committee has at least made it clear that suppression of democratic discourse and human rights cannot be justified on the grounds of national security:

> [T]he legitimate objective of safeguarding and indeed strengthening national unity under difficult political circumstances cannot be achieved by attempting to muzzle advocacy of multi-party democracy, democratic tenets and human rights; in this regard, the question of deciding which measures might meet the "necessity" test in such situations does not arise.[58]

---

[55] *The Sunday Times v. The United Kingdom*, 26 April 1979, Application No. 6538/74, para. 49.

[56] The definition of 'national security' is not usually closely scrutinised by courts. In cases such as the Binyam Mohamed case referred to earlier, it is often suspected and speculated in the media that the real aim behind the non-disclosure of the contested paragraphs in the judgment is to guard against national embarrassment rather than to guard national security.

[57] *Observer and Guardian v. United Kingdom*, 26 November 1991, Application No. 13585/88 (European Court of Human Rights), paras. 56–71.

[58] *Mukong v. Cameroon*, UN Human Rights Committee decision of 21 July 1994, Communcation no. 458/1991, para. 9.7.

The U.N. Sub-Commission on Prevention of Discrimination and Protection of Minorities has attempted to fill this void in its *Siracusa Principles*.[59] Principle B(iv) states:

> National security may be invoked to justify measures limiting certain rights only when they are taken to protect the existence of the nation or its territorial integrity or political independence against force or threat of force.
>
> National security cannot be invoked as a reason for imposing limitations to prevent merely local or relatively isolated threats to law and order.
>
> National security cannot be used as a pretext for imposing vague or arbitrary limitations and may only be invoked when there exists adequate safeguards and effective remedies against abuse....

A similar definition is found in the free speech organisation ARTICLE 19's *Johannesburg Principles*.[60] However, neither definition has been accepted in full by the courts who have instead preferred to leave the definitional question open.[61]

What Restrictions are "Necessary in a Democratic Society"

The question when a restriction is "necessary" in the interests of national security, public order or any other of the aims mentioned in Article 10(2) of the European Convention on Human Rights is harder to answer now than it was five years ago. Authoritative jurisprudence from the European Court of Human Rights used to set a high threshold and required Governments to demonstrate intent to incite violence, as well as a clear nexus between the expression it had restricted and a likelihood of violence. The late 1990s case of *Karatas v. Turkey* is instructive. The applicant in this case had been convicted for the publication of poetry that allegedly condoned and glorified acts of terrorism. The Court accepted as a matter of fact that in Turkey violent terrorist attacks occurred regularly. However, the Court emphasised that even in the context of regular threats to national security, there needed to be a causal connection between the applicant's poetry and any violence that occurred in the region. The Court stated:

---

[59] *Siracusa Principles on the Limitation and Derogation of Provisions in the International Covenant on Civil and Political Rights*, Annex, UN Doc E/CN.4/1984/4 (1984). Available for download at http://www1.umn.edu/humanrts/instree/siracusaprinciples.html.

[60] *Johannesburg Principles on National Security, Freedom of Expression and Access to Information*, adopted October 1995: www.article19.org.

[61] See, for example, the House of Lords judgment in *Secretary of State For The Home Department v. Rehman (AP)*, [2001] UKHL 47.

In the instant case, the poems had an obvious political dimension. Using colourful imagery, they expressed deep-rooted discontent with the lot of the population of Kurdish origin in Turkey. In that connection, the Court recalls that there is little scope under Article 10 § 2 of the Convention for restrictions on political speech or on debate on matters of public interest ... In a democratic system the actions or omissions of the government must be subject to the close scrutiny not only of the legislative and judicial authorities but also of public opinion.

Moreover, the dominant position which the government occupies makes it necessary for it to display restraint in resorting to criminal proceedings, particularly where other means are available for replying to the unjustified attacks and criticisms of its adversaries ... [E]ven though some of the passages from the poems seem very aggressive in tone and to call for the use of violence, the Court considers that the fact that they were artistic in nature and of limited impact made them less a call to an uprising than an expression of deep distress in the face of a difficult political situation.[62]

This judgment, and a string of the Court's other 'Turkish' cases on incitement to terrorism, ought to bar the enforcement of many of 'indirect incitement' laws discussed in the previous section but has not so far been invoked in any judicial proceedings.

Similarly, the European Court of Human Rights in the 1990s was a standard-setter on the issue of protection of sources. It's seminal *Goodwin* judgment has been referred to above;[63] and the Court continued its strong protection of journalists sources in cases such as *Roemen Schmit v. Luxembourg*,[64] in which it extended the principle of protection of sources to newsroom searches; and *Tillack v. Belgium*, in which it effectively overruled the European Court of Justice.[65]

However, in recent years, the Court has at times strayed from the strict line it set in the 1980s, 90s and early 2000s, and has appeared to allow some—particularly western-European—States a greater margin of appreciation.

The recent decision of the Court in *Leroy v. France* is a particular example. As stated above, the case concerned a cartoon of the Twin Towers published in a Basque weekly in the direct aftermath of 9/11, with the caption "we've all dreamt of it—Hamas did it" (the caption parodied a well-known advertising slogan). The newspaper received numerous letters and emails protesting at the cartoon and published these in its next issue along with

---

[62] 8 July 1999, Application No. 23168/94, paras. 50–52.
[63] Note 39.
[64] 25 February 2003, Application no. 51772/99.
[65] 27 November 2007, Application no. 20477/05.

the cartoonist's apology that he hadn't intended to be hurtful. However, criminal proceedings were instituted for condoning terrorism and the cartoonist was convicted and sentenced to a fine. The Pau Court of Appeal upheld the judgment of the first-instance court, holding that "by making a direct allusion to the massive attacks on Manhattan, by attributing these attacks to a well-known terrorist organisation and by idealising this lethal project through the use of the verb 'to dream', [thus] unequivocally praising an act of death, the cartoonist justifies the use of terrorism, identifies himself through his use of the first person plural ("We") with this method of destruction, which is presented as the culmination of a dream and, finally, indirectly encourages the potential reader to evaluate positively the successful commission of a criminal act." Further appeal was refused.

In a sparsely reasoned judgment, the European Court of Human Rights held that the conviction did not violate the right to freedom of expression. It considered that although the domestic courts had not taken the applicant's intentions into account, they had examined whether the context of the case and the public interest justified the possible use of a measure of provocation or exaggeration. The Court further considered that publication in the direct aftermath of 9/11 could be understood as a call to action, and it was this factor—the date of publication—that was crucial, particularly in a sensitive region such as the Basque country.[66] Referral to the Grand Chamber was refused.[67] *Willem v. France* is a similar decision: this case concerned a French mayor who had called for a boycott of Israeli products following atrocities committed by the Israeli army in Palestine. He was prosecuted and convicted under French law for inciting discrimination, and the European Court of Human Rights upheld the conviction in a similarly tersely reasoned judgment.[68]

The Third Section decision in *Sanoma v. the Netherlands* is another example. This case concerned the a stand-off between Dutch police and the editor of a magazine which resulted, in the early hours of the morning and following (briefly) the detention of the editor and threats by the police to shut down the magazine's premises and conduct a thorough search, in the handing over of a CD-rom with photographs of cars that had taken part in a street race. What was particularly concerning is that the police acted without any formal prior judicial scrutiny, and without proof of exhaustion of alternative sources of information. The Third Section of the

---

[66] Application no. 36109/03, Judgment 2 October 2008.
[67] Registrar press release 333, 21 April 2009.
[68] 16 July 2009, Application no. 10883/05.

European Court of Human Rights found that this scenario did not violate the applicant's rights, despite agreeing that the police and public prosecutors had displayed "a regrettable lack of moderation".[69] There is a withering dissent by Judge Power, who warns that "the majority merely wags a judicial finger in the direction of the Netherlands authorities but sends out a dangerous signal to police forces throughout Europe, some of whose members may, at times, be tempted to display a similar "regrettable lack of moderation". To my mind the judgment will render it almost impossible for journalists to rest secure in the knowledge that, as a matter of general legal principle, their confidential sources and the materials obtained thereby are protected at law."[70]

The case was accepted for review by the Court's Grand Chamber,[71] and a grand coalition of media groups and NGOs lodged an intervention indicating their strong concern that if this precedent stands, police forces and public prosecutors across Europe may consider themselves free to target journalists for information and the media may find itself the first resort—not the last—when the authorities begin investigations into newsworthy subjects.[72] The Grand Chamber, in a unanimous and strongly worded judgment, overruled the Third Section's decision, referring to the situation that had taken place as "scarcely compatible with the rule of law".[73] The Dutch judge in the Grand Chamber, who also sat in the Third Section and voted with the majority decision finding 'no violation', changed his mind on the basis that the Third Section decision ultimately set a very poor precedent. In his Concurring Opinion, he writes:

> "What would your answer have been if a similar case, with a comparable show of force by the police and the prosecution service, had been brought before us from one of the new democracies?" is a question which I have been asked by a colleague from one of those countries. "Would you still have allowed yourself to be satisfied by the involvement, at the eleventh hour, of a judge who has no legal competence in the matter?"

---

[69] 14 September 2009, Application no. 38224/03.
[70] Ibid.
[71] Registrar press release 721, 1 October 2009.
[72] The intervention has been lodged by the Media Legal Defence Initiative, ARTICLE 19, the Open Society Justice Initiative and the Committee to Protect Journalists, with an additional Statement of Support from The Associated Press, Bloomberg News, Index on Censorship, The European Newspaper Publishers Association (ENPA), Condé Nast Publications, Hearst Corporation, The National Geographic Society, The New York Times Company, La Repubblica, Reuters, Time Inc., The Washington Post, and The World Association of Newspapers and News Publishers (WAN-IFRA).
[73] *Sanoma Uitgevers B.V. v. the Netherlands*, Decision of 14 September 2010.

> A remark of similar purport was made in the dissenting opinion appended to the Chamber judgment: "In finding no violation, the majority merely wags a judicial finger in the direction of the Netherlands authorities but sends out a dangerous signal to police forces throughout Europe, some of whose members may, at times, be tempted to display a similar 'regrettable lack of moderation.'"
>
> That was ultimately the push I needed to be persuaded to cross the line and espouse an opinion opposite to that which I held earlier. I am bound to admit that the Grand Chamber's judgment provides clear guidance for the legislation needed and the way in which issues like these should be addressed in future.

While this indicates a helpful judicial awareness of the impact of ECHR decisions across the continent, it does not stand out as a shining example of legal reasoning. These kind of 'political' considerations in ECHR freedom of expression decisions may also help explain some of the inconsistency in its case law in this regard.

I should stress that my criticism of the European Court is not that it has permanently departed from its strong pro-speech jurisprudence. In its most recent judgment on the protection of journalistic sources, *Financial Times Ltd and Others v. the United Kingdom*, the Court goes back to the *Goodwin* standard and hands down a strongly worded judgment finding the UK in violation of its obligations.[74] But what is concerning is that the European Court has become unpredictable and has failed, in an increasing number of cases, to apply its own standards. It is interesting to note that many of the cases in which the Court allows States a greater margin are those against long-established democracies—France, the Netherlands—while its decisions in 'Turkish' cases, for example, have consistently applied a far stricter standard. This apparent inconsistency leads to the Court's own standards being called into question—a process that ultimately must be detrimental to the free flow of information and ideas. Highly respected practising lawyers as well as academics have expressed their concern at this process.[75]

In contrast, German Courts have been consistently staunch in their defence of constitutionally guaranteed rights at risk in the war on terror.

---

[74] 15 December 2009, Application no. 821/03.
[75] It is particularly concerning that this process is taking place alongside the apparent re-assessment by the Court of the importance of reputation and privacy, which has led to a sea-change in its assessment of Article 10 libel complaints that come to it. See, in particular, Gavin Millar QC, *Whither the spirit of Lingens*, European Human Rights Law Review, Issue 3 2009.

The decision of the Constitutional Court in the *Cicero* case in particular has been held up as an example of how courts should protect media freedom.[76] The case concerned a police raid on the publishers of the magazine *Cicero*, which had published an article about Al Qaeda leader al-Zarkawi which cited from a classified police document. The prosecutors accused the journalists concerned of aiding and abetting the leaking of state secrets and therefore argued that the search of *Cicero*'s offices was legitimate as it would help them identify the source of the leak. The Constitutional Court disagreed, holding that search and seizure orders against media houses are unconstitutional if they are "purely or mainly intended to detect the identity of an informant". The Court furthermore strengthened the degree of suspicion of involvement in crime required for a search to be legitimately conducted. It held that, in light of the constitutional guarantee of freedom of the press, mere publication of a classified document is not sufficient to create probable cause that the author is guilty of aiding and abetting the leaking of state secrets.

Conclusion

It is now commonly accepted that media freedom has suffered as part of the war on terror. The new incitement and 'apology' of terrorism laws have placed ever-greater restrictions on what can be said, and it is particularly small and minority publications that have felt the chill of these laws. The evidence I have cited in the opening few pages of this paper may be dismissed as anecdotal—but the issue is not. The threat hanging over journalists' heads who refuse to divulge their sources or who may have some sympathy with terrorists' causes—if not their methods—is very real and has an ongoing chilling effect on media freedom. This is particularly so for online journalists and those writing for small and minority publications. Moreover, the threats to other aspects of journalistic activity—to journalists' freedom of movement, their ability to have access to official information, to their sources, the searches of newsrooms, the use of surveillance, all in the name of fighting terror—has a pernicious effect on media freedom and is ultimately to the detriment of society as a whole.

Furthermore, the courts—including the European Court of Human Rights, the ultimate arbiter on human rights issues in Europe—can no

---

[76] BVerfG, NJW 2007, 1117—Cicero.

longer be relied on to provide uniform guidance on where the line is to be drawn. With the ongoing mushrooming of the Court's case-load and the separation of the court into different Sections, there has been a dilution of standards. Whatever the cause of this, it has been detrimental to the free flow of information and ideas.

But it would be wrong to point the finger solely at the Strasbourg Court. At a time when European governments tell their citizens that terrorism is one of the biggest threats they face, there ought to be space for an open and frank debate on all forms of terrorism and what causes it. Such debate needs a wide space within which different ideas and opinions can be voiced—including extreme ideas. Its ability to tolerate harsh criticism is the litmus test of any democracy. But this has not happened. Instead, laws have been adopted that outlaw any statements that might conceivably be construed as in support of terrorism and journalists are deterred from conducted in-depth investigations into the issue for fear that police will demand access to their research materials or will place them under surveillance. It is hard to see how any of this is in the public interest. Governments need urgently to take stock of the effect the war on terror has had on media freedom, and on human rights and civil liberties in general, and adjust course.

CONCLUSION: UTILISING A HUMAN RIGHTS FRAMEWORK

Merris Amos, Jackie Harrison and Lorna Woods

INTRODUCTION

The overarching theme of this book has been freedom of expression and the media, in particular, the application of legal standards to journalistic practice. Contributors have considered a variety of issues concerning media practice, media regulation and freedom of expression from different perspectives, and from this four sub-themes emerge. First, the question of whether or not the media should be regulated at all. Second if we are to accept some regulation of the media, the problems inherent in determining where to draw the line. Third, the difficulties involved in regulating a new and changing media. And finally, a discussion of how it is possible to ensure that all voices, who would like to be heard, are being heard. A connecting theme throughout has been the utility of applying the right to freedom of expression to all of these issues, and generally, the influence of a human rights framework to the work of the media. This chapter will conclude with a discussion of how the right to freedom of expression, and other important human rights, apply to all of these themes and rather than inhibiting media freedom, can, as some contributors have suggested, help achieve goals which might otherwise be difficult to realise.

SOME REGULATION OF THE MEDIA IS ACCEPTABLE

The first theme is the issue of regulation itself. All of the contributors to this book would seem to accept that there is a need for some regulation of the media. All would also accept the value of freedom of expression and the important role played in our society by the media. What separates them is determining where the line should be drawn. This is not an unusual conundrum. Regulation is fraught with risk and in some cases danger because regulation in a liberal democracy is both a first resort and a last resort. As a first resort, regulation can be used to promote a merit good that must be legislated for, such as public sector broadcasting. But of more concern is the use of regulation as a last resort where it is used to ameliorate media unaccountability with regard to their actions.

Tom Gibbons has set out the case for statutory regulation of the media as necessary to freedom of expression. He states that there "appears to be justification for at least some state interventions in speech activity, whether it is a matter of purposive policy, or of positive action to prevent interference with speech." An unregulated market might, for example, place media proprietors in a position to censor the flow of information and deny an outlet to particular information and opinions. He reminds us of the strength of media power—it has proved itself capable of gross invasions of privacy, bullying, discrimination and defamation. Other contributors share this concern to ensure that powerful voices do not dominate public discussion. Feintuck and Barnett highlight the role of impartiality requirements, whilst McGonagle and Gross have discussed issues of minority access to the media.

However, if regulation of the media is to be continued and expanded, there is need for caution as Peter Noorlander has warned in his chapter. There is always the danger of regulation, introduced for what seems like an acceptable purpose, being abused and used by the State in a way which was not envisaged—to the stifle the dissenting views of journalists, in the name of national security for example. Also, once some regulation is in place and accepted, the path to more regulation is slightly easier. Certain events, such as a terrorist attack, might encourage the adoption of more regulation to meet a particular objective such as the "prevention and detection of terrorism". Experience has shown that the UK is not immune from such measures and many will remember the statutory ban imposed in the 1980s on the broadcasting of words spoken by persons representing terrorist organisations, such as the IRA. Whilst this is no longer in place, there is now the offence of the "glorifica-tion of acts of terrorism" contained in the Terrorism Act 2006. As Noorlander has explained, this had a profoundly negative impact on the journalist Shiv Malik who was ordered under the Terrorism Act 2000 to produce material he had gathered in relation to a book he was writing about an individual suspected of terrorist offences.[1] It is clear that regulation should be regarded with some caution leading to the second theme, the problems with regulation and getting the balance right.

---

[1] *Malik v Manchester Crown Court* [2008] EWHC 1362 (Admin), [2008] 4 All ER 403.

The Problems with Regulation

Whilst it may be accepted that some regulation of the media is acceptable, in practice it is very difficult to get this right. In essence decisions must be made about what type of media activity is unacceptable and should be guarded against or even suppressed. In addition, there is a need to determine who should judge what is acceptable and what is not—who exactly the media should be accountable to. Some have faith in self regulation, such as the task performed by the Press Complaints Commission. Others disagree and would prefer to look to the courts and, in particular, the right to respect for private life as protected by the Human Rights Act 1998 (HRA), for more draconian remedies. Another position would be that exemplified by the Communications Act 2003, the Broadcasting Code for television and radio, and the work of Ofcom, the independent regulator and competition authority for the UK communications industries. Ofcom has, or is assumed to have, the independence of courts but also the specific knowledge of a specialist regulator.

One typical, highly contentious, obligation is the requirement of impartiality imposed upon all broadcasters in the UK, as regulated by Ofcom. One of the concerns Barnett discusses, although critically, is the notion that a "cloak of impartiality" has actually concealed a fundamental in-built establishment bias. The requirement of impartiality can also affect groups. Bernhard Gross in his chapter analysed the conditions under which asylum seekers and refugees can express their voice on British television news and although he does not criticise the impartiality requirement directly, he makes a convincing case that reporting on such issues is usually far from impartial, even in the rare instances where the individual asylum seekers and refugees are able to speak for themselves.

This example illustrates that in practice, impartiality can also be very difficult to implement. Barnett identifies some of the practical difficulties for the BBC maintaining impartiality in a changing world and the notion of radical impartiality where "interviews with members of the Taleban and the far-right British National Party would sit alongside those speaking out against Europe or against immigration." To a similar effect Mike Feintuck highlights the difficulties of applying the impartiality requirement in practice drawing upon the BBC's decision in 2009 not to broadcast the Disasters Emergency Committee's appeal relating to Gaza. He concludes that "the BBC's position on the DEC Gaza appeal was tenuous to the point of implausibility". Nonetheless, despite its difficulties, both recognise that the impartiality requirement contributes, albeit imperfectly, to an informed or diverse public sphere.

In addition to impartiality, regulation brings with it numerous other definitional problems. For example, how should "user generated content" be defined if it is to be regulated or, conversely, excluded from regulation? Central to the balancing of freedom of expression with other interests is the 'public interest' but, what is meant by a "public interest publication"? Some may recall a particularly poor start to the legal definition of a public interest publication when Lord Woolf, in Gary Flitcroft's privacy claim, suggested that the public interest in this context was what the public was interested in, here details of Flitcroft's extra marital affair.[2] Furthermore, how should "taste and decency" restrictions, themselves imposed in the public interest, be imposed? IT culd be argued that such requirements so vague that journalists will self censor rather than run the risk of a complaint to an external regulator. Those who take a robust approach to taste and decency may find themselves reprimanded, or excluded from having a voice in the media. A recent example was the finding by Ofcom that radio presenter Jon Gaunt had breached rules 2.1 and 2.3 of the Broadcasting Code. These rules are designed to protect the public from harmful and offensive material including offensive language and discriminatory treatment or language. The breach took place during his interview with a councillor concerning the Redbridge Council's decision to ban smokers from becoming foster parents. During the interview he called the councillor a "Nazi", "ignorant pig" and "health fascist". Neither Gaunt, his employer Talksport, or his many supporters including the human rights NGO Liberty, believed he had breached the Code but, as discussed later in this chapter, the matter eventually was resolved by the High Court in favour of Ofcom.[3]

It seems that some form of legal pragmatism is the only answer to the problem of determining the limits of regulation. Case by case and issue by issue a balance must be struck between protected interests and the desirability in a liberal democracy of freedom of expression. From this perspective the independence of media regulators is of central importance. This requires independence not only from the industry regulated but also from governmental and other media pressure. Matters are further compounded by the fact that the form and reach of what is considered to be "the media"

[2] *A v B* [2002] EWCA Civ 337, [2003] QB 195.
[3] *Gaunt v Ofcom* [2010] EWHC 1756 (Admin).

is constantly changing and evolving. This leads to the third theme of this book, how to regulate a new and changing media.

How to Regulate a New and Changing Media

If we accept that some regulation of the media is permissible, an additional problem is whether or not this regulation should be applied to all the new forms of communication. Many will remember the days when the media consisted of the print media, radio and television, and a limited selection at that. Today there is internet, mobile phones, international media, a huge range of radio and television broadcasters as well as content produced by private individuals. The role of the journalist is also changing. Whilst regulation may seem inappropriate or impossible in such an environment, there are, as Harrison notes, concerns about leaving content provision to the dictates of the market.

For example, are the rights of minorities both in terms of content and the right to participate adequately protected in such an environment? Lorna Woods and Jackie Harrison in their chapters have discussed in depth the problems presented by user generated content, especially when seen as a mechanism for ameliorating the shortcomings of the professional media when content is assessed for diversity or representativeness. Formerly the public was only allowed to speak when a professional journalist sought them out. Now the audience's participation in news extends to their ability to create content and not to wait for the professional to approach them. But does this need to be moderated? The experience of the BBC, as Jackie Harrison has explained, would suggest that it does. Often the content is unsuitable. Organised, co-ordinated and large scale protest is easier to organise via this medium. There is the problem of hate speech, bullying with texts and emails and the complete absence of an ethical code of conduct. Also raised is the question of the limits of acceptable speech and the means used for determining where that line, assuming it exists, should be drawn.

Distinctions are also opening up between regulation of the "old" media and the "new" media—should they all be subject to the same rules or is this not desirable or even possible? Some argue that the divisions between regulation of the two are anomalous, especially those who are concerned about the rights of the audience and the public sphere. Others suggest that such a distinction results in those subject to regulation being at a disadvantage in terms of compliance costs. Others suggest that these divisions are inevitable given the continually changing nature of the media. But it is also important to consider the possibility that the old media, subject to some regulation are actually at an advantage. Figures reported in the *British Journalism Review* showed that 61 percent of survey respondents trusted BBC journalists to tell the truth but only 15 percent trusted red tops like *The Sun*.[4] While the link between public trust and regulation may need further investigation, Barnett notes in his chapter that surveys of public opinion consistently show very strong public support for the existing regime of broadcasting impartiality. A question which arises in relation to the new sources of information at our disposal is whether or not we still need trusted broadcasters—with such a variety of sources, is it not possible for us to find the truth for ourselves? Both Harrison and Woods are sceptical of this argument.

Part of the problem about the discussion concerning new media regulation is that 'new media' as a term might cover a range of communicative activities, as well as involving a range of actors. It seems then that the different situations (between public and private communications, professional and amateur, and content and infrastructure) may require different regulatory responses. In many ways, the issues surrounding the regulation of the new media are the same as those concerning the regulation of the traditional media, although boundaries might be drawn in different places. It must be judged as a last resort and is acceptable because it is used to ameliorate media unaccountability with regard to its actions. Regulation is pragmatically undertaken in reaction to perceived risks. The identification of those at risk as a result of actions by the media is a matter of what is acceptable to civil society and what is not. However, civil society is not always open and can be censorious of those we regard as "others". It is important to ensure that as many voices as possible are heard. This leads to the subject matter of theme four.

How to Ensure that as Many Voices as Possible are Heard

It is important to ask if the media, new or old, regulated or unregulated, merely support the status quo. Do alternative voices have a platform within the media? Or, are journalists bringing unchallenged assumptions to their editorial judgments? McGonagle has reviewed a range of instruments aimed at protecting the rights of minorities. Whilst the system is

---

[4] S. Barnett, "On the road to self-destruction" *British Journalism Review* 19 (2008), 5.

flawed, there is some basis for suggesting some rights of access. Bernhard Gross' examination of the limited ability of asylum seekers and refugees in this country to get the story across from their perspective to a wide audience, illustrates this problem in practical terms. It is difficult to think of a less powerful group within British society—as he has noted, they are talked about but rarely speak for themselves. Even if they are allowed to speak, it is difficult for them to make themselves understood. It is clear that increased access or opportunity does not necessarily translate into increased understanding.

In this new information age, it is clear that large sums of money are no longer necessary for private individuals to have a voice. However, as Jackie Harrison has illustrated, where private individuals use a forum such as the BBC to express their views, the same constrictions can apply as user generated content is very carefully moderated, perhaps reflecting the impact of the site or, as Woods more generally suggests, concerns about liability. Within this flood of user generated content, might there be the murmurings of civil change which are moderated out of existence? As has been argued by a number of contributors, user generated content is not a universal panacea. Despite the number of voices, it is possible that we still need reliable news sources. As Mike Feintuck questions whether we can expect individuals to be able to gather their news from a variety of sources, of different perspectives and quality, and piece together an accurate picture. Jackie Harrison has concluded that user generated content has a tendency towards soft journalism and human interest—stories of crime, calamities and accidents as well as pictures of much loved pets frolicking in the snow rather than portraying the range of perspectives that we might otherwise expect from the multiple voices speaking.

A Human Rights Framework

One framework in which we can analyse the problems raised by these four themes is that of human rights. Although the legal human rights framework we have at present in the UK is very rudimentary, consisting of the Human Rights Act 1998 (HRA) which gives further effect in domestic law to the European Convention on Human Rights (ECHR), it can offer some answers and offer future guidance. It is also important to note that even if a human right is not given protection in domestic law, the idea of human rights can provide a useful starting point in relation to many questions concerning the media and journalistic practice.

Regulation of the Media within a Human Rights Framework

The first issue concerns the regulation of the media, both new and old. As many of the contributors to this book have suggested, regulation must have a clear objective. This is reflected in the drafting of Art.10 of the ECHR, the right to freedom of expression. The right is set out in the first paragraph: "everyone has the right to freedom of expression". But it is limited by an express recognition in the last sentence of that paragraph concerning the need to regulate some forms of media and, more generally, by the second which provides that the exercise of this freedom, since it carries with it duties and responsibilities, may be restricted, so long as the restriction is necessary in the interest of a number of different objectives. Regulation in accordance with such objectives can apply to all publications and broadcasts, regardless of whether or not it is published by a public sector broadcaster, privately owned newspaper, magazine or an individual's web based blog.

In freedom of expression terms, if regulation is to be imposed, which will always constitute an interference with freedom of expression, what must be identified is the objective to be achieved and then measures must be adopted which are no more than necessary to accomplish that objective. There may well be disagreement about the objective. Certain objectives are clearly acceptable and are set out in Art.10 itself: national security; public safety; prevention of disorder or crime; protection of morals; protection of reputation. We have defamation laws to protect reputation, other laws to punish contempt of court, to protect national security, and, controversially, a judge made law to protect privacy. As the European Court of Human Rights has held

> Article 10 of the Convention protects journalists' right to divulge information on issues of general interest provided that they are acting in good faith and on an accurate factual basis and provide 'reliable and precise' information in accordance with the ethics of journalism. Under the terms of paragraph 2 of Article 10 of the Convention, freedom of expression carries with it 'duties and responsibilities', which also apply to the media even with respect to matters of serious public concern. Moreover, these 'duties and responsibilities' are liable to assume significance when there is a question of attacking the reputation of named individuals and infringing the 'rights of others'.[5]

Proportionate regulation to protect the "rights of others" is potentially very broad and the question must always be asked, what are the particular

---

[5] *Ukraina-Tsentr v Ukraine*, ECtHR, Application no.16695/04, 15 July 2010.

rights that it is the state is trying to protect? There could be a number of possibilities: the right to entertainment? The right to accurate information? The right to be protected from biased news? Or the right of an individual to a source of accurate and unbiased information so as to allow them to exercise to the fullest extent their democratic rights? British courts have considerable sympathy with the latter objective. This was reflected in the claim brought by Animal Defenders International against the broadcasting ban contained in the Communications Act 2003 which prevented them from running their planned television advertisement "My mate's a primate" as it was deemed to breach the ban on political advertising. Whilst this was not a case directly concerning a restriction on the media, the comments of the House of Lords are instructive as to how it might consider any future regulation of the media to achieve a similar objective. Lord Bingham, stated as follows:

> It is highly desirable that the playing field of debate should be so far as practicable level. This is achieved where, in public discussion, differing views are expressed, contradicted, answered and debated. It is the duty of broadcasters to achieve this object in an impartial way by presenting balanced programmes in which all lawful views may be ventilated. It is not achieved if political parties can, in proportion to their resources, buy unlimited opportunities to advertise in the most effective media, so that elections become little more than an auction.[6]

Provided it can be demonstrated that a particular restriction on freedom of expression and thereby freedom of the media is genuinely connected to the objective of ensuring a level playing field for debate in this way, and no more than necessary in the circumstances, it would be lawful and compatible with the Art.10 right to freedom of expression. The European Court of Human Rights (ECtHR) also has considerable sympathy with this position. It has held that it is the "essence of democracy to allow diverse political programmes to be proposed and debated, even those that call into question the way a State is currently organised, provided that they do not harm democracy itself".[7] It has also held that the audiovisual media, such as radio and television, have a particularly important role in this respect. "Because of their power to convey messages through sound and images, such media have a more immediate and powerful effect than

---

[6] *R. (on the application of Animal Defenders International) v Secretary of State for Culture, Media & Sport* [2008] UKHL 15, [2008] 1 AC 1312. Contrast the judgment of the ECtHR in *TV Vest and Rogaland Pensjonistparti v Norway*, Application no 21132/05, 11 December 2008.

[7] *Manole v Moldova*, Application no 13936/02, 17 September 2009 at [95].

print."[8] With respect to the requirement of impartiality imposed upon a
state broadcaster, it has held as follows:

> A situation whereby a powerful economic or political group in a society is
> permitted to obtain a position of dominance over the audiovisual media and
> thereby exercise pressure on broadcasters and eventually curtail their edito-
> rial freedom undermines the fundamental role of freedom of expression in a
> democratic society as enshrined in Article 10 of the Convention, in particu-
> lar where it serves to impart information and ideas of general interest, which
> the public is moreover entitled to receive ... This is true also where the posi-
> tion of dominance is held by a State or public broadcaster.[9]

In the Court's opinion, "genuine, effective exercise of freedom of expression does not depend merely on the State's duty not to interfere, but may
require it to take positive measures of protection, through its law or practice". This was because, given the importance of what is at stake under
Article 10, the State must be the ultimate guarantor of pluralism.[10] It has
held that in the field of audiovisual broadcasting, the above principles
place a duty on the State to ensure "first, that the public has access through
television and radio to impartial and accurate information and a range of
opinion and comment, reflecting *inter alia* the diversity of political out-
look within the country and, secondly, that journalists and other professionals working in the audiovisual media are not prevented from imparting
this information and comment."[11]

Nevertheless, it is also clear that the ECtHR will take a hard look at the
application of these principles in practice and it is not keen on blanket
bans where individual consideration is dispensed with by broadcasting
laws. For example, in *TV Vest v Norway*[12] it concluded that the fine imposed
on a television broadcasting company for breaching the prohibition on
political advertising was incompatible with Art.10. The short broadcasts
sought to portray the values of the Pensioners Party and encouraged viewers to vote for them. The Court found that the political nature of the adver-
tisements that were prohibited called for strict scrutiny on its part and
circumscribed the national margin of appreciation.[13] Whilst referring to

---

[8] *Manole v Moldova* Application no 13936/02, 17 September 2009, at [97].
[9] *Manole v Moldova*, Application no 13936/02, 17 September 2009 at [98].
[10] Ibid., at [99].
[11] Ibid., at [100].
[12] *TV Vest and Rogaland Pensjonistparti v Norway*, Application no 21132/05, 11 December 2008.
[13] At [64].

the justifications of pluralism and quality and preventing the financially powerful having greater influence, the Court was not convinced these applied in the present case. It found that the Pensioners Party were not financially powerful and further held:

> On the contrary, while the Pensioners Party belonged to a category for those protection the ban was, in principle, intended, the Court... is not persuaded that the ban had the desired effect. In contrast to the major political parties, which were given a large amount of attention in edited television coverage, the Pensioners Party was hardly mentioned. Therefore, paid advertising on television became the only way for the Pensioners Party to put its message across to the public through that medium. By being denied this possibility under the law, the Pensioner Party was at a disadvantage compared with other major parties which had obtained edited broadcasting coverage, and this could not be offset by the possibility available to use other, less potent, media.... it has not been contended that the specific advertising at issue contained elements that were capable of lowering the quality of political debate.[14]

The Problems with Regulation within a Human Rights Framework

But it is clear that even if there is proportionate regulation, in order to achieve a specified objective, there will still remain difficulties of definition and interpretation. Who is going to be the final arbiter on the meaning of the rules put in place—the meaning of impartiality for example? Whilst a freedom of expression analysis might tell us that preservation of an impartiality requirement for at least one public service broadcaster is a proportionate interference to ensure there remains at least one source of trusted, accurate information so as to allow the people of the United Kingdom to participate fully in political, social and cultural life, who is going to decide when the line has been crossed and a broadcaster has not been impartial? Some would say that these questions are so important that a safety net should be provided by the law with the courts adjudicating as to when the line has been crossed. Others would argue that this should be the preserve of Ofcom with the safeguard of judicial review and the Human Rights Act 1998 if Ofcom gets it wrong. There are also those who believe self-regulation is the most appropriate in such circumstances as the risk of a legal remedy imposes a "chilling effect" on broadcasters. It might be that a combination of all three systems works best. What is important from a human rights perspective is that the limits on freedom

---

[14] At [73]–[74].

of expression are accessible to those affected, sufficiently precise and are not applied in a way which is arbitrary.

The recent case brought by Jon Gaunt demonstrates that definitional problems will always remain where there is regulation or a law in place. As already discussed, Gaunt argued that the interview he conducted, and the comments he made, were not offensive or harmful and that Ofcom's decision to the contrary amounted to a violation of his right to freedom of expression. The High Court concluded that its task was to decide the question for itself and, having considered the evidence, it agreed with Ofcom finding that this constituted no material interference with Gaunt's freedom of expression at all as this was not protected expression. In the opinion of the court "[a]n inhibition from broadcasting shouted abuse which expresses no content does not inhibit, and should not deter, heated and even offensive dialogue which retains a degree of relevant content."[15]

The Importance of Effective Remedies for Violations of Human Rights

Whilst Art.10, the right to freedom of expression, can play a part in ensuring proportionate regulation of the media, it is important to remember that a human rights framework does not only guarantee respect for the right to freedom of expression. An important aspect of human rights protection is to ensure effective remedies before national authorities for violations of all human rights given further effect by the HRA. For example it is clear that there must be some regulation of the media in order to ensure effective protection for the right to respect for private life as protected by Art.8. As noted by Amos, under the HRA it is now possible for an individual to seek a remedy from a court under the tort of modified breach of confidence where there has been an interference with their private life.[16] It is also possible to seek a remedy from Ofcom for a breach of that part of the Broadcasting Code protecting privacy[17] or a remedy from the Press Complaints Commission (PCC) for a breach of the privacy guarantee contained in the Editor's Code of Practice.[18]

But although there are now three official avenues for complaint about an invasion of private life, there is still the presence of dissatisfaction with the current system. Given the costs involved in seeking a remedy from a court, in particular it is thought that the PCC does little to ensure that

---

[15] *Gaunt v Ofcom* [2010] EWHC 1756 (Admin).
[16] See for example *Campbell v MGN Ltd* [2004] UKHL 22, [2004] 2 AC 457.
[17] Section 8.
[18] Section 3.

there is actually an effective remedy for invasions of privacy by the print media. The lack of effective remedies for invasions of privacy by the media was a strong theme in evidence presented to the House of Commons Culture Media and Sport Committee during its inquiry into press standards, privacy and libel.[19] Max Mosley used his appearance before the Committee to complain vehemently about the PCC and make a case for legislation requiring editors and journalists to give people about whom they write not just the opportunity to comment, but also notice of their intention to publish so that such people would have time, if appropriate, to seek injunctions preventing publication. He has also lodged an application with the ECtHR seeking a ruling that the UK government's failure to enact such legislation amounts to a breach of its positive duty under Art.8 and a failure to afford an effective remedy for invasions into private life.

Not going as far as Mosley would like, the Committee recommended that the PCC amend the Code to include a requirement that journalists should normally notify the subject of their articles prior to publication, subject to a public interest test, and should provide guidance for journalists and editors on pre-notifying. Whilst it concluded a legal requirement would be ineffective, it recommended that failure to pre-notify should be made an aggravating factor in assessing damages for breach of Art.8. With respect to the operation of the PCC, it concluded that self-regulation of the press was preferred to statutory regulation and should continue. But it stated that "for confidence to be maintained, the industry regulator must actually effectively regulate, not just mediate. The powers of the PCC must be enhanced, as it is toothless compared to other regulators."[20] It remains to be seen whether Mosley will succeed before the ECtHR in establishing that better regulation of the UK press is necessary in order to ensure Art 8 rights are adequately protected and effective remedies are provided for the violation of all Convention rights, not just Art.10.

Human Rights and Regulating a New and Changing Media

To some extent, the new media is already regulated in the same way as the traditional media as it is bound by the general law and this reflects content standards found in the Broadcasting Code and also the PCC Code. As already discussed by Woods, it is possible to commit an offence under s.127 of the Communications Act 2003 by publishing on Twitter something

---

[19] *Press standards, privacy and libel* Second Report of Session 2009–2010, HC 362-I (London: TSO, 2010).

[20] at [79].

grossly offensive or of an obscene or menacing character. A recent example was the conviction of Paul Chambers under s.127 of the Communications
Act 2003 for tweeting "Robin Hood Airport is closed. You've got a week . .
otherwise I'm blowing the airport sky high!"[21] Control in this manner is
not just limited to those using Twitter and has reached other areas of the
new media. In November 2010 a man was charged with soliciting murder
and other offences in relation to a blog listing MPs it was claimed had
voted for the invasion of Iraq. Psychiatrist and prolife campaigner Patricia
Casey is currently suing The Irish Times for defamation over a reader's
comment published on its website. It was recently reported that a 15 year
old girl has been arrested on suspicion of inciting religious hatred after
allegedly burning the Qur'an and then posting video footage of the act on
Facebook.

The benefits of a human rights framework for the new media are similar
to those outlined in relation to the traditional media. There is a right to
freedom of expression enshrined in domestic law which new media defendants can utilise in their defence. Whilst new media defendants may not
enjoy the privileged position of traditional media defendants before the
courts, a human rights framework requires consideration of the exact circumstances in order to ensure that the interference with freedom of
expression is proportionate. However, given the failure of Twitterer Paul
Chambers to successfully defend his conviction under s.127 of the
Communications Act 2003, it could be that the new media ends up as dis-
appointed with the HRA as the traditional media.[22]

Nevertheless, it is important to remember that Art.10 protects not only
information or ideas which are "favourably received or regarded as inof-
fensive or as matter or indifference, but also to those that offend, shock or
disturb. Such are the demands of pluralism, tolerance and broadmindedness".[23] Furthermore, a democratic society requires "tolerance and broadmindedness in the face of controversial expressions."[24] The ECtHR
has confirmed that Art 10 applies to Internet forum postings and that
depending on the content, it is willing to treat these as matters of general
interest particularly if these are unbiased. It has also held that "journalistic

---

[21] Further examples include the arrest of a Conservative Councillor in Birmingham on
10 November 2010 for posting a message on Twitter stating "Can someone please stone
Yasmin Alibhai Brown to death?" And the police suspension of the anti-police blog
Fitwatch on 15 November 2010 as it was giving advice about avoiding arrest to students.
[22] It was reported in November 2010 that he was seeking judicial review of his conviction on freedom of expression grounds.
[23] *Sarristo v Finland*, ECtHR, Application no. 184/06, October 12, 2010 at [54].
[24] *Cox v Turkey*, Application no 2933/03, 20 May 2010.

freedom" covers possible recourse to a degree of exaggeration, or even provocation.[25] As suggested by Woods it is not necessary to be a journalist working for the traditional media in order to enjoy the enhanced freedom of expression which has been afforded to the media. The ECtHR has held:

> The function of the press includes the creation of forums for public debate. However, the realisation of this function is not limited to the media or professional journalists. In the present case, the preparation of the forum of public debate was conducted by a non-governmental organisation. The purpose of the applicant's activities can therefore be said to have been an essential element of informed public debate. The Court has repeatedly recognised civil society's important contribution to the discussion of public affairs ... The applicant is an association involved in human rights litigation with various objectives, including the protection of freedom of information. It may therefore be characterised, like the press, as a social "watchdog" ... In these circumstances, the Court is satisfied that its activities warrant similar Convention protection to that afforded to the press.[26]

But the ECtHR has not been so supportive of the new media where it considers that the boundary between responsible journalism and irresponsible journalism has been crossed. It has held that "[i]n a world in which the individual is confronted with vast quantities of information circulated via traditional and electronic media and involving an ever-growing number of players, monitoring compliance with journalistic ethics takes on added importance."[27] The requirement that journalists, whether new media or old, act in good faith, on an accurate factual basis providing reliable and precise information in accordance with the ethics of journalism has been held to play "a particularly important role nowadays, given the influence wielded by the media in contemporary society: not only do they inform, they can also suggest by the way in which they present information how it is to be assessed.[28] One example was the judgment of the Court in *Pasko v Russia*[29] where it held that the military journalist claimant had been convicted as a serving military officer, and not as a journalist, of treason through espionage for having collected and kept, with the intention of transferring it to a foreign national, information of a military nature that was classified as a State secret. It concluded that his conviction was

---

[25] *Fattullayev v Azerbaijan*, Application no 40984/07, 22 April 2010 at [89] and [91].

[26] *Társaság a Szabadságjogokért v Hungary* Application no 37374/05, 14 April 2009 at [27].

[27] *Stoll v Switzerland*, Application no 69698/01, 10 December 2007 at [104].

[28] *Stoll v Switzerland*, Application no 69698/01, 10 December 2007 at [104].

[29] Application no.69519/01, 22 October 2009.

proportionate. Where a crime is serious, the ECtHR has not automatically found that the compulsory handover of journalistic material is incompatible with Art.10.[30] A similar conclusion might be reached were any criminal proceedings to be brought in relation to disclosures by new media websites such as WikiLeaks.[31]

It is also important to note that Article 10 can protect international media operating within the UK. It has been confirmed by the ECtHR that Art 10 rights are enshrined regardless of frontiers and that no distinction can be drawn between the protected freedom of expression of nationals and that of foreigners. "This principle implies that the Contracting States may only restrict information received from abroad within the confines of the justifications set out in Article 10. The scope of Article 10 of the Convention includes the right to impart information."[32]

The Role of Human Rights Principles in Ensuring all Voices are Heard

Human rights can also provide some guidance to efforts to ensure that all voices are heard. As noted above, it is a strong principle of freedom of expression jurisprudence that all voices are protected by freedom of expression including not only those which are favourably received but also those that offend, shock or disturb the state or any sector of the population. "Such are the demands of pluralism, tolerance and broadmindedness without which there is no 'democratic society'.[33] However, whilst it is possible for anyone to join Twitter, Facebook, or set up a website or a blog, access to the traditional media is often more difficult. As Tarlach McGonagle has explained, positive duties—requiring the state to do something rather than refrain from doing something, are not yet well developed either in British or European human rights law. For example, it has been held by the House of Lords that the right to freedom of expression does not entitle anyone to make free television broadcasts.[34] The European Court of Human Rights has also recently held that privately owned newspapers must be free to exercise editorial discretion in deciding whether to publish articles, comments and letters submitted by private individuals. It concluded that the State's obligation to ensure the

---

[30] See also for example *Sanoma Uitgevers B.V. v The Netherlands*, Application no. 38224/03, 31 March 2009.

[31] See for example the approach of the Court in *Stoll v Switzerland*, Application no. 69698/01, 10 December 2007.

[32] *Cox v Turkey*, Application no 2933/03, 20 May 2010 at [31].

[33] *Fattullayev v Azerbaijan*, Application no. 40984/07, 22 April 2010 at [86].

[34] *R. (Prolife Alliance) v BBC* [2003] UKHL 23, [2004] 1 AC 185.

individual's freedom of expression did not give private citizens or organisations an "unfettered right of access to the media in order to put forward opinions".[35]

There are a few limited exceptions. It might be that the press is in the hands of a private or state monopoly. If there is a public broadcasting system, the ECtHR has held

> ...a positive obligation arises under Article 10. The State, as the ultimate guarantor of pluralism, must ensure, through its law and practice, that the public has access through television and radio to impartial and accurate information and a range of opinion and comment, reflecting *inter alia* the diversity of political outlook within the country and that journalists and other professionals working in the audiovisual media are not prevented from imparting this information and comment. Where the State decides to create a public broadcasting system, the domestic law and practice must guarantee that the system provides a pluralistic audiovisual service. In this connection, the standards relating to public service broadcasting which have been agreed by the Contracting States through the Committee of Ministers of the Council of Europe provide guidance as to the approach which should be taken to interpreting Article 10 in this field.[36]

It might also be the case that a formerly public space has become privately owned thereby limiting opportunities for those who would like to present a message in person either by distributing leaflets and posters, or demonstrating. In *Appleby v UK*[37] the applicants complained that the new town centre of the town of Washington was located within an area owned by a private company and that this private company had refused to allow them to collect signatures on any land or premises owned by the company. A part of their argument was that there was a positive duty on the state under Art.10 to secure the exercise of their rights within this private property. The Court agreed that genuine and effective exercise of freedom of expression did not "depend merely upon the State's duty not to interfere, but may require positive measures of protection, even in the sphere of relations between individuals".[38] But whilst it conceded that demographic, social, economic and technological developments were changing the ways in which people move around and come into contact with each other, "the Court is not persuaded that this requires the automatic creation of rights of entry to private property, or even, necessarily, to all publicly owned

---

[35] *Saliyev v Russia* Application no. 35016/03, 21 October 2010 at [52].
[36] *Manole v Moldova*, Application no 13936/02, 17 September 2009 at [107].
[37] Application no. 44306/98, 6 May 2003.
[38] at [39].

property". This might be different where the bar on access to property has the effect of "preventing any effective exercise of freedom of expression or it can be said that the essence of the right has been destroyed". Here the Court did not exclude the possibility that a "positive obligation could arise for the State to protect the enjoyment of the Convention rights by regulating property rights. A corporate town where the entire municipality is controlled by a private body might be an example".[39] In the present case it was not satisfied that the applicants could claim that they were, as a result of the refusal of the private company, effectively prevented from communicating their views to their fellow citizens. But the importance of the judgment lies in the fact that the principle has been established, were the situation to ever arise.

With respect to the process of applying for a broadcasting licence in the UK, it is clear that the decision whether or not to issue a licence is regulated by Art.10 as it affects the freedom to impart information and ideas.[40] It has also been established that the right to receive information basically prohibits a Government from restricting a person from receiving information that others wish or may be willing to impart to him or her, whether through the use of technical equipment or otherwise. It may be that a person wishes to receive television programmes from their native country. "[W]hile such news might be the most important information protected by Article 10, the freedom to receive information does not extend only to reports of events of public concern, but covers in principle also cultural expressions as well as pure entertainment. The importance of the latter types of information should not be underestimated, especially for an immigrant family with three children, who may wish to maintain contact with the culture and language of their country of origin."[41]

In addition to Art.10, other important human rights principles also come into play in this context, in particular, the principles of equality and non-discrimination. It has been a suggested by a number of contributors to this book that the media essentially supports the status quo and it is difficult to hear alternative voices presenting another point of view. If this is the case, improving the diversity of voices is an objective which could be pursued, legally or politically, within a regulatory framework. This could be an objective pursued positively or negatively. It is possible

---

[39] at [47].
[40] *Meltex Ltd and Mesrop Movsesyan v Armenia*, Application no 32283/04, 17 June 2008.
[41] *Mustafa and Tarzibachi v Sweden*, Application no. 23883/06, 16 December 2008 at [44].

that the media is indirectly discriminating against certain groups—their treatment of all stories and contributors in the same way results in a disproportionate negative impact on some. If this is the case, existing anti-discrimination laws might provide some guidance. If this were to be an objective pursued positively, it might be necessary to impose a legal requirement on some media to ensure diversity of viewpoint although this might conflict with the requirement of impartiality. But it also has to be appreciated that with the many new opportunities for access to the media now available, such a requirement might be seen as a disproportionate interference with freedom of expression.

Conclusion

Effective human rights standards are crucial to the operation of the media, both new and old. As the contributors to this book have demonstrated, the issues are far more complex than the simple formula that that media has an untrammelled right to freedom of expression. Any regulation of the media requires a consideration of the objective to be achieved and proportionality but also an acceptance that regulation is not simple, and there will always been disagreements over whether the regulator has actually got it right. The new media, whilst benefiting from the right to freedom of expression, is also clearly subject to some level of regulation. But human rights standards can play an important role in ensuring that alternative voices contribute to the public debate. The following quote, from a judgment of the ECtHR, is universally applicable to all of those reporting and commenting on matters of public interest:

> The pre-eminent role of the press in a State governed by the rule of law must not be forgotten. Although it must not overstep various bounds set, *inter alia*, for the prevention of disorder and the protection of the reputation of others, it is nevertheless incumbent on it to impart information and ideas on political questions and on other matters of public interest. Freedom of the press affords the public one of the best means of discovering and forming an opinion of the ideas and attitudes of their political leaders[42].

---

[42] *Kuliś and Różycki v Poland*, Application no. 27209/03, 6 October 2009 at [30].

UNITED NATIONS INTERNATIONAL COVENANT ON CIVIL AND POLITICAL RIGHTS

Article 19
1. Everyone shall have the right to hold opinions without interference.
2. Everyone shall have the right to freedom of expression; this right shall include freedom to seek, receive and impart information and ideas of all kinds, regardless of frontiers, either orally, in writing or in print, in the form of art, or through any other media of his choice.
3. The exercise of the rights provided for in paragraph 2 of this article carries with it special duties and responsibilities. It may therefore be subject to certain restrictions, but these shall only be such as are provided by law and are necessary:
   (a) For respect of the rights or reputations of others;
   (b) For the protection of national security or of public order (ordre public), or of public health or morals.

COUNCIL OF EUROPE

The European Convention on Human Rights

Article 10
1. Everyone has the right to freedom of expression. this right shall include freedom to hold opinions and to receive and impart information and ideas without interference by public authority and regardless of frontiers. This article shall not prevent States from requiring the licensing of broadcasting, television or cinema enterprises.
2. The exercise of these freedoms, since it carries with it duties and responsibilities, may be subject to such formalities, conditions, restrictions or penalties as are prescribed by law and are necessary in a democratic society, in the interests of national security, territorial integrity or public safety, for the prevention of disorder or crime, for the protection of health or morals, for the protection of the reputation or the rights of others, for preventing the disclosure of information received in confidence, or for maintaining the authority and impartiality of the judiciary.

INDEX